Civic Engagement in the Wake of Katrina

THE NEW PUBLIC SCHOLARSHIP

SERIES EDITORS

Lonnie Bunch, *Director, National Museum of African-American History and Culture*

Julie Ellison, *Professor of American Culture, University of Michigan*

Robert Weisbuch, *President, Drew University*

The New Public Scholarship encourages alliances between scholars and communities by publishing writing that emerges from publicly engaged and intellectually consequential cultural work. The series is designed to attract serious readers who are invested in both creating and thinking about public culture and public life. Under the rubric of "public scholar," we embrace campus-based artists, humanists, cultural critics, and engaged artists working in the public, nonprofit, or private sector. The editors seek useful work growing out of engaged practices in cultural and educational arenas. We are also interested in books that offer new paradigms for doing and theorizing public scholarship itself. Indeed, validating public scholarship through an evolving set of concepts and arguments is central to **The New Public Scholarship.**

The universe of potential contributors and readers is growing rapidly. We are teaching a generation of students for whom civic education and community service learning are quite normative. The civic turn in art and design has affected educational and cultural institutions of many kinds. In light of these developments, we feel that **The New Public Scholarship** offers a timely innovation in serious publishing.

DIGITALCULTUREBOOKS is an imprint of the University of Michigan Press and the Scholarly Publishing Office of the University of Michigan Library dedicated to publishing innovative and accessible work exploring new media and their impact on society, culture, and scholarly communication.

Civic Engagement
IN THE Wake OF Katrina

——————————— ❧ ———————————

Amy Koritz and George J. Sanchez

EDITORS

*The University of Michigan Press
and The University of Michigan Library
Ann Arbor*

Copyright © by the University of Michigan and the
University of Michigan Library 2009
All rights reserved
Published in the United States of America by
The University of Michigan Press
Manufactured in the United States of America
⊗ Printed on acid-free paper

2012   2011   2010   2009   4   3   2   1

A CIP catalog record for this book is available from the British Library.

Library of Congress Cataloging-in-Publication Data

Civic engagement in the wake of Katrina / Amy Koritz and George J.
Sanchez, editors.
    p. cm. — (The new public scholarship)
    Includes bibliographical references and index.
    ISBN 978-0-472-11698-0 (cloth : alk. paper) — ISBN 978-0-472-
03352-2 (paper : alk. paper)
    1. New Orleans (La.)—Social conditions—21st century.
2. Hurricane Katrina, 2005—Social aspects—Louisiana—New Orleans.
3. Disaster relief—Social aspects—Louisiana—New Orleans—History—
21st century. 4. Community life—Louisiana—New Orleans—History—
21st century. 5. City and town life—Louisiana—New Orleans—
History—21st century. 6. Political participation—Louisiana—New
Orleans—History—21st century. 7. New Orleans (La.)—Social life
and customs—21st century. 8. New Orleans (La.)—Cultural policy.
9. New Orleans (La.)—Intellectual life—21st century. I. Koritz,
Amy, 1955– II. Sanchez, George J.
  HN80.N45C58   2009
  307.3'41609763350905 11—dc22   2009018642

DEDICATION

To the people of New Orleans and those who joined with them to rebuild the homes and communities of this city.

❧❧

To those still displaced from those homes and communities.

❧❧

To those who have found new homes and are building new communities in New Orleans.

Acknowledgments

This volume owes its existence to George J. Sanchez's willingness to come to New Orleans in the spring of 2006. That event, in turn, only occurred because Julie Ellison invited him to present at a September 2005 conference sponsored by Imagining America: Artists and Scholars in Public Life in New Brunswick, New Jersey. Nor would I have met George at that conference had not Julie insisted that I attend it at her organization's expense since at the time I was holed up in rural North Carolina with my in-laws wondering if I still had a job. Once George arrived in New Orleans he recognized what none of us immersed in the urgency of daily life in a devastated city could see: there was work happening in New Orleans that needed to be shared. It was George who first suggested this volume, and it was his willingness to devote resources not available to me at Tulane to its completion that made it possible. Although Julie no longer directs Imagining America, she is coeditor of the University of Michigan Press series that has given this book a home and the experiences recorded within it a voice and audience. I owe the deepest thanks to both George and Julie. I would finally like to acknowledge the efforts of the contributors to this volume, all of whom took time away from the pressing needs of their families, communities, and organizations to meet, think, draft, revise, and respond to the requests of the editors with generosity and grace.

This volume would not have been produced without the vision, determination, and networks of Amy Koritz. Having been displaced with her family by Hurricane Katrina, Amy understood that her return to her adopted city and her job at Tulane University required a new reckoning with the struggles of others in New Orleans to rebuild lives, reconnect with communities, and rebuild the city. As part of that refashioning of her work, I was fortunate enough to be invited by Amy to come to New Orleans for the very first time to help make sense of the new Latino immigrant communities that were growing in that post-Katrina region. Amy was my guide, along with several of the contributors to this volume, to the city that once was and the city that was becoming New Orleans. What made that connection possible was the national network of scholars and artists that is Imagining America, and particularly Julie Ellison, who was its first and founding director. She encouraged us to make this connection and put together this volume to feature the voices of those at the forefront of the work of rebuilding in New Orleans. The new director of Imagining America, Jan Cohen-Cruz, has been equally as supportive of these productive networks and collaborations, and I am joyful for her voice in this volume. Three dedicated research assistants at the University of Southern California helped me put this volume together and worked tirelessly on its behalf. Adam Bush, Margaret Salazar, and Barbara Soliz are each up-and-coming scholars, and their dedication to academic excellence, civic engagement, and racial equity is what makes working with graduate students such a fulfilling experience. What I experienced in New Orleans, certainly as an outsider to the city but as a supporter of sustained civic engagement, is an unparalleled dedication to the people and communities in Louisiana by a host of academics, community organizers, and professional activists. They welcomed me into their world and allowed me to make my small contribution to their efforts. For their openness and willingness to share their stories, I will forever be grateful.

We would both additionally like to acknowledge the support of our families. Bob, Ben, and Daniel Gaston have never failed to provide for Amy a reminder of the really important things in life. Without their humor and understanding, patience, impatience, and willingness to pick up the slack at home, everything I do would have less meaning, less flavor, less laughter.

Debra Massey Sanchez, after much worry, allowed George to participate in a project in New Orleans just months after Hurricane Katrina and put up with all the travel and work involved in getting this project done with great love and support. She is a constant reminder to me of what true love is all about and why it is so important for each of us to find the person that makes life meaningful and passionate.

Contents

Civic Engagement in the Wake of Katrina

Introduction

Amy Koritz and George J. Sanchez

New Orleans is a place where the "slaves of the city" still
ask "who will betray us today."
—Brenda Marie Osbey

Democracy must be reborn in each generation. Education
is the midwife.
—John Dewey

The local community must be the microcosm of our
pluralistic, inclusive democracy, and the realization of our
democratic ideals. Community is, in fact, democracy
incarnate, where culture is woven into the fabric of our
daily lives, not worn as a decoration on its surface, or
observed from afar as the province of the privileged few.
—Sondra Myers

Everything that happened at Charity during the storm was
a failure . . . everything bad was a failure of the system.
Everything good was a success of individuals.
—Joel Rene Morrissey, chief resident at Charity Hospital

ON AUGUST 29, 2005, THE CITY OF NEW ORLEANS and the surrounding Gulf
Coast region was hit by a monstrous hurricane named Katrina, which exposed the underlying racial and economic inequalities and public corruption that mark so many cities in the United States at the beginning of the

twenty-first century. Over the next few days, as the rest of the United States and the world witnessed the lack of adequate planning and preparation, which left thousands of residents to struggle for their very survival in the wake of Katrina, residents of New Orleans realized that they had experienced one of the most catastrophic failures of public investment that had ever been perpetrated on a resident citizen population in the history of the United States. Now, three years past those tragic days at the end of the summer of 2005, it is clear that the U.S. federal government and local state, parish, and city governments still have not provided the economic and social support necessary to reconstruct New Orleans to any semblance of what it once was. Yet with 70 percent of its prestorm population now in the city, those individuals who today call New Orleans home continue to hope for support in rebuilding the homes, lives, and institutions necessary for the "Big Easy" to once again become a beacon of distinctive culture and resounding fortitude.

By focusing on individuals and organizations involved in civic engagement work, this volume offers a window into one aspect of this recovery. Civic engagement work before Hurricane Katrina was not easy given the broad structural inequalities and palpable history of racism and political corruption in the region. In 2004, Louisiana had the second-highest rate of poverty in the nation and the fifth-lowest rate of median household income, with almost 37 percent of its black residents considered impoverished.[1] The flooding caused by Hurricane Katrina and the breaks in the city's levees not only exposed residents in various neighborhoods to potential death and destruction; it also decimated neighborhoods in the long term, leading between 30 and 40 percent of the city's population to seek permanent or semipermanent exile in other cities. Some civic engagement projects stopped in the wake of Katrina because the very neighborhoods where engagement took place had disappeared.

Yet, as several of this volume's essays make clear, civic engagement work has rebounded tremendously in the rebuilding process, with new forms of democratic citizenship flourishing in ways that most did not think possible—and that were often *not* possible—pre-Katrina. We believe that there is much to be learned from closely examining civic engagement in the wake of Katrina in an effort to go beyond pat answers about how to deal with natural disasters or survive in the wake of extreme tragedy. Indeed, Katrina exposed the kind of community fissures that complicate most efforts at civic engagement and the possibilities for citizen participation that can arise when traditional politics devolve into inaction and stalemate. We undertook this volume partly to ask ourselves whether it is even possible for civic engagement work to cope with a disaster that is rooted in a long history of racial injustice, economic disparity, and political malfeasance.

As the editors of this volume, our paths to putting together this book couldn't have been more different. Neither of us was born in New Orleans, but we are both intimately involved in civic engagement issues. Amy Koritz is a longtime professor in the English Department at Tulane University in New Orleans. She came to civic engagement in higher education almost inadvertently. Having been asked by a provost in the late 1990s to lead a project to improve the educational experience and retention of first-year students, she determined that connecting them powerfully to their immediate environment was probably the most effective means of achieving this goal. As a result, she began instituting programs that introduced students to New Orleans, enabling them to learn more about its compelling culture and deep problems. The project ended with the tenure of that provost, but by that time it was evident how significant an impact civic engagement could have on college students. By the time Katrina struck in 2005, Koritz was persuaded that most institutions of higher education were neglecting their obligation to the public good by failing to address how undergraduate education prepares students to be effective citizens as well as productive workers. The aftermath of Katrina transformed this conviction into an imperative.

George J. Sanchez is not a resident of New Orleans and had never visited the city before Hurricane Katrina. Invited to give a lecture at Tulane University the spring after Katrina hit, he was struck by the experience, intensity, and sadness that pervaded the community of civic engagement workers he met while there. And, like Professor Koritz, he was convinced that the stories of survival and recovery he was hearing deserved a wider, more national audience. As a scholar of the history of Los Angeles, he had experienced the similar sense of shock, despair, and energy that accompanied that city's effort to rebuild itself in the aftermath of the 1992 Los Angeles riots. But he was also acutely aware that as a newcomer to New Orleans he had much to learn and absorb about the uniqueness of the region and its peoples.

Many features of New Orleans history, politics, and culture are unique to it and must be explained to those unfamiliar with the contours of the city. First of all, New Orleans is above all else a city of neighborhoods—a fact that proved critical to the unfolding of civic engagement work before and after Hurricane Katrina. The spatial organization of Orleans Parish (the Louisiana version of a county) can be traced back to the French arpent system.[2] This system created long, narrow plots of land, each of which had access to the only transportation route available, the Mississippi River. The city's streets still reflect the geography of these early plantations, as does its organization into wards. For many native New Orleanians, their ward defines their primary loyalty, and various wards have long associations with particular populations; the Seventh Ward, for example, was historically home to the skilled craftsmen of the building trades. Stretching back toward Lake Pontchartrain and slightly downriver from the French Quarter, this area was settled by free people of color and sustained a strong intergenerational network of masonry workers, ironworkers, bricklayers, and carpenters that facilitated the development of an African American and Catholic middle class locally referred to as Creole. The Lower Ninth Ward, with which the entire country became familiar when the wall of the Industrial Canal, which borders its western edge, collapsed, was overwhelmingly poor and African American but also had a higher rate of owner-occupied houses than the city as a whole (59.0 as opposed to 46.5 percent for Orleans Parish).[3] Devastated by flooding, this community is called "lower" not because it is on lower ground but because it is farther down the Mississippi River than the rest of the Ninth Ward. The ward system is complicated by an array of neighborhood names that reflect different historical formations, some physically descriptive (such as the Garden District) and others referencing real estate developments (Pontchartrain Park, Lakeview, Gentilly Woods), streets and landmarks (Audubon, Carrollton), or local designations whose history has long been forgotten by those who live in and use them now (Gert Town, Irish Channel).

The geography of New Orleans is best understood by reference to the Mississippi River since the natural levees formed by the annual flooding of the river created the high ground on which the city was first built. This high ground (the "sliver by the river") suffered considerably less flooding than other parts of the city, was the first to rebound following Katrina and is generally more affluent than many low-lying neighborhoods. The neighborhoods farther from the river were settled as the ability to drain swampland and protect the city from flooding increased. The most damaged white neighborhood of New Orleans, Lakeview, was developed in the early twentieth century on newly drained land near Lake Pontchartrain. This community rests five to seven feet below sea level and took on five to fifteen feet of water when the adjacent Seventeenth Street Canal was breached. In comparison, the French Quarter is nine feet above sea level

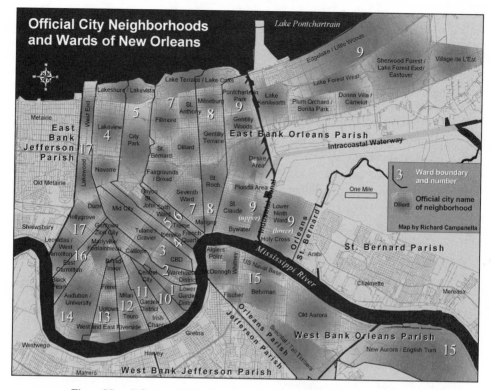

Fig. 1. New Orleans neighborhoods. (Map by Richard Campanella.)

and did not flood at all. Although the confidence of scientists and the avarice of developers combined to increase settlement by both whites and blacks in low-lying Orleans Parish throughout the twentieth century, the fact that the majority of the population was African American and historic housing patterns ensured that much of the higher ground was inhabited by whites meant that the impact of the storm and its aftermath was racially skewed.

Moreover, the lesson drawn by many New Orleanians from the multiple failures of government during Hurricane Katrina was that they are on their own. Local and state governments failed to prepare for and address the needs of citizens without access to cars, credit cards, and social networks outside the city or to facilitate their evacuation. Government was also directly responsible for the horrible conditions faced by those in the

Superdome and Convention Center in the days following the flooding. Although the victims were tax-paying citizens of a city, state, and country that acknowledge their responsibility to attend to the needs of communities in crisis, none of these entities was able to do so in a timely and efficient manner. While it is easy to argue that the corruption and incompetence that have long plagued New Orleans and Louisiana contributed mightily to these failures, which they no doubt did, to do so risks ignoring the equally inept federal response.

On one level, the increase in civic engagement following Katrina that Richard Campanella documents in his contribution to this collection can be attributed to the failure of government-run institutional and bureaucratic support systems and processes to engage and communicate with their constituents. Large nonprofit relief organizations such as the Red Cross, however, didn't seem to perform much better. The stories of success that came out of the receding floodwaters tended to feature individuals or small grassroots groups that came together in the face of a compelling need. And this pattern of institutional shortfalls and individualized achievement in the realm of civic engagement held true in higher education as well.

The institutions of higher education in New Orleans have unique histories that reflect the uneven growth of the city, and these disparities affected their recovery paths in the wake of the disaster. Higher education in New Orleans is dominated by the remnants of Jim Crow and the city's deeply rooted French Catholic traditions. It is home to the only historically black Catholic university in the country, Xavier University of Louisiana. It contains two public universities. One, the University of New Orleans (UNO), has historically served white students, while the other, Southern University of New Orleans (SUNO), is part of the Southern University System established by the state for African American students. Dillard University, the other private Historically Black College or University (HBCU) in New Orleans, emerged from Protestant roots to become a liberal arts college. The remaining major universities in the city, Loyola and Tulane, are majority white institutions. Loyola, like Xavier, is a Catholic university. Tulane, the only research institution in the city, historically served New Orleans' white elite.

The response of the universities to the devastation of New Orleans following Katrina varied widely. Under eleven feet of water for several weeks, SUNO is still struggling to rebuild. Dillard University, located in the Gentilly section of the city, took on eight feet of water and was unable to reopen its campus for a year. While Xavier also suffered flooding, it was not as extensive, and classes resumed on its campus in the spring of 2006. Loyola and Tulane suffered the least damage to their physical facilities (with the exception of Tulane's Medical School) because they are located on higher ground far from the levee breaches. Students and faculty at both schools returned to campuses minimally marked by flooding and wind damage. All of these universities, however, took a heavy financial hit, and all responded in part by laying off significant numbers of faculty and staff. Tulane also undertook a major restructuring of its schools, combining the sciences and engineering; separating the social sciences, arts, and humanities in their own new School of Liberal Arts; and wiping out a third of its doctoral programs, including those in economics, political science, sociology, English, and French. The manner in which the administrations of Loyola, Tulane, UNO, and SUNO handled these changes led to their censure by the American Association of University Professors (AAUP) in 2007.

Despite high levels of internal turmoil, the universities recognized their role as institutional citizens of a city in crisis and attempted to respond. The success of this response so far has been mixed. Xavier and Dillard are gathering resources to help rebuild their surrounding communities. Amy Koritz's institution, Tulane, emphasized community service by requiring all undergraduates to complete two service learning classes in order to graduate. It also established a new center focused on urban communities and an institute devoted to education policy. At the same time, however, it dismantled its program in civil engineering (the folks who build levees) and did away with doctoral programs in many of the disciplines that concentrate on urban environments. Because this kind of inconsistency is endemic in higher education, it suggests one way in which the crisis facing New Orleans can serve as a clarifying moment for higher education nationally. The very real demands of the bottom line required that any program too expensive and without adequate prestige or a strong enough constituency to justify its continued support be ruthlessly excised. The fact that many of these programs were the ones most needed to further the institution's stated commitment to improving its surrounding community was ignored. In consequence, we now have a structurally instantiated imperative (and, for some, a moral one) without the reservoir of knowledge and expertise needed to meet it, at least in the liberal arts.

To be a faculty member in a humanities discipline under such circumstances is not, except in degree, much different from being a faculty member in the humanities at most research universities in this country. And it is in this respect that the lessons of *Civic Engagement in the Wake of Katrina* are most generalizable. Despite the increased rhetoric and student requirements, civic engagement so far remains marginal to the way in which faculty members are evaluated and rewarded. For most faculty members and academic administrators, this is as it should be. As a research university, the dominant view at Tulane remains that peer-reviewed scholarly publication within a discipline is the only appropriate measure of professional productivity. Certainly teaching matters, as does service, but both are relatively less important. Further, Edward Zlotkowski's observation that "the agenda of a faculty member's discipline often takes precedence over his or her commitment to institutional priorities" holds true.[4] Thus, here, as elsewhere, the ability of an administration to insist on civic engagement by its faculty, even if the will to do so is present, remains limited. For a faculty member to choose civic engagement in the face of weak institutional support and a discipline-focused culture of setting priorities and allocating respect would seem close to suicidal. What the crisis of Katrina did, however, was present that choice starkly to the consciences of individuals. For some, the result has been a significant movement toward engagement. For others, it has been business as usual.

The consciences of individuals, however crucial to a just society, are an inadequate substitute for competent and responsive bureaucracies that are engaged and flexible enough to understand and address the needs of their constituencies in times of crisis. It is important to consider whether the failures that plagued New Orleans in 2005—and continue to do so—are unique to this place and circumstance or indicative of more widespread problems in the values and priorities that drive public agencies and large nonprofit institutions. Shortly after the storm, *Time* magazine quoted Louisiana representative Jim McCrery, who complained, "I've talked to the White House staff. I've talked to FEMA [Federal Emergency Management Agency]. I've talked with the Army. And, of course, I've talked with the state office of emergency preparedness. And nobody, federal or state, seems to know how to implement a decision, if we can get a decision."[5] This pervasive inability to act on the part of well-educated civil servants and their leaders begs for analysis. One such analysis was provided early on by the sociologist Harvey Molotch, who observed that in a well-functioning bureaucracy crisis provokes "a kind of panic of empathy that trumps organizational habit and individual postures."[6] Bureaucrats throw out the rule book and have faith that their superiors will support their decisions. In the aftermath of Katrina, this did not happen. Instead bureaucrats fell back on routine.

In higher education, similar issues emerged. The culture of competitive individualism that governs the careers of scholars and researchers encourages an uneasy combination of personal aggressiveness and organizational conformity that may not be in the best interests of Dewey's vision of education in a democracy. Like other professionals with obligations to the larger public good—clergy, health care workers, civil servants—educators are often caught between a path to professional advancement that rewards careerist behavior and the public's expectation that we serve a higher purpose. Postdiluvial New Orleans saw both. There were professors and students from around the country who made, and continue to make, real contributions to the city's recovery; in this volume, the essays on the Gulf South Youth Action Corps and *HOME, New Orleans* illustrate just two instances out of many. At the same time, the nonprofit sector in New Orleans was rife with reports of "drive-by" research and opportunistic grant writing that did not even attempt to engage local expertise.[7] Well-intentioned people can have honest disagreements about the value of such work, but there can be little question that local academics struggling to put their professional lives back together would have benefited enormously from being written into projects that they had neither the time nor energy to develop themselves, and to which they could have made real contributions. This too is a form of civic engagement.

For John Dewey, civil society's power to frame the problems and priorities to which expert professionals devote their energies determined whether those experts were playing their proper role in a democracy. He reasoned that ordinary citizens were best qualified to know their own concerns, even if the experts were best able to develop effective responses to them. His fear, however, was that expert professionals were losing their sense of connection and obligation to this population, instead developing their own insular caste and subculture. Thus, he warned, "A class of experts is inevitably so removed from common interests as to become a class with private interests and private knowledge, which in social matters is no knowledge at all."[8] Universities do the crucial work of reproducing and maintaining our society's pool of expertise. Do they have an allied obligation to ensure that ordinary citizens have the information and skills needed to direct the energies of experts in ways that best serve their families and communities? To the extent that Dewey is right in asserting that education is the midwife of democracy, educators bear a responsibility to ordinary citizens not shared by other professionals. This is the responsibility to ensure that citizens have the tools to insist on a socially effective use of expertise, not in its technical application but in defining the broad goals, and judging the success, of its application. To the extent that this responsibility is in real conflict with the understanding of professional expertise that guides the careers of many academics, we in academia have a problem.

Constructive civic engagement on the part of higher education, however, also requires community partners with the capacity and commitment to partner with university teachers and researchers in good faith. In New Orleans, effective citizen-driven action has frequently been inhibited by a lack of organizational capacity in distressed communities exacerbated by a political culture of insider patronage. The past and continuing poverty of the region plays a part in this circumstance. According to the Bureau of Governmental Research, a local, private, nonpartisan group, the percentage of government-subsidized rental households in New Orleans is holding steady at pre-Katrina levels. Sixty-five percent of the metropolitan region's very low income households live in the city as opposed to 70 percent prior to the storm.[9] The economic profile of New Orleans has changed little. The racial profile has shifted slightly, reducing the majority held by the African American population and increasing the Hispanic population.[10] Although pockets of well-organized civic action emerged, they were often driven by middle-class professionals with a stake in a specific neighborhood or issue.

Despite the high-profile posturing of government officials in the wake of natural and man-made disasters, weakly organized long-term responses seem to be characteristic of our era of neoconservative politics and colorblind racism. In the immediate aftermath of the 1992 Los Angeles riots, for example, under the watch of the first President Bush, the federal government also promised to revitalize South Central Los Angeles, while local government leaders enacted a plan to "Rebuild L.A." Most of the federal government's plan, however, consisted of blueprints already available to enact a "Conservative War on Poverty," consisting of the promotion of enterprise zones, a "Weed and Seed" program light on seeds but heavy on the incarceration of minority youth, and the privatization of school choice to allow parents to send their children to private schools with public dollars. Peter Ueberroth's Rebuild L.A. initiative also emphasized private initiatives over public sector improvements, and neither did much to slow down the rapid loss of jobs available to South Los Angeles residents. What Los Angeles needed, much like what New Orleans needs today, was an initiative along the lines of the Works Progress Administration (WPA) of the 1930s to resolve chronic joblessness, the lack of economic opportunity, and crumbling public infrastructure. Instead government officials have consistently relied on a private sector with little long-term commitment to bringing about fundamental change or social equity.[11]

Higher education enters into this situation primarily with short-term supplementary labor and expertise. While some civic organizations have developed ongoing relationships with university faculty members or programs (e.g., the relationship between Broadmoor and the Harvard School of Government described by Pat Evans and Sarah Lewis in this volume), the emerging model for university engagement in the city is a one-to-three-week "residency" where students and their faculty mentors contribute to a project defined by or in consultation with a nonprofit organization with sufficient administrative capacity to organize and help supervise such projects. For local universities, the dominant models remain single-day service projects and semester-long service learning assignments or internships.

Both general recovery efforts in New Orleans and the interventions of higher education through volunteerism have occurred in an era of neoliberalism in the United States that emphasizes privatization of the public sphere or what Lisa Duggan calls "the transfer of wealth and decision-making from public, more-or-less accountable decision-making bodies to individual or corporate, unaccountable hands."[12] In the wake of Katrina, most of the recovery work has been outsourced, from debris removal to levee reconstruction, with politically connected corporations reaping benefits without necessarily being subject to adequate public scrutiny. Likewise, university project managers and volunteer students are asked to perform vital services that were formerly performed by paid government employees, a situation that pushed at least one New Orleans historian, Lawrence N. Powell, to ask, "Can the methods of a nineteenth-century barn raising drag a twenty-first century disaster area from the mud and the muck?"[13] In what Powell refers to as a "market-focused recovery," how do individuals interested in sustained civic engagement navigate these ideological waters?

Civic engagement, under these conditions, will be understood by students to consist primarily of charity work and what might be termed "laboratories of practice." In the arts and humanities, in particular, it is extremely difficult to conceptualize and maintain partnerships that might enable students and professors to embark on sustained, reciprocal action in the surrounding community. The infrastructure required by such partnerships is beyond the capacity of individual faculty members without external funding, and university units charged with facilitating and overseeing engagement too often focus on short-term experiences. The complex reasons that make it difficult for universities to involve students in forms of engagement that model ongoing, collective, and collaborative action also threaten the ability of the arts and humanities disciplines to remake themselves so as to support such a goal. Despite ongoing efforts by many, including Ira Harkavy of the University of Pennsylvania, David Scobey of Bates College, and Julia Reinhardt Lupton of the University of California at Irvine, the ability of higher education to do otherwise is apparently limited.[14]

In New Orleans, these dominant forms of university-based engagement reinforce the tendency to organize civic action around the short-term goals of private voluntary associations and nonprofit organizations or around the pedagogical objectives of individual courses. What is missing is an ongoing dialogue that connects education with multidisciplinary strategies for addressing community needs and building on community assets. Perhaps this absence simply reflects the widespread laissez-faire attitude toward the public sphere that assumes it is nobody's responsibility in particular and certainly not that of higher education. Perhaps it is an unintended consequence of the confluence of a student focus on marketable credentials and a faculty reward system that encourages individual achievement at the expense of group endeavor. The danger, though, is that in the absence of concerted action universities will end up teaching students that civic engagement is ancillary to their lives as citizens.

Nevertheless, the ongoing push toward increased civic engagement in higher education is a positive development that should be supported through analysis of the dangers it poses as well as the potential it embodies. One critical question to ask is to what extent this rhetorical and actual advocacy of the civic responsibility of higher education also contributes to increased privatization of the public sphere. For example, government officials used the flooding that devastated the New Orleans school system as an opportunity to experiment with the privatization of the public system, more readily offering charter school startups than restoring long-standing, if always struggling, neighborhood schools. Individual actors from higher education are often critical to this trend toward privatization, offering short-term expertise to desperate parents and underfunded teachers willing to accept any help to get schools open and operational. The general trend toward privatization of community institutions can therefore be fundamentally supported in a time of recovery without thinking through the long-term implications for neighborhood survival and public responsibility. Indeed, this usually happens in such a way that local actors end up denigrating the public sector, if not the public sphere entirely, seeing the role of government in recovery and restoration as minimal or restricting, while enhancing the reputation of privatized solutions that have little chance of successfully remaining in place in the long run.[15] These fundamental issues need to be addressed by all who work in civic engagement, but they are especially urgent in a time of crisis and recovery when the failings of government seem so obvious. Crises should not prevent us from carefully examining the long-term consequences of private efforts, including those of higher education.

This volume is organized in part chronologically, in part by theme or emphasis. Given the diversity of voices, projects, and methodologies represented in this collection, we were pleasantly surprised by the relative coherence that emerged in the issues raised and the approaches to civic engagement taken by the authors. Most contributors tend, for example, to work toward building on the assets of a community rather than toward correcting its perceived deficits. This approach assumes that community members are knowledgeable about their own strengths, able to assess their community's weaknesses realistically, and interested in achieving collective goals that will benefit themselves and those around them. It assumes that civic engagement is always a two-way street, requiring deliberation and decision making on the part of all participants not just the experts. With roots in the community-organizing and education philosophies and practices of Saul Alinsky, Myles Horton, and Paolo Freire, such asset-based models of community development attempt to build social capital and expand the voices and agency of community members in their own shared future. Because university researchers, particularly in the social sciences, have often focused on reporting, analyzing, and putting forward solutions to the problems of communities not their own, an approach to civic engagement that challenges this model also challenges the ways in which university faculty members understand their roles in the places they study. Arguably, however, asset-based approaches to communities are well suited to the arts and humanities as currently practiced. Asset-based community development, with its focus on dialogue, shared learning, and respect for multiple perspectives, overlaps methodologically with the participatory pedagogies and attentiveness to the voices of the marginalized and disadvantaged common in these disciplines.

Although the contributors include social scientists, community organizers, and nonprofit leaders, more than half would identify themselves as artists or humanists. As such, they tend to place particular value on creative expression, dialogue, and the complex interrelations of place, history, and personal experience. They see the work of civic engagement in terms of relationships and discourses rather than institutions and outcomes. This emphasis on process, while not discounting the importance of completing projects and producing results, can lead to definitions of success that assign greater weight to participant-defined goals and qualitative measures of growth. Thus, the arts community in New Orleans has embraced the role of the arts in providing spiritual sustenance and healing, outcomes appropriately evaluated by subjective measures. Too often, though, those working in other sectors—such as housing, health care, the environment, or family services—perceive the arts and culture as secondary concerns to be addressed only after the many pressing issues in their own domains have been tackled. Overwhelmingly the contributors to this volume would disagree. They have, for example, seen the power of creative expression to strengthen youths' belief in their own agency, help them resist peer pressure, and find the support and information they need to make better choices. Neglecting such programs might, in fact, make it less likely that we would ever successfully address many of those other needs.

At the same time, for most local university-based artists (with the exception of those in Xavier University's Community Arts Program) the predominant mode of civic engagement rests on the "outreach" model. What, though, might change in the education and experience of university students in the arts and humanities if civic engagement did not stop with tutoring children, making famous artists and writers available for workshops in public schools, or providing free performances of Shakespeare's plays to local students? The implications of projects such as Mat Schwarzman's Creative Forces theater troupe and the multipartner community arts network of *HOME, New Orleans,* for how we think about the content and format of arts and humanities education are interesting and profound. What might a college curriculum in theater look like that was less oriented toward Broadway and Hollywood and more focused on the schools and community centers where so many ordinary citizens in fact experience the arts?[16]

This question, of course, gives rise to several others that transcend the arts and humanities disciplines. In multiple selections and a variety of contexts in this volume, contributors question the proper balance between respect for professional knowledge and open-door participation in planning and decision making. They acknowledge and worry about the fact that some of them have benefited professionally from the attention and sympathy extended to New Orleans after the floods. They also express concern over the ways and degree to which outside experts have exploited the laboratory provided by disaster in the service of their own agendas. These concerns raise questions that should be central to how university-based actors see their roles in communities. At the same time, just as academics will sometimes allow personal goals to outweigh their obligations to engage in equitable and mutually beneficial partnerships with communities, so will nonprofit and community leaders sometimes let the immediate goals of their organizations or their personal agendas blind them to the need for a larger perspective based on the multiple kinds of knowledge that universities bring to the table. Balance, well seasoned with transparency, is everything.

Finally, we would like to comment on the question of scale. There is a bias in this volume toward small-scale, close to the ground engagement, perhaps at the expense of projects involving larger, more established institutions or policy- and advocacy-oriented organizations. Despite Carole Rosenstein's plea to the arts community to focus on the policy implications of its programs and goals, as well as the fact that neighborhood associations do enter the policy arena, often effectively, the bias here is toward projects that enable individual voices to be heard. For artists and humanists, it may be difficult to proceed otherwise since the act of creative expression and the interpretive tools of close reading are skewed so markedly toward individual experience. The inevitable tension between the complex particularity of experience and the abstract requirements of policy documents poses a challenge to civic engagement in the arts and humanities. To what extent does preserving and valuing the experiences of small groups and individuals hamper our ability to participate significantly in conversations that might in fact impact policy? Perhaps civic engagement should take place on an integrated continuum of scales, self-consciously balancing the importance of grassroots and direct service contexts with broader and larger scale attempts to address issues requiring structural changes and legislative action.

These themes and questions surface in very different ways in a volume that combines contributions from teachers and scholars in higher education with those of nonprofit leaders and community activists. Including this range of voices and positions both conveys the array of strategies and activities undertaken on the ground and places the university in its proper context as one among many actors. For some contributors, however, the extreme dislocation of their experience surfaces in modes of discourse that transcend their social or institutional location. Particularly in the first section, "Coping with Disaster," readers will see on occasion the rhetorical consequences of having to negotiate between personal loss and uncertainty and professional norms of discourse. The eclecticism within and among these selections, which range in content from data-focused exposition to personal witness and in tone from objective analysis to emotional urgency, accurately reflects the disorderly process of making sense of catastrophe. While these contributors are positioned within universities, the centrality of that place to their sense of what needs to be conveyed to a national audience in this volume varies widely.

The insecurity of the role of higher education in organizing and launching successful responses to the needs of people struggling to rebuild becomes evident in the second section, "New Beginnings." Neither the visionary energy nor the specific programs and initiatives developed to lend immediate comfort and assistance to a damaged and rapidly changing population were the products of university leadership. While individuals situated in universities played a role in all of them—as consultants, collaborators, or documenters—the conception and implementation of these new beginnings emerged much closer to the ground. Small nonprofit organizations or faith-based groups in close contact with the needs and possibilities facing individuals and their families provided the urgency to implement responses, put programs in place quickly, and advocate for resources from sources of funding. It was here, not in the larger, better-resourced institutions of the city, that a "panic of empathy" took over. The need to act and act quickly motivated a powerful and often effective array of responses that provide multitudes of teachable moments for those of us in higher education.

Finally, and most hopefully, however, the crisis caused by this disaster has led to new connections, imaginative and productive collaborations, and a broadened appreciation for the role of culture in the rebuilding of communities. For the many times that those working in higher education failed to respond quickly or effectively to urgent needs, for the many times that opportunism and individual gain trumped strategic action for a larger good, there were an equal number of innovative and committed attempts to bring the knowledge and resources of intellectual and creative expertise to the communities of New Orleans. Perhaps it is in the final section of this collection, "Interconnections," that the astounding possibilities of genuine university-community partnership emerge. Even here, however, the reader will be hard pressed to find a single message, a unified platform for launching effective civic engagement. This necessary eclecticism of effort, however, need not translate into fragmentation. If the humanities, in particular, have a role to play in the emerging landscape of university-community collaborations in New Orleans—and perhaps nationally—it may well be in providing the interpretive glue that will surface, explain, and strengthen, through participation in the work of civic engagement, the connective tissue needed to secure a vibrant public sphere.

NOTES

The chapter-opening epigraphs are quoted from the following, respectively: Clyde Woods, "Katrina, Trap Economics, and the Rebirth of the Blues," *American Quarterly* 57:4 (December 2005): 1015–16; Harry C. Boyte, "A Different Kind of Politics," Dewey Lecture, University of Michigan, November 1, 2002; Imagining America: Artists and Scholars in Public Life, "The End of the Beginning: Report on the First Two Years," 2001, 4; and Joel Rene Morrissey, interview, "I-10 Witness Project," http://i10witness.org.

　　1. Woods, "Trap Economics," 1010.

　　2. Much of the information in this and the following paragraph comes from the work of Richard Campanella, particularly his most recent book, *Geographies of New Orleans* (Lafayette: Center for Louisiana Studies, 2006).

　　3. Greater New Orleans Community Data Center, Pre-Katrina Data Center Web site, www.gnocdc.org/prekatrinasite.html.

　　4. Edward Zlotkowski, "The Disciplines and the Public Good," in *Higher Education for the Public Good: Emerging Voices from a National Movement*, edited by Adrianna J. Kezar, Anthony C. Chambers, and John C. Burkhardt (San Francisco: Jossey Bass, 2005), 147.

　　5. Ripley, Amanda. "How Did This Happen?" *Time*, September 4, 2005.

　　6. Harvey Molotch, "Death on the Roof: Race and Bureaucratic Failure," in *Understanding Katrina: Perspectives from the Social Sciences*, September 20, 2005, http://understandingkatrina.ssrc.org.

　　7. As a local folklorist quoted in the *Chronicle of Higher Education* put it, "Y'all couldn't even pick up the phone and see if we can collaborate?" Jennifer Howard, "Stories from the Storm," *Chronicle of Higher Education*, September 14, 2007, A10–11.

8. John Dewey, *The Public and Its Problems* (Denver: Alan Swallow, [1927] 1960), 207.

9. Bruce Eggler, "La. Policies Concentrate Poverty," *Times-Picayune*, September 17, 2007, B1.

10. The numbers are difficult to pin down because they are still in flux. According to the Census Bureau's 2006 figures, the Orleans Parish population was then approximately 59 percent African American. See the Greater New Orleans Community Data Center's Web site for more information (gnocdc.org).

11. See Melvin L. Oliver, James H. Johnson Jr., and Walter C. Farrell Jr., "Anatomy of a Rebellion: A Political-Economic Analysis," in *Reading Rodney King, Reading Urban Uprising*, edited by Robert Gooding-Williams (New York: Routledge, 1993), 132–35, for the best analysis of the immediate government response in the aftermath of the 1992 Los Angeles riots.

12. Lisa Duggan, *The Twilight of Equality? Neoliberalism, Cultural Politics, and the Attack on Democracy* (Boston: Beacon, 2003), 12.

13. Lawrence N. Powell, "What Does American History Tell Us about Katrina and Vice Versa?" *Journal of American History* 94:3 (December 2007): 874.

14. For one analysis of why this might be the case, see Barbara Holland, "Institutional Differences in Pursuing the Public Good," in *Higher Education for the Public Good: Emerging Voices from a National Movement*, edited by Adrianna J. Kezar, Anthony C. Chambers, and John C. Burkhardt (San Francisco: Jossey Bass, 2005), 235–59.

15. See George J. Sanchez, *Crossing Figueroa: The Tangled Web of Diversity and Democracy*, Imagining America: Foreseeable Futures, no. 4 (Ann Arbor: Imagining America, 2005), for a fuller description of this dilemma for civic engagement work in our era.

16. Those interested in learning more about community-based arts should consult the many articles posted on the Community Arts Network Web site, www.communityarts.net. See also Arlene Goldbard, *The Art of Community Cultural Development* (Oakland: New Village, 2006).

SECTION 1

———— ❧❧ ————

Coping with Disaster

Amy Koritz

WHEN I RETURNED TO NEW ORLEANS in January 2006, Richard Campanella was one of the first people I found at my university who was actively engaged in studying and supporting recovery efforts. As a geographer who is fascinated with the intersection of physical and cultural space, Rich had been cruising the city on his bicycle, counting business openings and documenting other signs of recovery. He had also been following the public controversy over whether or not the city of New Orleans should reduce its footprint, consolidating the smaller population it now had on higher ground. His scientific training gave him an acute appreciation for the discouraging data on soil subsidence and wetlands loss that made all of South Louisiana more vulnerable to hurricanes. At the same time, he knew from his study of the history of New Orleans how deeply attached its people are to this place. His thinking about how to adjudicate the competing imperatives of science and home led finally to an op-ed piece in the local paper. This column both challenged the data being used by those, such as the geologist Timothy M. Kusky, who argued that New Orleans was too vulnerable to natural disaster to justify rebuilding at all and acknowledged the often irrational nature of the stance that argued for rebuilding all of New Orleans exactly where it was before the storm.[1] Coming from a discipline itself torn between the hard sciences and the softer end of the social sciences, he used all the tools available to him as a geographer to try to gain an understanding of the complexity of the civic engagement after Katrina. He also knew that these tools alone were not enough.

Richard Campanella inhabits the creative margins of the university. His primary appointment is in an interdisciplinary research center focused on the environment, where disciplinary turf is not defended quite so vigorously as elsewhere. Both Pat Evans and Sarah Lewis likewise occupy ancillary locations within the complex bureaucracy of higher education. Sarah is a graduate student. Engaged in an apprenticeship by turns inspiring and disillusioning, she hopes to one day join the ranks of tenure-line professors and thereby move into serving the central educational mission of higher education. Pat Evans's background and current position are altogether different. She has never held an academic appointment, does not hold a terminal degree in any discipline, and has taken a career path that violates all professional decorum. Pat has managed political campaigns, produced documentary films, worked in government agencies, and participated in efforts to mediate ethnic strife in Cyprus and the Baltic. She eventually returned to New Orleans and founded the International Project for Nonprofit Leadership. Although it is housed in the University of New Orleans, this program's focus is on building the capacities of nonprofit and community-based organizations.

A native New Orleanian with family roots in the city that go back generations, Pat felt personally the horrible loss of memories, histories, places, and people that afflicted New Orleans. I first met her at a meeting of Unified Non-profits, a sort of support group for people working in the nonprofit sector that emerged after the storm to provide a place to exchange information, leads on jobs, funding, or space and to share the pain of caring for too many needs with too few resources. Pat and I were often the only people from higher education in the room. But this is not to suggest that those in the local universities were disengaged. Many were, like us, trying to use the tools we had to get the work done that we saw before us. One of these was Michael Mizell-Nelson. Trained as a historian, he felt an imperative to document and preserve the massive dislocations unfolding before him. In establishing the Hurricane Digital Memory Bank, a collaboration with the Center for History and New Media, Michael attempted to provide a location to house the vast array of stories, images, and experiences that make up Katrina's legacy in New Orleans. He had earlier written and produced a documentary film on the history of the streetcar lines in the city and was familiar with the use of digital technologies in archiving and distributing historical information for public use. My memory of reconnecting with him following the storm consists of several informal, almost random conversations, episodes in the struggle many of us back in the city faced in finding the place in its recovery that would allow our skills to best serve the needs of our communities. The difficulty of achieving this match was often extraordinary. Some of this frustration emerges in Michael's essay as he describes the problems he and his colleagues faced in locating funding for their work while managing the financial, physical, and emotional challenges of putting their lives back together in a ruined city.

In some ways, those academics whose area of research focused on New Orleans prior to the storm benefited from the disaster. What previously looked like a local and parochial interest suddenly took on national importance. For many local professors, however, the work they pursued post-Katrina was really a mode of coping with tragedy. We fell back on what we knew how to do as the vehicle for our response to a community in crisis. Sometimes this work became therapeutic, enabling us to deal constructively with our own sense of loss and lack of control over our environment. Scholarly and creative productivity merged with personal and social needs to engage, get out of ourselves, and contribute something that made sense to us. Rebecca Mark's long poem/prose composition detailing the evacuation of her family blends the poet's commitment to emotional truth with the historian's need to bear witness. One section of a series of "Katrina Poems" written in 2005 and 2006, this piece details the confusing, stressful reality of having to remake one's life on an almost daily basis as the storm and its aftermath unfolded. The trajectory of her family's movement—east, north, west, then east and north again—was replicated in many variations by thousands of the displaced. It is hard to recover the deep uncertainty that afflicted this population in the weeks and months immediately following the levee breaches. Rebecca's piece reminds us that civic engagement is the work of individuals with families, relatives, homes, pets—the complicated personal webs that each of us inhabits.

The essays in this section reflect modes of coping with disaster that vary with the personalities, professional skills, intellectual interests, and personal circumstances of the contributors. They embody the diversity of languages and experiences the authors brought with them to that disaster and therefore also a multiplicity of ways of making sense of worlds being remade by it before their eyes. The scope and meaning of civic engagement in the wake of Katrina encompasses all of these perspectives. It includes the clearheaded scholarship of Rich Campanella. It embraces the impassioned mixture of professional imperatives with personal outrage and loss conveyed by Sarah Lewis, Pat Evans, and by Michael Mizell-Nelson. It also acknowledges the need to bear creative witness to the individual experience of dislocation found in Rebecca Mark's contribution. These selections embody most closely the tension between the scholarly protocols of analytic distance and the passionate immediacy of circumstance that often motivates civic engagement.

NOTE

1. An expanded version of this piece appeared as Richard Campanella, "Geography, Philosophy, and the Build/No-Build Line." *Technology in Society* 29, no. 2 (April 2007): 169–72.

"Bring Your Own Chairs"

CIVIC ENGAGEMENT IN
POSTDILUVIAL NEW ORLEANS

⚜——————————————————————⚜

Richard Campanella

August 28, 2005: Dr. Ivor Van Heerdon, a scientist at Louisiana State University, states unequivocally in a CNN interview that New Orleans "is definitely going to flood. . . . This is what we've been saying has been going to happen for years." After his prediction comes true the next day, Van Heerdon emerges as the most prominent of a small number of university-based scientists who break from academic confines and engage vigorously in the civic arena.[1]

On the morning of August 29, 2005, Hurricane Katrina's residual category 5 surge of Gulf of Mexico water penetrated a network of man-made navigation and drainage canals and inundated the heart of the sea-level-straddling New Orleans metropolis. It overtopped, undermined, or disintegrated certain levees and flood walls along those waterways, transforming the otherwise weakening category 2 or 3 wind event into a fatal deluge of unprecedented proportions. Nearly every hydrological sub-basin on Orleans Parish's eastern bank of the Mississippi River, plus all those in neighboring St. Bernard Parish and one in Jefferson, drowned in brackish water, starting from their below-sea-level nether regions and progressing to areas as high as three to four feet above sea level. Hundreds of citizens perished; tens of thousands of survivors waded to high ground or waited on rooftops for helicopter rescue.

August 29 through early September 2005: In the ultimate display of civic engagement, hundreds of Louisianans rescue thousands of their fellow citizens by boat and vehicle under potentially deadly conditions. Federally, only the Coast Guard matches their timely heroism.

Nearly a million residents of the metropolitan region who had evacuated earlier watched with the rest of the stunned world as the apocalypse unraveled on television. It was not until September 4, after a harrowing week of human suffering, government failures, and individual heroism, that the last of the stranded citizens were evacuated to safety—and an unknown future. The effect of this searing shared trauma may never be fully appreciated, but it played heavily into the passionate public discourse that followed.

August 31, 2005: Ms. Mae's Bar on the corner of Napoleon and Magazine reopens and soon becomes a meeting place for neighbors who weathered the storm. It is the first of hundreds of local establishments to serve as civic engagement nodes.[2]

The "lost September" of 2005 found scattered New Orleanians grappling with the lower tiers of Maslow's hierarchy of needs, ranging from immediate matters of food, clothing, and shelter to long-term uncertainties about loved ones, homes, jobs, possessions, and finances. Residents of less-damaged Jefferson Parish and the West Bank of Orleans Parish trickled back during September's second week, while harder-hit East Bank Orleans and St. Bernard Parish residents awaited word from officials. Then category 5 Hurricane Rita struck, destroying coastal southwestern Louisiana, reflooding parts of New Orleans, and further delaying reinhabitation. It was not until early October that significant numbers of residents and basic services tenuously returned to unflooded areas. Even then, Hurricane Wilma—the third category 5 tempest in two months, which affected the Yucatan and Florida peninsulas—further shook residents' faith in the city's drastically compromised infrastructure. Only about 100,000 New Orleanians of the pre-Katrina population of approximately 450,000 occupied their homes by the last quarter of 2005. A city that was formerly predominantly African American and working class or poor was now mostly white, better educated, and professional. As in a frontier town, men outnumbered women, elders were few, children were practically nonexistent, and transient laborers seemingly materialized out of nowhere, toiling off the books from dawn to dusk and sleeping in cars and tents.

October 2, 2005: After a monthlong absence for the first time since 1718, religious services return to New Orleans. "People from every walk of life, dressed in their Sunday best or in blue jeans, packed every pew in the historic St. Louis Cathedral," reported the Times-Picayune. *A poll later showed that Louisianians gave highest marks to religious organizations (followed by nonprofits) in their hurricane response, far ahead of all levels of government.*[3]

For all the tragedy and uncertainty, life in New Orleans in the autumn of 2005 proved extraordinary. At once reeling and resilient, the reconvening community exhibited the qualities of a frontier town crossed with a dysfunctional third world city. While mold and silence enveloped the flooded ruins of much of the city, higher-elevation areas buzzed with the sounds of saws and hammers. Historic Magazine Street became the "village's" bustling new main street, with 16 percent of its businesses reopening within six weeks of the storm and over 90 percent by Christmas.[4] "Welcome Home" banners were draped across eager storefronts; proclamations of rebuilding appeared on billboards and in graffiti; and placards offering house gutting, house shoring, roof repair, and legal services ("Saw Levee Breach? Call Us Now!") cluttered intersections to such a degree that local governments banned them for public safety. Locals reclaimed the once-touristy French Quarter as a place to conduct business, bank, worship, convene, eat, shop for groceries, recreate, and reside (albeit temporarily). Patrons at local restaurants ordered staples off paper menus for cash only, waited patiently on short staffs, and took it in stride when blackouts interrupted their dinners. Flaky utilities, limited hours at grocery stores, curfews enforced by soldiers with M-16 rifles, and other occupationlike conditions turned mundane errands into achievements. In the flooded region, what passed for good news was the moldy piles of personal possessions heaped unceremoniously in front of gutted houses, a sign, at the very least, of life. Violent crime, once pervasive, disappeared almost entirely as its perpetrators, drawn disproportionately from the social classes affected most fundamentally by the catastrophe, remained evacuated.

October 9, 2005: The city's first post-Katrina jazz funeral wends its way through the Seventh Ward, commemorating a famed Creole chef who died during the evacuation. Unique traditions such as second-line parades, Mardi Gras Indians, and Carnival celebrations offer opportunities for citizens to reengage with each other through civic rituals.

Fig. 2. Cityscapes of resiliency, cityscapes of engagement. (a) first post-Katrina jazz funeral, October 2005; (b) "No Surrender—Yet," declares a hair stylist on Magazine Street, November 2005; (c) the Unified New Orleans Plan "Community Congress" planning meeting, December 2006 (note the artist capturing the event at lower right); (d) poignant graffiti in the Fifth Ward, December 2005. (Photos by Richard Campanella.)

A cityscape of resiliency emerged as the first autumn cool fronts mercifully ended the hyperactive 2005 hurricane season. Those fortunate enough to return home seemed to recognize the history they were both living and making, and they moved about with a sense of purpose. Human interaction was electric: emotional reunions erupted in noisy, crowded coffee shops, which, along with restaurants and houses of worship, served as important social and civic engagement nodes. Conversations began with "So how'd you make out?!" continued with war stories and reconstruction visions, and ended with "Stay safe!" Strangers at adjacent tables joined in conversations and debates and left with exchanged phone numbers and e-mail addresses. Patrons pecked away at wireless-enabled laptops—the unsung technological heroes of post-Katrina New Orleans—to reestablish social, educational, and professional networks or fight with insurance adjusters and the Federal Emergency Management Agency (FEMA). Everyone dropped Dickensian lines: a tale of two cities . . . best of times, worst of times. . . .

Best of times? In some strange ways, it was. Citizens were intensely engaged with each other with a view toward overcoming tragedy and solving mutual problems. Of course, those who lived in that *other* city, and were suffering the *worst of times*, were largely absent from the inspiring postdiluvial tableau. Their stories played out beyond the Orleans Parish limits.

Each morning presented new and unpredictable adventures through unchartered waters, and everyone agreed that only one source could reliably guide the way: a fresh copy of *Times-Picayune*. The venerable daily, long a target of local adoration as well as disdain, was now everyone's darling, having heroically covered the apocalypse firsthand ("We Publish Come Hell AND High Water") and reported on the recovery with journalistic objectivity blended with proactive investigation and steadfast demands for accountability. Citizens purchased the "T-P" at vending machines (home delivery was still months away) or navigated its Byzantine nola.com Web page and devoured the latest news like the figure in Richard Woodville's *War News from Mexico*.

Autumn 2005 to the present: A steady stream of faith-based groups, college classes, students on break, and civic and professional organizations from across the nation arrange "voluntourism" visits to the city, helping to gut houses, clean parks, and build homes in union with local citizens. The remarkable phenomenon is viewed as a triumph of civic spirit over bureaucratic lethargy.

High-stakes concerns about flood protection, contamination, health, education, residents' right to return, economic recovery, coastal restoration, and myriad other postdiluvial issues drove the energized public discourse. To help address the litany of problems, Mayor C. Ray Nagin had formed, on September 30, 2005, the Bring New Orleans Back Commission (BNOB) inside what the *New York Times* described as "the heavily fortified Sheraton Hotel on Canal Street, a building surrounded almost constantly by cleanup crews as well as beefy private security guards armed with weapons."[5] That hotel, as well as the First Baptist Church in one of the few unflooded sections of Lakeview, would serve as venues for scores of public meetings attended by thousands of concerned citizens.

Committees and subcommittees tackled a wide range of topics, but one topped the list and inspired the most passionate response: should the city's urban "footprint"—particularly its twentieth-century sprawl into low-lying areas adjacent to surge-prone water bodies—be "shrunk" to keep people out of harm's way? Or should the entire footprint "come back" in the understanding that federal levee failure, not nature, had ultimately caused (or, rather, failed to prevent) the deluge? That fundamental question fell under the domain of the BNOB's Urban Planning Committee.

November 2005: In response to high levels of public interaction, the Times-Picayune *launches a special column (called "Meetings") entirely devoted to announcing meetings and another listing key contact information ("Meetings and Websites").*

As a geographer and longtime New Orleans researcher, I pondered the footprint question and sketched out a methodology to try to answer it. It involved measuring four important variables—residents' desire to return, structural safety, historical and architectural significance, and environmental and geographical safety—and mapping out the results to inform decisions on neighborhoods' futures. Encouraged by a conversation with a stranger in a coffee shop—civic engagement in its rawest form—I contributed it to the e-mail circuit. It made its way to the chairman of the BNOB, which resulted in an invitation to present it to the Urban Planning Committee and eventually to publish it as a guest editorial in the *Times-Picayune*. The essay appeared precisely as representatives from the Urban Land Institute (ULI) arrived in town to advise the BNOB on, among other things, the footprint issue.

I later learned that ULI members had "hotly debated" my proposed methodology but decided not to endorse it because of the difficulty of measuring the first variable (desire to return).[6] I was told that the proposal did help frame the footprint question as a balancing act between undeniable scientific realities, on one hand, and cherished cultural and humanistic values on the other. Subsequent public meetings with capacity crowds and long lines of testifiers proved that this balancing act weighed heavily on everyone's mind. "In a city that has seen a resurgence of civic activism since [Katrina]," wrote the *Times-Picayune*,

> more than 200 people attended the [ULI] meeting to voice their opinions about what shape New Orleans should take in the future. The resounding refrain: Learn from our history. Many residents told the 37-member Urban Land Institute panel to use the original footprint of the city—along the Mississippi river and its high ridges—as a guide for land use.[7]

Those two hundred people, however, were mostly residents of the "high ridges" they recommended for prioritization. Residents of low-lying areas, mostly flooded, were sparsely represented at the meeting but nevertheless managed to engage through their political representatives, the Internet, and commuting. Their stance (shared by many in higher areas) was firm: the entire city will return, and the footprint will remain precisely as before the storm.

December 2005: The recently formed Citizens for 1 Greater New Orleans, launched largely by wealthy uptown women, commences a determined, no-nonsense effort to consolidate parochial levee boards and unify redundant tax assessors. The group gathers 46,600 signatures by mid-December and eventually succeeds spectacularly in both aims.[8]

When the ULI finally issued its recommendations to the BNOB—via a long PowerPoint presentation that was at once wordy and carefully worded—it gently advocated footprint shrinkage through the allocation of recovery investments first to the highest and least-damaged areas and only later to the depopulated flooded region. The news hit the front page of the *Times-Picayune* in the form of an intentionally confusing map of three purple-shaded "investment zones" in which Investment Zone A, despite its optimistic label, was recommended for delayed rebuilding at best and possibly for conversion to green space.[9]

The wordsmithing and mapsmithing fooled no one. "Don't Write Us Off, Residents Warn: Urban Land Institute Report Takes a Beating," scowled the headlines after the recommendations sunk in. The article continued:

> Elected officials and residents from New Orleans' hardest-hit areas on Monday responded with skepticism and, at times, outright hostility to a controversial proposal to eliminate their neighborhoods from post-Katrina rebuilding efforts.
>
> Even Mayor Ray Nagin . . . said he is reserving judgment on [whether] to abandon, at least for the near term, some of the city's lowest-lying ground. . . . During the meeting, Nagin reiterated his intention to ultimately "rebuild all of New Orleans. . . ."
>
> [City Council member Cynthia] Willard Lewis spoke with particular disdain for ULI's "color-coded maps" which divide the city into three "investment zones": areas to be rehabilitated immediately, areas to be developed partially, or areas to be re-evaluated as potential sites for mass buyouts and future green space. Those maps, she said, are "causing people to lose hope," and others to stay away.[10]

Indicating the reductionist power of maps—a reoccurring theme in the footprint debate—one local politician, "noting that she was wearing a pink blouse . . . said sarcastically that she should have worn purple, the map color used by ULI for sections of the city that suffered the worst flood damage."[11]

December 2005: Uptown woman launches Levees for Greater New Orleans, later known as levees.org, to promote federal accountability for the Katrina flood and improved protection from future storms. The organization represents citizen engagement in matters traditionally left to engineers and scientists.

Mayor Nagin found himself in a bind since ULI's advice was intended specifically for the benefit of his BNOB. He assured an agitated public that "once the recommendations are finalized . . . it will be up to the commission members and the community to evaluate it, kick the tires, say we like this and we don't like this."[12]

Kick its tires the community did. The ULI report ratcheted up civic engagement in post-Katrina New Orleans markedly. It, as well as a similar consultation from the Philadelphia-based design firm Wallace, Roberts and Todd, became gist for further rounds of highly attended and increasingly polemical BNOB meetings during December 2005 and January 2006.

December 8, 2005: Tulane University president Scott Cowan issues a "Renewal Plan" for post-Katrina recovery, declaring that Tulane, long considered aloof and disengaged from local realities, "will play an important role in the rebuilding" and that students will "develop a [mandatory] commitment to community outreach and public service through the creation of a Center for Public Service."[13]

Finally, on January 11, 2006, the Urban Planning Committee of the BNOB unveiled its final recommendations. Like ULI, the group (sometimes referred to as the Land Use Committee) communicated its findings through a hefty PowerPoint presentation rather than traditional literary methods. Entitled the "Action Plan for New Orleans: The New American City," the sixty-nine-page presentation's dizzying array of proclamations, factoids, bulleted lists, graphics, and platitudes seemed eager to placate all sides while sacrificing lucidity in the process. Audience members hungry for a clear answer to the footprint question grew agitated at the recommendation of a moratorium on building permits until May 2006 for heavily damaged neighborhoods. During those four months, residents themselves would have to demonstrate their neighborhood's "viability," a recommendation that cleverly placed the burden of proving neighborhood wherewithal on the backs of the most vocal full-footprint activists. Further insight into the BNOB's position regarding the footprint question came in the form of a map, revealed halfway through the presentation, entitled the "Parks and Open Space Plan." It depicted Orleans Parish with the usual cartographic overlays of street networks and water bodies. At the bottom of its legend was a dashed green line indicating "Areas for Future Parkland," which corresponded to a series of six large circles sprinkled throughout certain low-lying residential neighborhoods.

January 2006: Local television stations bring back on-air editorials, "a vanished practice on most local TV newscasts around the country," while one station launches a nightly civic education and activism forum for "the sheer need to [address] the issues that all of us are going through right now. . . . People who are being asked to make decisions on [rebuilding] need more than just a sound bite."[14]

The next morning, the *Times-Picayune* featured the map on its front page. The newspaper's adaptation transformed the dashed circles, which cartographically suggested a certain level of conjecture and abstraction, into semiopaque green dots labeled "approximate areas expected to become parks and greenspace." The dots covered so much terrain with such apparent cartographic confidence that many readers interpreted them to represent discrete polygons rather than dimensionless abstractions merely suggesting some neighborhood parks. *If my house lies within the "green dot,"* many readers presumed, *it will be "green spaced" into wetlands.* Just as citizens in November had seized on ULI's "purple investment zone" map as the parapraxis of that organization's underlying footprint philosophy, citizens now saw this "Green Dot Map" as a Freudian slip revealing the BNOB's hidden agenda. The response was livid. Said one man to committee chairman Joseph Canizaro, whose day job as a major real estate investor was not viewed as coincidental by some skeptical citizens, "Mr. Joe Canizaro, I don't know you, but I hate you. You've been in the background trying to scheme to get our land!"[15]

"4 MONTHS TO DECIDE," blared the *Times-Picayune* headline; "Nagin Panel Says Hardest Hit Areas Must Prove Viability"; "City's Footprint May Shrink."[16] The infamous Green Dot Map entered the local lexicon even as it motivated residents of heavily damaged neighborhoods to demonstrate "viability" and save their neighborhoods. *Green space*, a benign notion elsewhere in urban America, became a dirty word in postdiluvial New Orleans.

Early 2006: Women of the Storm, a consortium of mostly upper-income citizens, marches on Washington, DC, with iconic blue umbrellas in hand. They demand congressional engagement to resolve New Orleans' troubles, arranging specifically for congressional visits to the damaged city.

What ensued, starting in late January 2006, was one of the most remarkable episodes of civic engagement in recent American history. Scores of grassroots neighborhood associations, civic groups, and homeowners' associations formed organically sans professional expertise and usually with zero funding. Web sites went up, e-mails circulated, and signs popped up on once-flooded lawns (Broadmoor Lives! I Am Coming Home! I Will Rebuild! I Am New Orleans!), and impromptu venues were arranged. One association in the heavily flooded Lake Bullard neighborhood, lacking a decent venue but not an ounce of determination, demurely asked attendees to "bring their own chairs."[17] Despite their tenuous life circumstances and other responsibilities, New Orleanians by the thousands joined forces with their neighbors and volunteered to take stock of their communities; document local history, assets, resources, and problems; and plan solutions for the future.

February 2006: The first post-Katrina Mardi Gras unfurls with small but enthusiastic and predominantly local crowds. The festivities demonstrate the city's ability to handle major functions. The national and international reaction, initially skeptical, is transformed into one of endearment and admiration. This annual ritual is its own form of civic engagement.

So many grassroots neighborhood planning associations were formed that umbrella associations arose to coordinate the dealings among them. One, the Neighborhood Partnership Network, listed at least seventy fully active neighborhood organizations within Orleans Parish alone, while many more in poorer areas strove to coalesce.[18] Their names formed a veritable "where's where" of famous New Orleans places—the French Quarter Citizens, Inc.; Audubon Riverside Neighborhood Association; Bouligny Improvement Association; Faubourg St. Roch Improvement Association; Algiers Point Association—but also included less famous modern subdivisions more likely to occupy lower ground and suffer higher flood risk—the Lake Bullard Homeowners Association, Inc.; Venetian Isles Civic and Improvement Association; Lake Terrace Neighborhood Property Owners Association.

In some cases, such as that of the stellar Broadmoor Improvement Association, professional help arrived from outside (Harvard University), and funding aided the planning process. Many associations eventually produced fine neighborhood plans and, perhaps more importantly, empowered their members to meet their neighbors and learn about their environs, past and future, to degrees unimaginable a year earlier.

One crude way to measure this civic engagement is to compute the number of times the terms *civic association* or *neighborhood association* appeared in *Times-Picayune* articles or announcements as queried through Lexis-Nexus. Before the storm, when roughly 450,000 to 455,000 people lived in the city, those key words appeared at a steady pace of 40 to 45 times per month. That rate dropped to zero during the lost September of 2005 but returned to normal rates by early 2006 despite the dramatic drop in population. After January 2006—when the Green Dot Map inadvertently

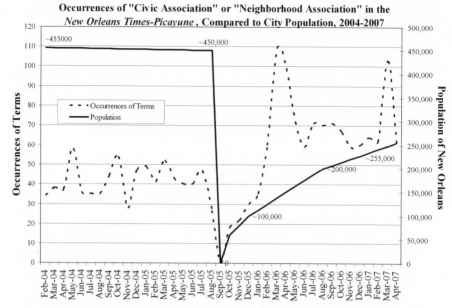

Occurrences of "Civic Association" or "Neighborhood Association" in the *New Orleans Times-Picayune*, Compared to City Population, 2004-2007

Months prior to and after Hurricane Katrina (August 29, 2005)

Fig. 3. This graph plots the pre- and post-Katrina city populations against the frequency of appearance of the terms *neighborhood association* or *civic association* in local newspaper announcements. By this measure, civic engagement on the part of New Orleanians increased roughly four to seven times (relative to population) following Hurricane Katrina. (Analysis and graph by Richard Campanella.)

kick-started the grassroots planning effort—the terms appeared up to 103 times per month before stabilizing by summertime to around 70. When the figures are normalized for population differences, neighborhood associations were literally "making news" in post-Katrina New Orleans at least four times, and up to seven times, the rate in prediluvial times *despite* the new hardships of life in the struggling city.[19] A statistical sampling of 362 "meeting" announcements posted in the *Times-Picayune* between November 2005 and April 2007 (from a total population of over 1,000) revealed that fully 48 percent represented neighborhood association meetings and another 19 percent represented civic groups unaffiliated with specific neighborhoods.[20]

In a later editorial on "the curse of the Green Dot," *Times-Picayune* columnist Stephanie Grace reflected on the episode. "You know the Green Dot," she reminded her readers.

> In a move that will go down as one of the great miscalculations of post-Katrina planning, [the ULI and BNOB] designated the off-limits areas with green dots. Around town, people picked up the paper that morning and saw, for the first time, that their neighborhoods could be slated for demolition. To say they didn't take the news well is an understatement.
>
> "People felt threatened when they saw the green dot," LaToya Cantrell, president of the Broadmoor Improvement Association, would say months later. "All hell broke loose." . . . City Councilwoman Cynthia Willard-Lewis, who represents the hard-hit Lower 9th Ward and Eastern New Orleans, said the green dots made many of her African-American constituents flash back to the civil rights era, thinking they would need to fight for equal access all over again. *The maps, she said soon after they were unveiled, "are causing people to lose hope."*[21]

Ironically, the very recommendations that motivated the formation of grassroots associations—the Green Dot Map, the permit moratorium, and the threat of "green spacing" if neighborhood viability were not demonstrated by May 2006—ended up torpedoing the very commission that issued them. Mayor Nagin, embroiled in an election campaign that attracted national interest, rejected the advice of his own commission. Fatally undermined despite its worthwhile contributions beyond the footprint issue, the BNOB disbanded unceremoniously. Talk of footprint shrinkage among the mayoral candidates became the proverbial "third rail" of local politics in large part because certain engaged citizens and their representatives had, for better or worse, yelled it off the table.

Spring 2006: Mayoral campaign attracts international interest and galvanizes civic engagement among both returned and displaced New Orleanians. Yet it remains high even after Mayor Nagin is reelected on May 20.

After Mayor Nagin cinched reelection in the closely watched race, the great footprint debate largely disappeared from public discourse. The mayor's "laissez-faire" repopulation and rebuilding stance, which was more of a default position than an articulated strategy, settled the footprint question by saying, in essence, *let people return and rebuild as they can and as they*

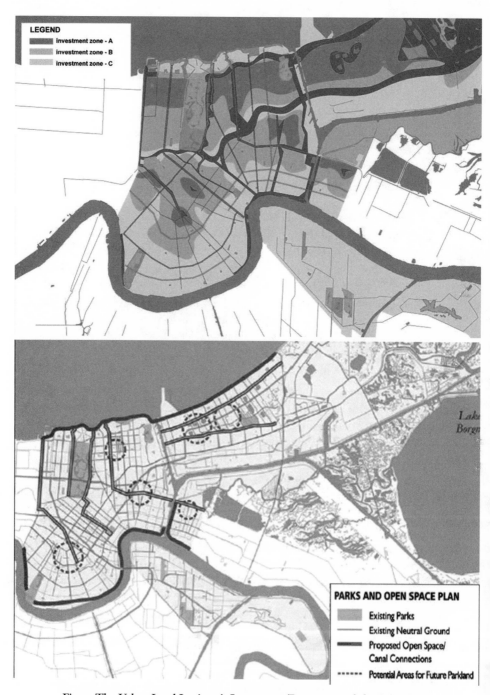

Fig. 4. The Urban Land Institute's Investment Zone map and the Bring New Orleans Back Commission's Parks and Open Space Plan (which appeared on the front page of the *Times-Picayune* and became known as the Green Dot Map) brought the controversial issue of "footprint shrinkage" to the forefront of civic discourse. (Maps by the Urban Land Institute and Bring New Orleans Back Commission.)

wish, and we'll act on the patterns as they fall into place. Federal complicity bore responsibility as well: FEMA's updated Advisory Base Flood Elevation maps—which drive flood insurance availability and rates—turned out to be largely the same as the old 1984 maps, thus seemingly communicating federal endorsement (as well as actuarial encouragement) to homeowners deliberating on whether to rebuild in low-lying areas. Road Home (a state-administered recovery program) monies provided no special incentive to do otherwise, and no federal compensation fund awaited those homeowners and businesses that would have been affected by a hypothetical footprint-shrinkage decision.

The entire city *could* come back, but what that city would look and function like still remained an open question. Additional planning efforts would ensue, provoking more civic engagement among meeting-weary New Orleanians.

August 29, 2006: The first anniversary of the storm is marked with a wide range of civic remembrances. The front page of the prior Sunday's Times-Picayune *salutes the past year's civic engagement, reporting "Katrina Generates Wave of Activism; Myriad Groups Aim to Reshape Region."*[22]

One new planning effort sprang from the New Orleans City Council, which, historically competitive with the mayor's office and concerned about losing ground to Mayor Nagin's BNOB, belatedly joined the discourse. "With more and more New Orleans neighborhoods launching post-Katrina planning efforts on their own," wrote the *Times-Picayune,* "the City Council is trying to bring some order and overall direction to the process."[23] It hired Paul Lambert and Sheila Danzey from Miami to convene citizens throughout the flooded region and draw up a series of neighborhood plans. The planners scheduled simultaneous meetings with scores of neighborhood associations even as the public still mulled over the findings of the earlier BNOB and ULI efforts. Some wags described the overlapping efforts as "plandemonium."

November 2006: In a city reputedly more interested in musical escapism than civic discourse, a local radio station switches from a classic rock format to all-talk programming led by local hosts. Reason: "post-Katrina information-hunger."[24] *A 2007 television ad promoting the new format featured a Broadmoor flood victim recounting how the Green Dot Map had motivated her to participate in civic engagement.*

Adding to the confusion was yet another planning effort, this one paid for with private foundation monies. The Unified New Orleans Plan (UNOP) endeavored to "weave together" and fill in the gaps in all the previous plans by producing a series of "district plans" and a broad plan for not just the flooded areas but the entire city. The UNOP effort initially met resistance from council members, who favored their own Lambert-Danzey planning team, while the grassroots neighborhood associations, staffed almost entirely by local volunteers with everything to lose rather than paid, out-of-town professionals, expressed impatient skepticism about everything. Civically engaged citizens grew cynical not because of lack of commitment but because too many uncoordinated efforts and competing meetings were chasing too few tangible resources to allow for honest-to-goodness problem solving.

Late 2006: With returning citizens come a small but extremely violent number of criminals. While the city's returned population doubles between last quarters of 2005 and 2006, murders and overall violent crimes increase nearly sixfold. Murders of two particularly civically engaged citizens—a black male music teacher and a white female filmmaker—incite a massive March against Crime on January 11, 2007, and help add crime fighting to the list of problems addressed through civic engagement.

The ample resources of the UNOP nevertheless empowered it to arrange three "Community Congress" megaevents in December 2006 and January 2007. Thousands of citizens gathered in the Morial Convention Center, linked through satellite feeds to groups of displaced New Orleanians in Atlanta, Dallas, and Houston, to discuss and vote on priorities using real-time electronic balloting. The resultant Citywide Strategic Recovery and Rebuilding Plan, as well as a plethora of UNOP district plans, hit the streets in draft form in early 2007 about the same time that Mayor Nagin appointed a world-renowned disaster recovery expert, Dr. Edward Blakely, as chief of the city's Office of Recovery Management. In March 2007, "Recovery Czar" Blakely unveiled yet another plan, which called for seventeen "rebuild," "redevelop," and "renew" nodes to be located throughout the city marking spots for intensive infrastructure investment. Striking more focused and modest chords than the grandiose visions of earlier plans, Blakely's proposal aimed

> to encourage commercial investment—and with it stabilize neighborhoods—rather than defining areas that are off-limits to rebuilding. One

such previous plan, advanced in early 2006 by Mayor Ray Nagin's Bring New Orleans Back Commission and backed by the widely respected Urban Land Institute, drew howls from residents who found their neighborhoods represented on maps by green dots that denoted redevelopment as perpetual green space.[25]

Once again, citizens engaged, calling meetings among themselves to discuss Blakely's proposal. (This explains the March 2007 spike in neighborhood meetings in Figure 3.) While a general consensus of support for Blakely's plan emerged, citizens wondered how it might affect all the parallel planning efforts. Would their civic engagement be for naught? Officials assured citizens that all the other ideas—those offered by the BNOB, the ULI, the City Council's Lambert-Danzey team, the UNOP, and particularly the myriad grassroots groups—would help guide and inform the final allocation of resources. This remains to be seen. If history is any guide, grandiose recovery plans rarely come to full fruition. The true benefit of civic engagement in post-Katrina urban planning may have been alluded to deep into the 394-page UNOP tome:

> The citizens of New Orleans have invested their time, their hearts and their vision in creating a plan for their neighborhoods and their city. . . . New Orleans now has an educated army of "citizen-planners" who have found their voice and worked tirelessly over the many months of planning.
> In return, the City must now and forever invest in its citizens as shareholders [and] stakeholders in the City. . . . A formal process for citizen engagement must be developed and implemented to facilitate neighborhood recovery and future development, and to ensure that citizens continue to have a voice in the City's future.[26]

Even beyond the rudimentary social benefits of civic engagement, the various planning efforts succeeded in spawning scores of fine ideas for the betterment of the city—*specific* ideas, with extensive documentation, ranging from bike lanes to green space to flood control and crime prevention. Many may eventually come to fruition even if "the plan" as a whole (be it the UNOP's, BNOB's, or any other) never ends up serving as the metaphorical "blueprint" or "road map" it was envisioned to be. Ed Blakely's Office of Recovery Management seemed to affirm this notion (of post-Katrina planning documents serving as handy rosters of project ideas rather than genuine guiding documents) when, in early 2008, it described

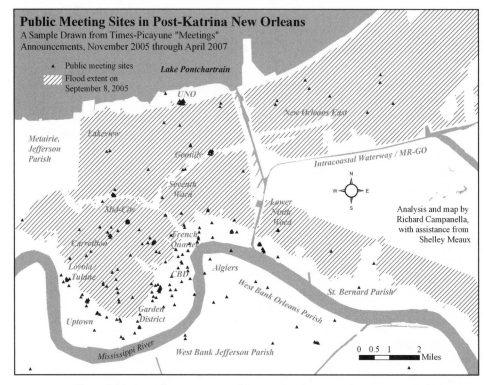

Fig. 5. This map plots over 350 public meeting locations drawn in a stratified manner from over one thousand announcements in the *Times-Picayune* from November 2005 through April 2007. Two-thirds of these meetings were called by neighborhood associations or civic groups. When overlaid on the flood zone, we see that nearly as many meetings were held in flooded-damaged areas as in spared areas. (Analysis and map by Richard Campanella with assistance from Shelley Meaux.)

its 117 upcoming rebuilding projects as having mostly been "gleaned from post-flood neighborhood planning efforts, including the Unified New Orleans Plan."[27]

We should not be surprised that civic engagement flourished in the wake of the Katrina catastrophe. Crises often spawn eager participation in civic affairs; few things motivate like a threat. Yet the magnitude of post-Katrina civic engagement dwarfs that which followed Hurricane Betsy in 1965 or the hurricanes of 1947 or 1915 and almost certainly tops the level of engagement triggered by recent earthquakes, fires, and storms nationwide.

What may distinguish New Orleans' civic engagement experience is the visceral fear among many citizens that a genuine, full-scale, metropolitan death may ensue if citizens allow current trends to continue without intervention. When hundreds of thousands of citizens collectively realize that their salvation (levee repair, coastal restoration, flood-loss compensation, neighborhood improvement, and crime fighting) lies largely in the hands of detached, lumbering authorities, *they engage*—oftentimes passionately—in the civic arena.

Authorities, then, would do well to read this historic blossoming of civic engagement as a measure of the sheer gravity of New Orleans' problems and the fierce determination of New Orleanians to "bring their own chairs" and solve them.

NOTES

For the purposes of this chapter, *civic engagement* is defined as occurring when individuals voluntarily venture out of their private spheres and participate in a public forum in order to learn about, address, and/or resolve a communally held problem. Typical examples include involvement in neighborhood associations, weighing in at "town hall" meetings, speaking at public hearings, editorializing in local newspapers, writing letters to representatives, and organizing to paint schools or clean parks. Civic engagement takes places in a variety of venues: in city halls, school basements, houses of worship, art museums, coffee shops, or the streets. It also may occur through publications, on the Internet, or in voting booths. Although one would be naive to assume that all people who engage in the aforementioned activities have purely altruistic motives, this essay excludes activities that involve the obligatory participation of compensated individuals or the pursuit of commercial gain. Sales pitches by insurance companies or housing contractors soliciting work are not considered civic engagement even if citizens attend, learn from, and ultimately benefit from the interaction.

1. CNN Online, "Chertoff: Katrina Scenario Did Not Exist; However, Experts for Years Had Warned of Threat to New Orleans," September 5, 2005, http://www.cnn.com/2005/US/09/03/katrina.chertoff/.

2. Ramos Dante, "What's a Bar's Best Defense? To Stay Open," *Times-Picayune*, August 31, 2005.

3. "New Study Reveals Louisianians' Post-hurricane Attitudes," *LSU News*, November 30, 2005, http://appl003.lsu.edu/UNV002.NSF/(NoteID)/445F7344 A01DF40E862570C900705A0E?Open Document.

4. Richard Campanella, "Street Survey of Business Reopenings in Post-Katrina New Orleans," CBR white paper funded by National Science Foundation Award 0554937, May 2006 and January 2007, www.kerrn.org/pdf/campanella2.pdf.

5. Gary Rivlin, "New Orleans Forms a Panel on Renewal," *New York Times*, October 1, 2005, A11.

6. Personal communication, ULI member, November 2005.

7. Martha Carr, "Citizens Pack Rebirth Forum: Experts Urged to Use N.O. History as Guide," *Times-Picayune*, November 15, 2005, A1.

8. Bruce Eggler, "Drive to Unify Levee Boards Revs Up: 46,600 Sign Petition, Citizens Group Says," *Times-Picayune*, December 15, 2005, A1.

9. Urban Land Institute, "New Orleans, Louisiana: A Strategy for Rebuilding, an Advisory Services Program Report," November 12–18, 2005, map, p. 45 of PowerPoint file.

10. Frank Donze, "Don't Write Us Off, Residents Warn: Urban Land Institute Report Takes a Beating," *Times-Picayune*, November 29, 2005, A1.

11. Ibid.

12. Ibid.

13. Tulane University, Office of the President, "Tulane University—A Plan for Renewal," http://renewal.tulane.edu/renewalplan.pdf.

14. Dave Walker, "TV Editorials Return: WWL and WDSU Start Weighing In on Hot-Button Issues, *Times-Picayune*, January 30, 2006, Living Section, C1.

15. Gordon Russell and Frank Donze, "Rebuilding Proposal Gets Mixed Reception: Critics Vocal, but Many Prefer to Watch and Wait," *Times-Picayune*, January 12, 2006, 1.

16. Frank Donze and Gordon Russell, "4 MONTHS TO DECIDE: Nagin Panel Says Hardest Hit Areas Must Prove Viability; City's Footprint May Shrink; Full Buyouts Proposed for Those Forced to Move; New Housing to Be Developed in Vast Swaths of New Orleans' Higher Ground," *Times-Picayune*, January 11, 2006, A1.

17. "Meetings," *Times-Picayune*, September 30, 2006, Metro Section, B4.

18. Neighborhood Partnership Network, http://www.npnnola.com/associations. Many of these associations predate the storm but renewed their efforts afterward.

19. Analysis by the author using Lexis-Nexus to search for the occurrence of *civic association* or *neighborhood association* in the full text of the *Times-Picayune* from February 2004 through April 2007. Lexis-Nexus is a searchable archive of newspaper articles and other journalistic content. Strategically searching this archive for certain keywords relating to a particular phenomenon is a way to characterize the nature or perception of that phenomenon through the dimension of time.

20. Analysis by the author.

21. Stephanie Grace, "Will Plan Lift the Curse of the Green Dot?" *Times-Picayune*, April 1, 2007, Metro-Editorial Section, B7, emphasis added.

22. Michelle Krupa, "Katrina Generates Wave of Activism: Myriad Groups Aim to Reshape Region," *Times-Picayune*, August 27, 2006, A1.

23. Bruce Eggler, "N.O. Is Paying Consultants to Help Neighborhoods Plan: Advisers Will Work to Build Consensus," *Times-Picayune*, April 10, 2006, Metro Section, B1.

24. Dave Walker, "Rockin' the Ages: In the Ever-Turbulent World of Local Music Radio . . ." *Times-Picayune*, November 19, 2006, Living Section, C1.

25. Michelle Krupa and Gordon Russell, "N.O. Post-K Blueprint Unveiled: Plan Puts Most Cash in East, Lower Ninth," *Times-Picayune*, March 29, 2007, A1.

26. Unified New Orleans Plan, "Citywide Strategic Recovery and Rebuilding Plan, 2007," 148, http://www.unifiedneworleansplan.com/uploads/UNOP-FINAL-PLAN-April-2007-15744.pdf.

27. Michelle Krupa, "City Hall Begins a Building Boom," *Times-Picayune*, February 23, 2008, B1–3.

A Reciprocity of Tears

COMMUNITY ENGAGEMENT AFTER A DISASTER

Pat Evans and Sarah Lewis

ON AUGUST 29, 2005, HURRICANE KATRINA made landfall on the Mississippi Gulf Coast, bringing with it the pounding wind and rain that destroyed modest family homes and federal levees alike. Faced with unprecedented strains on infrastructure, public services, and emergency response resources, thousands of New Orleanians—often those too poor to flee the city as Katrina approached—were stranded without food, water, or medical care. It was one of the most widespread and highly televised human rights crises in modern American memory.

Such is the beginning of nearly every publication aimed at understanding New Orleans' physical and cultural recovery from Katrina. The storm itself is portrayed as a dramatic deus ex machina and a starting point for analyzing community organizing, planning priorities, and the myriad daily difficulties of a city ripped apart by floodwater. When the city's pre-Katrina social conditions are discussed, it is almost exclusively in relation to the racial and economic disparities that exacerbated the flood's effects on vulnerable populations.

To be sure, such inequalities did threaten the quality of life of far too many New Orleanians pre-Katrina, in many cases causing the poor to shoulder a disproportionate amount of storm-related hardship. However, to focus only on the demographics of the disaster overlooks the culture and social capital that existed before the storm. Built on centuries of a shared landscape and bolstered by local nonprofits and community activists, New

Orleans' pre-Katrina neighborhoods were a dense web of traditions and relationships. Whether focused on food, festivals, or simply a common streetscape, it is the city's neighborhoods themselves that serve as the building blocks for recovery and should guide post-Katrina community engagement.

A Blended Voice

The job of a citizen is to keep his mouth open.
—Günter Grass

The challenge of addressing community engagement in post-Katrina New Orleans is a humbling one. The scope, immediacy, and emotion-laden nature of the subject ensure that any author would find it nearly impossible to distill a salient argument from the combination of scholarly research and personal experience. For those of us straddling the line between our own generations-long family traditions in New Orleans and the insistent, daily experience of living in a community struggling for an image in which to recreate itself, the prospect is truly daunting. Add the task of combining two such perspectives and you get a potential quagmire, so it is with a certain degree of awe that we now put pen to paper or fingers to computer keys, earnestly attempting to write about "civic engagement in the wake of Katrina." We share our observations with some hesitancy. Ours is a blended voice of a front line practitioner and an aspiring academic, both rooted in the institutional resources of the university and the solidity of on the ground experience. We should, perhaps, begin by introducing ourselves.

Pat Evans has worked in media, government, and community building for forty-five years. Beginning her professional life as a documentary filmmaker at WBRZ-TV in Baton Rouge, she went on to a variety of positions within state government, working to pass landmark legislation that changed rape laws, family violence laws, child support laws, and laws affecting the elderly. In occupied Cyprus, she worked to assess and develop bicommunal projects between Greek and Turkish nonprofit organizations, and convened a week of intensive training for Serb, Muslim, and Croat nongovernmental organizations (NGOs) in Sarajevo. Pat also brought her skills to Estonia, Latvia, and Lithuania as an in-residence coordinator for the U.S. Baltic Foundation, offering education, training, and technical assistance in capacity building and advocacy to nearly one hundred Baltic NGOs.

Returning home to her native Louisiana in 1999, Pat founded the International Project for Nonprofit Leadership (IPNL) at the University of New Orleans (UNO), where she continues to direct the project. It provides a continuum of capacity-building offerings, including graduate education, certificate training, technical assistance, and consultancy to the nonprofit sector. Through its Urban Routes initiative, IPNL works with neighborhood groups in Treme and Central City, two of New Orleans' most culturally rich and economically depressed African American communities. In this capacity, IPNL is a catalyst, convener, connector, coordinator, collaborator, and capacity builder. It is community development one neighborhood at a time, combining capacity building and community building, neighborhoods learning to rely on each other, working together on concrete tasks, and becoming aware of their collective and individual assets, in the process creating human, family, and social capital.

In contrast, Sarah Lewis is a doctoral candidate in UNO's Department of Planning and Urban Studies. Also a native New Orleanian, Sarah spent three years working for the Louisiana Regional Folklife Program, where she worked with community groups to document and present their cultural traditions. Her work with this program spanned a broad range of topics, from New Orleans' skilled building artisans to local quilters and textile artisans. Following Hurricane Katrina, Sarah cofounded Common Knowledge, a nonprofit project that promotes accessible public information by providing New Orleanians with a road map to permitting and other municipal processes and documents the changing face of the city's built environment.

Community Building

Connectedness is the mother of all skills.
—Alexis de Tocqueville

How does a university initiative connect to the community in the first place? We will begin with a short description of IPNL's method. It uses an approach known as "appreciative inquiry" (AI) developed by David Cooperrider and his associates at the Weatherhead School of Management at Case Western Reserve University. It calls the community together in an inaugural meeting with the university. The university listens. The community identifies itself and what works in the community, in essence communicating what it appreciates about itself. This approach is based on the assumption that whatever the community wants more of already exists there. It reframes the question so often asked when we undertake civic engagement from "What are the problems?" to "What works?"

This type of community building buttresses a network of resources; it is most effective when it is interactional and transactional. Social theorists note that a "web of affiliation" knits a community together and helps turn an aggregation of people living together in the same neighborhood into a cohesive moral unit. It provides a sense of purpose and identity for individuals. Such work is particularly crucial in contemporary America, where the domain of civil society has been steadily encroached on by big business and big government and the preferred forum for disseminating information or discussing community concerns might be the shopping mall rather than the public park.

Community building is, by its very nature, expressive. It speaks to people's need to express their values, faith, and commitments through work, prayer, volunteerism, and philanthropy. It is a capricious loudness, and there is an undeniable personal element to community engagement that must be grasped. It is based on the fundamental goal of obliterating feelings of dependency and replacing them with attitudes of self-reliance, self-confidence, and responsibility. It is not the provision of a finite work product but rather helping individual neighborhoods build the capacity to do their own work. Looking over our experiences in New Orleans, and with an eye toward successful community building in the impoverished neighborhoods of other U.S. cities, we find that the most successful of these projects share a number of characteristics:

1. They are focused on specific initiatives in a manner that reinforces and builds social and human capital. This process involves neighbors working with neighbors on specific, productive projects. The work serves to build friendship, mutual trust, institutions, and capacity, the social capital that is essential to building a community of support for families and residents.

2. They are community driven with broad resident involvement. If social capital is to be built, if attitudes of dependency are to be replaced with those of self-reliance, community residents must do it for themselves. Community participation is not enough. The community must play the central role in devising and implementing strategies

for its own improvement. This does not mean that outside facilitators cannot help, but it does mean that the agenda must be set by community members rather than facilitators.

3. They must be comprehensive. Quality of life is not limited to single issues such as housing, schools, jobs, crime, or infrastructure. While it is impossible to tackle all community concerns at once, an assessment of neighborhood concerns and assets can provide a guide to the issues that are most important to community members. Following a brief planning period, it is crucial to begin results-oriented work swiftly. You cannot overestimate the power of "building your monuments early" as small successes foster enthusiasm and hope.

4. They are asset based. Assisting residents in an inventory of neighborhood assets is in itself a powerful device for building trust and exploring community concerns.

5. They are tailored to the size and condition of the neighborhood. The core unit of a neighborhood should not exceed ten thousand people. Working on this highly focused scale builds on the natural face-to-face interactions that support friendships and mutual trust.

6. They are collaboratively linked to the broader community. Partnering with universities and other outside institutions brings in resources otherwise unavailable to neighborhood residents.

7. They consciously change institutional barriers between universities and their surrounding communities.

It is a quotidian affair, this business of civic engagement, and there is no escaping the dailiness of it. It requires an experimental mind-set and the willingness to work by trial and error. More often than not, it is an iterative process replete with small successes and temporary setbacks. Like folk culture itself, it builds on everyday life and oral tradition but must constantly adapt to changes in culture and community if it is to remain relevant. To borrow an analogy from New Orleans' great musical tradition, "It ain't Beethoven. It's jazz."

Engagement: The Role of the University

Our responsibility transcends pragmatism. We must help our cities become what we aspire to be on our campuses—a place where human potential can be fully realized.
                    —Richard Levin, President, Yale University

The neighborhoods of America's cities invigorate the creative spirit and provide homes and opportunities to thousands of families. However, over the past three decades city dwellers across the country have become all too familiar with the scourge of deindustrialization and the jobs it has sucked from city economies. In this new environment, universities are increasingly significant elements of urban job markets, in some cases representing the largest employers in individual cities. With their significant landholdings, large urban universities also wield tremendous power regarding the physical landscape of their host cities. Conversely, as top-notch faculty and students are drawn to safe, vibrant communities, the success of large urban universities is closely wedded to the quality of life in their surrounding cities.

As institutions tremendously tied to their locations, universities have a vested interest in the health of their host cities, and it is not surprising that many undertake community-based service projects. Traditionally, this community work has tended to take the form of stand-alone projects or studios aimed at addressing narrowly tailored concerns, for example, literacy programs, design initiatives, sociological analyses, and small business assistance. These are links between a walled academy and the city streets.

The benefit for impoverished communities varies, partially because the personal social interactions necessary to implement such programs often prove difficult to negotiate. Disparities in education and power represent one primary obstacle facing university employees who undertake community-based projects in inner cities.[1] Community members, many of whom have experienced previous collaborations with university groups, are often wary of outside "experts" who offer advice on community development.[2] Some view academics as opportunistic do-gooders who use their work with "the poor" to gain grant money and prestige.[3]

In recent years, however, a new paradigm has begun to influence university-community partnerships, one that considers consistent civic engagement to be a morally imperative institutional priority. This model—in stark contrast to the short-term nature of individual projects—has been prominently championed by Yale University president Richard Levin. After assuming the presidency of Yale in 1993, Levin created the institutional foundations for an enduring community partnership that crossed the lines of academic semesters and grant-funding cycles. The university, he argued, "needed to develop a comprehensive strategy for civic engagement, infrastructure to support the strategy, and make a substantial, long-term commitment to its implementation."[4] As an employer, the university supported the local economy by providing financial incentives for faculty and staff to buy homes within New Haven. Under Levin's leadership, the Yale and New Haven communities have begun to overcome long-standing distrust and address the needs of surrounding neighborhoods.

This type of holistic, collaborative engagement, while it is becoming more common, remains marginalized at far too many universities. An academic culture of theoretical inquiry and scholarly publishing leaves little room for the protracted, empathic relationship building that is the yeoman's work of community engagement.

And yet we persevere, those of us attempting to build capacity at the neighborhood level. We choose to do so, aware that our on the ground efforts are unlikely to earn us quick promotions or academic accolades, out of a dedication to serve the greater needs of a civil society. Association with the university, while sometimes constrictive, provides a degree of legitimacy that can help us voice neighborhoods' concerns to seats of power or more directly to argue that neighborhood leaders deserve a place at the decision-making table themselves. It is precarious and delicate, straddling this line between academia and activism, but the potential payoffs are huge.

Engagement Post-Katrina

A crisis is a terrible thing to waste.
—Paul Romer, Economist

As Katrina made its way across the Gulf Coast, New Orleans was faced with unimaginable destruction of its physical and social resources. The city experienced a disaster, and sluggish institutional response at all levels of government made it a catastrophe. New Orleans was laid bare, wounded, revealed, and its wounds were vividly depicted via television news. The nation's attention and compassion were briefly focused on our city.

Local universities responded to the disaster in several ways. Not surprisingly, in the hours and weeks after the storm they began to address the logistical concerns associated with securing and repairing buildings, temporarily relocating academic programs to undamaged facilities, and providing information for displaced students. At our own university, for example, a call center was immediately established in Baton Rouge. With the university's e-mail system down and information difficult to disseminate, faculty and staff manned the center and provided up-to-date advice for students. Back on campus, administrators worked tirelessly to restore power and coordinate mold remediation in flooded buildings.

Just as quickly city leaders engaged prominent university officials to participate in the creation of a blueprint for recovery. For example, Tulane president Scott Cowan became part of the Mayor's Bring New Orleans Back Commission (BNOB), the body charged with drafting recommendations for everything from land use to tourism and health care. He was later appointed to the New Orleans Redevelopment Authority, a state body that controls the disposition of city-owned land and promises to have tremendous power over who is able to purchase properties seized due to tax delinquency or turned over to the state via widespread buyout plans. Alex Johnson, the head of Delgado Community College, was also a member of the BNOB and served on the City Council's similar commission, the New Orleans Hurricane Advisory Committee. Norman Francis, president of Xavier University, became the chairman of the governor's Louisiana Recovery Authority and serves on the board of the New Orleans Building Corporation, which guides development on the city's own land. Timothy Ryan, a prominent local economist and chancellor of UNO, also advised the mayor and held board memberships at the local Chamber of Commerce and United Way.

As large local institutions, universities played significant roles in early visions for the city, and school leadership articulated a newfound dedication to urban issues. Tulane University created new community service requirements for its undergraduates and announced plans to create a new urban studies program. For its part, the University of New Orleans strategically focused its anthropology and geography curricula around urban concerns. Adjacent to the Gentilly and Lakeview neighborhoods—two of the hardest-hit areas—UNO also directed its urban planning staff to assist community groups in developing their recovery plans. These collaborative planning efforts, which have outlasted several formal government planning initiatives, included documentation of infrastructure conditions, proposals for housing and community design, and surveys to determine the portion of pre-Katrina residents who planned to return.

For its part, pursuant to Chancellor Timothy Ryan's directive that UNO assist New Orleans neighborhoods in their recovery, the International Project for Nonprofit Leadership stepped up the kind of community building it had been doing before the storm. In the weeks after Katrina, when information and communications systems were down, IPNL organized six different sites to serve as "recovery stations" where returning residents could receive and post information about needs and services. In the hard-hit Lower Ninth Ward, IPNL increased the ability of the Lower

Ninth Ward Neighborhood Empowerment Network Association (NENA) to lead the comeback of the neighborhood by drafting a capacity building plan, conducting board development, and offering ongoing technical assistance on staff development.

Despite their express support for community service, local universities' overall sustained participation in neighborhood-level community building has been inconsistent. Initially two significant factors were the damaged facilities and displaced faculty that limited local schools' ability to reach out to their surrounding communities. Decreased enrollment and unanticipated expenses further increased the stresses on university resources. However, even in light of their substantial challenges, New Orleans' universities made post-Katrina restructuring decisions that directly hindered their ability to serve the city's neighborhoods.

At UNO, the most significant of these changes was our administration's decision to dissolve the College of Urban and Public Affairs (CUPA), the academic unit that housed our urban planning and public administration programs. While both degree programs were retained, the university placed them in separate academic units, threatening a good deal of the synergy that stemmed from a shared dedication to community building. The termination of two public administration professors in an effort to save money further limited the university's capacity to serve its surrounding neighborhoods.

As the primary community outreach arm of the university, CUPA had developed name recognition with many neighborhood groups, nonprofits, and city agencies. The dissolution of the unit created understandable confusion on many levels, with some community members wondering whether the degree programs had been wiped out altogether. For community-building work, where constancy is key, decisions like this one threatened residents' trust that their university-based collaborators would be in it for the long haul. For instance, even as UNO staff helped the Lakeview neighborhood develop a broad recovery plan, steering committee members brought up rumors that the school's planning program had been cut.

External funding opportunities also influence the nature of university involvement in post-Katrina New Orleans. Spurred by empathy and the desire to help rebuild a great American city, large private funders have dedicated significant resources to community-based projects in Katrina-affected areas. However, with few exceptions these grants have provided support for citywide initiatives and pseudo-government-planning efforts rather than neighborhood-level engagement. The highest-profile funding agency has been the Rockefeller Foundation, which donated $3.5 million dollars to the Greater New Orleans Foundation for the completion of a Unified New Orleans Plan (UNOP). Another $500,000 dollars was donated to America Speaks, a national citizen participation company that held three large public input sessions—facilitated by a computer-enabled voting system and simulcast in several cities throughout the southeast—in conjunction with the effort. The planning initiative, which employed well-known planning firms from around the country along with some local planners from UNO and elsewhere, drafted a recovery plan for the city. However, following completion of the plan the majority of these planning groups left the city entirely and moved on to new endeavors.

Rockefeller's investment in New Orleans continues to be substantial, and the foundation recently announced a grant of more than $500,000 to defray staffing and other expenses at the city's Office of Recovery Management. In addition, the foundation has pledged more than $2 million for a fellowship program, housed at the University of Pennsylvania, that uses New Orleans as a laboratory for training young development professionals. In each case, the foundation's money has targeted short-term, citywide initiatives over the types of time-intensive, neighborhood-specific work that constitutes true community building. While these projects may be powerful first steps toward reviving New Orleans' urban vitality, they cannot substitute for the protracted community building that builds trust between neighbors and helps residents develop the capacity to improve their own neighborhoods.

Like private foundations, in its support for Katrina-related research the federal government has tended to favor external researchers over local scholars with on the ground expertise. Through grants from the National Science Foundation (NSF), which funds roughly 20 percent of the nation's academic research, federal tax dollars have supported Katrina-focused initiatives in nearly every state in the union. In fact, of the $15,731,651 granted for Katrina research as of the summer of 2007, only $1,216,220, less than 8 percent, went to universities based in New Orleans. Local universities lost out on this federal funding for many reasons—political, perhaps, or capacity based—but a key one was the fact that the government's initial grant deadlines passed before many local scholars had returned home from their evacuations. Negotiating temporary housing and with their offices, books, and files inaccessible, New Orleans' scholars were distinctly disadvantaged.

With millions of research dollars focused on studying the region and service-minded academics eager to conduct projects in New Orleans, the city has been teeming with outside scholars. In fact, in the summer after Katrina it sometimes seemed that actual New Orleanians were matched one-to-one by those who had come to study our recovery. There have been some success stories in blending neighborhood building and outside academics, most notably the collaboration between Harvard University and the Broadmoor neighborhood. Harvard students spent months on the ground in Broadmoor, developing relationships and working with the Broadmoor Improvement Association to map the neighborhood, create a community center, and complete a preliminary neighborhood plan. The relationship between Broadmoor and Harvard continues.

It is important to note, however, that this collaboration was not a random one. Walter Isaacson—a prominent Harvard graduate, cochair of the Louisiana Recovery Authority, and board member at Tulane University—grew up in Broadmoor and has a strong affinity for the neighborhood. Currently president of the Aspen Institute, Isaacson's behind the scenes networking has been a powerful influence on Harvard's focus on Broadmoor. Neighborhoods without such prominent former residents, outspoken remote champions for their recovery, have been significantly less successful in garnering sustained assistance from outside universities rather than the short-term, studio-type projects that often create scholarly work products but few tangible benefits for neighborhoods.

Community Building on Neighborhood Terms

These Americans are peculiar. If in a local community a citizen becomes aware of a human need, which is not met, he there upon discusses the situation with his neighbors. Suddenly, a committee is formed. And a new committee is established. It is like watching a miracle. These citizens perform these functions without a single reference to any bureaucracy or any official agency.

—Alexis de Tocqueville

In the months after the storm, initial hazards to public safety became less intense. Roadways were once again clear of fallen trees, gas leaks had been addressed, and potable water had been restored to most of the city. But as New Orleanians began to return home to their neighborhoods, they found places both physically and emotionally fractured from the communities they had known. One such change was mail delivery, which did not return to flooded neighborhoods for many months.

In many ways, it was a new world, even for lifelong New Orleanians, and the daily tasks of receiving mail, purchasing groceries, and navigating from place to place became foreign. We were experiencing our city anew, and our lives were those of newly settled migrants. With this uncertainty came an increasing consciousness of the city's social and institutional framework. As Oscar Handlin describes it in *The Uprooted: The Epic Story of the Great Migrations That Made the American People*, "The customary modes of behavior were no longer adequate, for the problems of life were new and different. With old ties snapped, men faced the enormous compulsion of working out new relationships, new meanings to their lives, often under harsh and hostile circumstances."[5]

Much like immigrants, New Orleanians turned to their neighbors for aid in negotiating the new landscape. Many leaders recognized early what Father Luke Nguyen of Mary Queen of Vietnam Church eloquently articulated: "You can't wait for the government to raise you up. You have to pull yourself up, and once you get far enough they will come to you." Neighborhood internet groups exploded in popularity immediately after the storm, providing a forum for neighbors to share information regarding municipal services and reputable contractors and to begin discussing community priorities for the recovery process. In a city whose culture is firmly rooted in face-to-face interaction, neighborhoods also began to share information and develop visions for the future at meetings. The number of New Orleans neighborhood associations quickly grew to more than two hundred. In fact, in the year following Katrina resurrected and newly formed neighborhood associations were so numerous that CityWorks, a new nonprofit organization, spent months simply mapping their boundaries.

Some neighborhoods, often those that had experienced severe storm damage, created their own planning initiatives long before city-endorsed recovery planning began. One particularly notable example was the Lakeview neighborhood, which with the help of UNO planning faculty created the District 5 Neighborhood Recovery Group. The group soon developed a complex organizational structure, including seven committees that met each week to discuss, in turn, communications and community engagement; green space recovery and beautification; neighborhood planning, resources, and finances; infrastructure; crime prevention; and coordination between the area's various neighborhood associations. The Infrastructure Committee itself included seventeen distinct subcommittees.

The focus on the neighborhood as an organic unit of recovery reached up to the city's political leadership. In the city's 2006 mayoral race, which pitted incumbent Ray Nagin against state lieutenant governor Mitch Landrieu, Landrieu's campaign highlighted neighborhood bonds. His memorable television ad campaign featured various small groups of New Orleanians, racially and ethnically diverse. "We're neighbors, and we're voting for Mitch," they would say.

Early neighborhood self-organizing caught the eye of those orchestrating formal city plans. One example of this consciousness occurred at a meeting of the Louisiana Recovery Authority, where architect Steven Bingler laid out the framework for the Unified New Orleans Plan. "Nobody wants to bring in another planning process that overwhelms the existing neighborhood process," he said, "because the neighborhood planning process is so beautiful."

Despite Bingler's lauding of neighborhood-based planning, the process he and his colleagues devised was far from grassroots. Time-intensive, small-scale community engagement proved impossible for a project with significant time constraints and tremendous scope. And yet citizens continued to participate in unprecedented numbers. This participation was rooted in the ideas of neighborhood power that formed in the months immediately following Katrina. Citizens worked to ensure that their concerns were not left out of official plans. As local architect Alan Eskew noted, there was a fear that "all of a sudden they're going to look up and things are going to be decided." In turn, residents recognized that it was their participation that lent the Unified New Orleans Plan its authority. While supporting official adoption of the plan, one Claiborne area activist summarized this point of view, saying that "the legitimacy of the Unified New Orleans Plan draws from citizen participation." Jeff Thomas, a representative of the city's Office of Recovery Management, echoed his sentiments, noting, "The true success of the recovery, to date, is the neighborhood planning process."

Conclusions

> The statement that nothing is going on in New Orleans is not true. There's a lot going on in New Orleans. You just have to go to the neighborhoods to see it.
> —Arnie Fielkow, New Orleans City Council
> Member at Large

Since Katrina flooded more than half of the city's neighborhoods, planners, elected officials, and outside observers have lauded neighborhood self-organizing as the key to New Orleans' rebirth. It is the everyday citizens, supporting each other and constructing visions for the future, who make recovery possible. However, despite the lip service given to neighborhood organizing, city leaders have shied away from substantive work at the neighborhood level. At an early meeting of the New Orleans Redevelopment Authority, Ed Blakely, director of the city's Office of Recovery Management, explained his plan to work primarily at the citywide level. "We will doing everything citywide," he said, "because neighborhoods exist within the city." He went on to explain that he would not be dedicating much of his energy to individual neighborhoods, arguing, "I am not going to get down to the neighborhood level. I have other things to do."

Neighborhood organizations' ability to address local issues more effectively than city government itself became evident in January 2007, nearly a year and a half after Katrina, when a devastating tornado hit the once flooded Northwest Carrollton neighborhood. In the hours following this small-scale disaster, neighborhood leaders mobilized. Using the social ties, communications capacity, and knowledge of city services developed as a result of Katrina, neighborhood residents quickly assessed damage, directed traffic, corralled local media, found alternative housing for those whose homes had been damaged, and assisted schoolchildren in navigating the dangerous landscape. They did this in spite of, rather than in collaboration with, the city's disaster response. "It became painfully obvious that no one was in charge when a call to City Hall some twelve hours after the event yielded the answer, 'We don't know,'" explains Northwest Carrollton resident Karen Gadbois. "We felt like we were working against the clock to avoid the chaos that would ensue when 'help' arrived from the city."

The potential for neighbors to effectively collaborate on issues of common concern is not limited to postdisaster environments. In their book *There Goes the Neighborhood*, William J. Wilson and Richard P. Taub tell us that people have long been accustomed to making their own geography, whether in bricks and mortar or in that less visible yet most important feature of the city, the neighborhood.[6] Neighborhoods deal with change or the threat of change in different ways. Their reactions are in large part determined by the strength of their social fabric. "Strong neighborhoods often remain so in opposition to other groups of people," the authors conclude somberly, noting the double-edged sword that is community strength.

The book does offer a note of hope. When interests coincide, such as when Latinos and whites joined forces against an autocratic school council in Beltway (a neighborhood in Chicago), groups can form across racial and ethnic lines. And the ability to see that "coincidence of interest," the book suggests, is perhaps the city's best hope: "Cities need leaders who can somehow persuade middle- and low-income residents of the metropolitan region to make common cause, to realize that their lives inevitably intersect." We who work in community building are challenged to maintain this hope in part by maintaining both balance of mind and quickness of sympathy, what the poet Wilfred Owen called during the First World War "the eternal reciprocity of tears." Perhaps this is the work required of "civic engagement after Katrina."

NOTES

1. J. Shefner and D. Cobb, "Hierarchy and Partnership in New Orleans," *Qualitative Sociology* 25, no. 2 (2002): 273–97.

2. Larry L Rowley, "The Relationship between Universities and Black Urban Communities: The Clash of Two Cultures," *Urban Review* 32, no.1 (2000): 45–65.

3. Kenneth M. Reardon, "A Sustainable Community/University Partnership," *Liberal Education* 85, no. 3 (1999): 20–25.

4. Richard Levin, "Universities and Cities: Richard Levin—the View from New Haven." Lecture delivered at the Inaugural Colloquium of Case Western University, January 30, 2003.

5. Oscar Handlin, *The Uprooted: The Epic Story of the Great Migrations That Made the American People* (New York: Atlantic–Little, Brown, 1951).

6. William J Wilson and Richard P. Taub, *There Goes the Neighborhood: Racial, Ethnic, and Class Tension in Four Chicago Neighborhoods and Their Meaning for America* (New York: Knopf, 2006).

Not Since the Great Depression

THE DOCUMENTARY IMPULSE POST-KATRINA

Michael Mizell-Nelson

SHORTLY BEFORE KATRINA GRAZED NEW ORLEANS and touched off the levee failures that ruined the city, my wife and I hosted a small party for two couples with infants. Other families had provided our kids with a good deal of outgrown clothes and books, so we wanted to pass along these hand-me-downs, too. Following the flooding, one of those families left the city permanently even though their jobs and apartment had survived. The other couple, Helen Hill and Paul Gailiunas, lost their home and one of their jobs, but they returned in fall 2006 despite Paul's misgivings. Someone shot Helen to death early in January 2007 in a home invasion. The news spread internationally because she was a talented white filmmaker with friends throughout the world. Several days before her murder, Helen had spent more than one hour engaging our ten-year-old daughter in a discussion about vegetarianism and veganism. Everything reported about Helen's welcoming nature, creativity, and childlike artistry was true.[1]

This open-ended unnatural disaster and the many terrifying ways it continues to spool out can exhaust the most grounded of people. At times, Katrina's half-life seems eternal. In assembling the content for an online database project regarding hurricanes Katrina and Rita called the Hurricane Digital Memory Bank, I regularly measure personal and community losses throughout the Gulf Coast.[2] Obviously, New Orleans serves as this catastrophe's ground zero. Similarly, each individual's piece in the immense debris field stretching across the Gulf Coast from Texas to Alabama complicates the larger picture.

Flood Bowl Refugees and the Gray Area Epitomized

As flood bowl refugees, my family has lost and gained much.[3] We lost all of our material possessions downstairs in our rented townhouse across from the Seventeenth Street Canal.[4] However, we had evacuated with almost all of our photographs and videotapes. If ever I begin to consider our family as unfortunate, I need only glance at the three plastic tubs of our family history, intact and safe, and think of our former neighbor's photographs, water-soaked and mildewed, scattered across their lawn in an attempt to salvage some shreds from thirty years of history.

Obviously, our personal losses were relatively limited. The second floor did not flood, so our rented townhouse can be interpreted as having been either half full of floodwater or half empty depending on how the day is going. "Well, you're lucky," more than one person told us after they heard that we had only rented the townhouse, so these conversations often ended on this chipper note. Yes, we knew the neighborhood was a flood zone, and we couldn't afford to purchase a home anyway, so we had remained renters. Our kids understood it to be home, however, so this sense of being lucky was lost on them. We were fortunate that we could simply move, but that's when our Katrina crises began. Our status as renters means we are not eligible for the federally funded homeowner bailout, ill managed though it may be.

Although my wife and I continue in our careers, rapidly escalating credit card debt is needed to rebuild and cover our monthly bills. Since we lacked flood insurance, we received $2,500 from our renter's policy before State Farm dropped us. (The appeal process remains unsuccessful.) The payout barely covered our hotel and travel expenses before we were able to benefit from the kindness of family and friends. The Red Cross had proved unwilling to help us on several different occasions, so we ended up relying on both sets of our retired parents for immediate financial support. In returning to the city in late 2005, we had felt relieved, understanding that the rent subsidy program of the Federal Emergency Management Agency (FEMA) would shield us from the full impact of post-Katrina rents for as long as eighteen months. Accustomed to paying $1,100 in rent per month in August 2005, four months later we began to pay $2,000 for a dilapidated house without heat.[5] After providing two rental assistance payments, yet another federal agency failed us, much as the U.S. Army Corps of Engineers' levee system had. After FEMA continually denied our appeals and letters from the landlord, we absorbed the inflated rent without government aid.

Unfortunately, we had to turn once again to parents, who helped us to get together a down payment for a house. Our family's recovery is based on the retirement savings of two octogenarian couples whose childhoods were marked by the Great Depression. (While some retirement plans allowed Katrina survivors to borrow funds without penalty, ours did not.) A Small Business Administration (SBA) loan helped to some extent, and their below-market interest rates are greatly appreciated as we experience the monthly usury shock each time our credit card bills arrive. While finishing this essay, I learned that we now must pay an additional $350 per month toward our mortgage since our insurance and property tax rates have increased again. While the details of my family's story may suggest otherwise, I remain certain that we truly are among the fortunate. The story of a Honduran laborer who spent three weeks in an Orleans Parish prison on a bogus charge is another reminder that other people are much worse off. The prison booking agent had misinterpreted the first letter of his surname. The man's family had witnessed his arrest, but prison officials told them many times over that he had not been imprisoned. The family's hired attorney made no progress. While also an example of misfortune, he was lucky enough to have rented from a bilingual, compassionate landlord who intervened with parish prison officials. One can only guess how much longer he might have remained imprisoned. The charges were dropped.[6]

Such personal details are salient because in collecting information related to hurricanes Katrina and Rita, it is typically difficult to convince people that their Katrina stories, though not dramatic, are worth recording. It's especially hard to persuade residents from the middle and upper-middle classes that such details need to be preserved. The documentary gaze is fixed on New Orleans, 2005's ground zero, and the emphasis is typically on either dramatic stories of death, survival, and first responders or on criminal behavior, at street level rather than corporate. Extra effort must be made to record both the continuing impact of the 2005 hurricanes and the majority of stories that fall between the extremes of heroism and hooliganism. The mundane signs of life and struggle in post-Katrina New Orleans and Gulfport, Mississippi, as well as post-Rita Lake Charles, must survive if we are to create a more representative record. Nevertheless, far too many affected people describe their stories as "not worth recording."

Stories of battles with insurance companies, multiple tires flattened by stray roofing nails, and overtaxed roads and city services throughout the Gulf South must be preserved.[7]

Concerned about the scale of the disaster, as well as the vast number of stories to be recorded, historians at the University of New Orleans and the Center for History and New Media began planning the Hurricane Digital Memory Bank (http://www.hurricanearchive.org) a couple of weeks after the flooding. The resulting project is the most broad-based, open-access, searchable hurricane research database yet to be developed. Most of the other hurricane documentation efforts intend to create new material, usually audiotaped or videotaped oral histories and, maybe, transcriptions. Our initial area of focus is to make important documentation work available to as many people as possible. The project also seeks to preserve the vast array of materials "born digital" but unlikely to be saved. Online since early November 2005, the Hurricane Digital Memory Bank now houses about fifty thousand objects related to Katrina and Rita and their aftermaths. Most of these are accounts e-mailed to friends and family, digital photographs, audio and video footage, text messages, blog postings, and scholarly and student work. Writing created by high school, community college, and other students provides entry to the experiences of those less likely to have access to the Internet. These are some of the most detailed and valuable objects in the collection. Long-term preservation via servers in both Louisiana and Washington, DC, is an essential part of the plan.[8]

Flooding the City to Save It, or, an Embarrassment of Riches

The media has covered the plight of medical professionals and other white-collar workers in the wake of the great population upheavals along the Gulf Coast fairly well. However, many different professionals have benefited from the flooding, especially academicians and others connected to the world of nonprofit foundations. One might say that those connected to the realm of storytellers in a broad sense—journalists (not just Anderson Cooper), film documentarians, historians, sociologists, and so on—have reaped professional gains. Gulf Coast residents obviously tally these gains against their professional and personal losses. While not comparable to the fortunes of insurance industry professionals who experienced record profits in 2005, these career advances are significant nonetheless. The same week my wife and I learned of the jarring mortgage payment increase also brought news of a significant honor awarded to the online database project. Many scholars, journalists, nonprofit heads, and others whose city and professional lives have been affected by a natural and unnatural disaster have hit a cruel jackpot of sorts. "Before Katrina, I could not get funding to do A, B, or C. Now, I have funds to do all of that and more" is a theme of many conversations I have had recently with longtime nonprofit heads in the city. Those people whose sustenance depends on the world of nonprofits reported with delight whenever the Rockefeller Foundation's representative in New Orleans—another post-Katrina development—expressed interest in learning more about their programs. My experience is similar. While I could not secure funds for an online New Orleans history database beforehand, the aftermath of Katrina brought funding for the Hurricane Digital Memory Bank, which has led to another, pre-Katrina, New Orleans history database.[9] To paraphrase Woody Allen, those of us vested in the collecting and telling of stories might say that 80 percent of a project's success is having a disaster show up.

My work with the database project has provided excellent views of resident and visiting scavengers as we feed on the carcass of New Orleans. It's also a good perch for noting the improved fortunes of many other professions tied to the gathering of stories. Just the honorific awards dispensed in the aftermath of Katrina, considered as a group, should cause one to ask whether there is a tipping point when these accolades lose some of their meaning, and can we trust ourselves to recognize when we reach it? The New Orleans *Times-Picayune* newspaper received Pulitzer awards for public service and breaking news reporting, maybe the grandest example of the accolades washed in by the storm. (The public service award was also presented to Biloxi-Gulfport's *Sun Herald*.)

A *Times-Picayune* editor recently boasted that the widespread leveling effect of the flooding afforded newspaper staffers much closer connections to New Orleanians.[10] He claimed that he could meet with a Gentilly neighborhood resident, mention that he lived in adjacent Lakeview, and enjoy immediate rapport. Both neighborhoods were inundated, but Gentilly is far less affluent and white than Lakeview. Unless this imagined Gentilly resident received some professional accolades for the flooding of his house, I doubt that he would see their situations as being equal.

The paper's media critic—also a Lakeview resident—earlier had chastised Spike Lee's documentary *When the Levees Broke* for excluding Lakeview and thus too much of the white person's experience.

The tragic story of black New Orleans trapped in Katrina's path has found a supreme chronicler, but the flooded-out residents of Lakeview or Old Metairie who attend tonight's sold-out premiere at New Orleans Arena will spend all night sitting on a hard plastic chair and then wonder: "Where am I in this?"[11]

This became a theme for many white New Orleanians' reactions to a fine film. Lee presented the stories of black residents of Gentilly along with those of white residents of St. Bernard Parish and Uptown, but according to the critics, this was not enough. The *Times-Picayune*'s critic praised much of Lee's film, but his divisive comments—"*Levees* tells only half the story. Or, rather, 67.3 percent of it."—alluded to the African American majority population and demonstrated little of the post-Katrina rapport across neighborhood and racial boundaries.[12] Both the editor and the media critic share in two Pulitzer prizes awarded to the *Times-Picayune* because the newspaper's staff did its job well under horrendous conditions. If we are to believe these *Times-Picayune* employees, there is some imagined common ground in post-Katrina suffering that white journalists apparently identify when it is convenient but black documentary filmmakers ignore.

Another *Times-Picayune* employee found a problem with Oprah Winfrey, one of the nation's most powerful media figures; Columnist Chris Rose made himself over post-Katrina from an ironic celebrity chaser and New Orleans nightlife denizen to the voice of middle-class white New Orleans angst. Fueled by the individual stories his readers sent him, Rose's columns resonated with his audience, especially as the hopeful feelings of the first several months of rebuilding disappeared. During a dramatic admission of his experience with post-Katrina depression, Rose wrote:

> I was receiving thousands of e-mails in reaction to my stories in the paper, and most of them were more accounts of death, destruction and despondency by people from around south Louisiana. I am pretty sure I possess the largest archive of personal Katrina stories, little histories that would break your heart. I guess they broke mine.[13]

After reading Rose's similar comments in a *Chicago Reader* interview during one of his book tours, I decided to take the bait and see if he would be willing to use the mass e-mailing system he used for book promotions to let these readers know that their stories would be welcome in the Hurricane

Digital Memory Bank. Rose's repeated observations about the "largest archive of personal Katrina stories" could be interpreted as suggesting that his readers had entrusted him with precious, horrible documents and he did not know what to do with them. Not surprisingly, some willingness to place such material in a noncommercial archive was not how I should have interpreted those remarks. Rose's self-published collection of newspaper columns proved so successful that Simon and Schuster contracted with him to release an updated version in time for Katrina's second anniversary. Maybe those reader stories are awaiting publication in Rose's next book. He complained in his second anniversary column that Oprah's producers wanted to focus on the story of his depression and refused to allow him to mention his book. Their plans ran dead against Rose's desire to use the Oprah appearance to promote the book. It is difficult to discern where irony begins and ends in Rose's account of his dealings with Oprah's staff. Nevertheless, when one commemorates the second anniversary of a national tragedy by complaining about being denied a book plug on a show that has made many authors wealthy one of those tipping points may have been reached.[14]

The *Times-Picayune*'s nola.com Web presence assumed unprecedented prominence in the days immediately following Katrina. Instead of the less than 500,000 page views the newspaper attracted in the weeks before the hurricane, nola.com received 32 million page views in the week immediately after the flooding.[15] Since then the paper has caught up with other daily papers and incorporated even more of the world of online journalism and bloggers. It has also caught up in another regard. After almost two years of providing free access to its newspaper archive, the *Times-Picayune* needed to cover its costs. Access to archived news stories now costs $3.95 per article. The publishers certainly need to stay in business, but since the disaster and its economic ramifications are nowhere near an endpoint, it would be good if the Newhouse parent company would hold off on the charges until its customer base is on a sounder footing.[16]

The *Times-Picayune* sometimes exhibits a sense of ownership of the Katrina story that can irk the many groups seeking to document their pieces of this epoch. This is most evident among local bloggers who early on perceived themselves as helping to steer the New Orleans recovery via their online pulpits and efforts at wired activism. A large part of this work involved identifying errors of omission committed by the daily paper as well as problems with its online content. In the first year following Katrina, the bloggers shared a sense of collective joy over their work as cybercitizens. A few years into the troubled recovery, they now share more collective out-rage over the daily chaos. Too often the bloggers' realm is a closed circle of online friends speaking to one another. Some of the coarsest but most in-sightful exchanges regarding race and class in New Orleans are found in the work of neither the bloggers nor the *Picayune*'s print journalists but in the raw, often racialized comments posted by citizens throughout the vari-ous nola.com forums.[17]

Documenting the Documentary Impulse

Not since the Great Depression has the impulse to document recent his-tory been as evident and widespread as along the Gulf Coast in the years following Katrina. Arguably, not even 9/11 generated as much documen-tary interest. Oral history projects, documentary films, social science and hard science research studies, Web sites, commercially published and self-published books, blogs, and ceaseless media coverage are only some of the efforts that allow people to tell their stories. Before the flooding, far fewer outsiders expressed interest in the history and well-being of New Orleans. Following Katrina, disaster researchers, various media workers, and many others began to inundate New Orleans, mining the city for purposes that may simultaneously be selfless and self-serving. Newcomers and natives share the desire to document New Orleans' man-made tragedy as well as the natural disasters that devastated vast areas east and west of the city.

Ironically, those Louisiana and Mississippi public historians, oral histo-rians, and anthropologists best prepared to document the effects of Katrina on the communities they have been working with for decades are too often on the periphery. Their carefully planned, regionwide oral history pro-posal went unfunded. Meanwhile, arts organizations whose interviewers have limited backgrounds in oral history are much more likely to have been funded. For example, arts groups accustomed to using oral history as their primary source for interpreting the culture of a neighborhood or other group have been anointed by their funding agencies to document for the sake of posterity rather than performance. Several of the professional oral historians in the region are resigned to the situation when they should be collaborating with the newcomers.[18]

While the arts organizations recognize the importance of oral history interviews, FEMA deliberately sought to avoid the difficulty of including "the human element" among its documentation efforts. Shortly after the disaster, a New Orleans–based social scientist met with a FEMA official who agreed that oral history interviews should be part of the agency's documentation program. A higher official quashed these plans because it was felt that including the human element would complicate things. Instead, FEMA subcontracted a great deal of this work through the same national public history firms that have worked for years with the U.S. Army Corps of Engineers. This documentation work centers on creating yet another property database to join those maintained by insurers, realtors, property tax assessors, and others. Teams combed through neighborhoods to assess which homes were damaged enough to warrant FEMA demolition funds. These groups also assessed and documented the state of buildings in National Register Historic Districts. The least experienced members of these teams earned twenty dollars per hour while the senior members earned thirty plus a fifty-five-dollar per diem. The status of the area's infrastructure will soon be palpable via yet another database, but the experiences of the residents and former residents of these neighborhoods remain the concern of oral historians with far fewer resources.

Another serious issue arises once material is gathered. The urge to document often overrides the question of how people might locate these invaluable resources in the future. Preservation and access to such materials should be at the center of such projects, but too often they are afterthoughts. Traditional archives will preserve some of the material, but only scholars and journalists can readily use such resources. "We'll put it on the Web" is a typical response to questions of access. Internet postings allow visibility, but every individual organization that decides to place materials on a Web site without plans to make the material searchable via one or more databases adds yet another site that must be consulted for even basic research.

Many people assume that material placed on the Internet will be preserved for all time. This belief is frustratingly common among the general public and even among the newest recruits to the Grand Army of the Documentation. A related problem is that once a person has been interviewed in any form—by a newspaper reporter, academic researcher, and so on—he or she often believes history has been served. When I speak with such people about posting their stories or e-mails to the online database, they often say it's unnecessary because they have already been interviewed, although it's evident that most have no sense of where or when their stories will be made available for others to read—never mind themselves.[19]

Online Collecting Democratizes History

Many take comfort in knowing that their stories have been recorded, not unlike those who have enjoyed preparing a time capsule and then burying the material for one hundred years or so. Despite the evidence that such time capsules stand limited chances of being retrieved as planned, they remain quite popular.[20] In an effort to build upon the general understanding of time capsules, at times I cast the memory bank as a "timeless" capsule. One may file and forget the information, but one can also revisit the database and provide updates. Two of the best examples of the promise that online collecting and archiving offers can be seen in the regularly updated postings of New Orleans author and publisher Mary Gehman and special needs activist Courtney Giarrusso.[21]

The Hurricane Digital Memory Bank also seeks to document the regional, national, and international scope of what quickly developed into a national crisis. Coast Guard and National Guard units from throughout the United States spent more of September 2005 in the city than did most residents. The experiences of these and other nonresidents must be added to the documentary record. Outreach efforts have already resulted in the development of special collections, such as that of the 102nd Military History Detachment of the Kansas Army National Guard, as well as postings by individual National Guard members. Likewise, the stories of friends, relatives, churches, and entire communities that helped Gulf Coast evacuees must also be collected. Collection building and outreach present a staggering task that could seemingly reach no end.

Extraordinary efforts are required to record the accounts of those without access to the Internet, so people may submit their stories via our project's voice mail system (504-208-3883). Following Delfeayo Marsalis's welcome message and brief instructions, one can record a message for as long as ten minutes. As with Internet contributions, one may choose to remain anonymous. The memory bank is distributing tens of thousands of postcards so people can record short statements regarding their status during the prolonged recovery. After they mail their handwritten responses, postage paid, to the History Department at the University of New Orleans, their statements are scanned and added to the database.[22]

New Media and New Documentarians

Most impressive is the creativity that individuals bring to this online archive project in using a new medium to express themselves.

Fig. 6. Mr. Ramsey's suit for Mardi Gras 2006 commemorated the lost history of the Corner Bar. The names of all the old bars that no longer exist post-Katrina are listed on his suit. (From Courtney Egan, "Mr. Ramsey's New Suit." Hurricane Digital Memory Bank, object 28422, June 8, 2007, 4:58 p.m., http://www.hurricanearchive.org/object/28422.)

Fig. 7. The caption for this entry in the Hurricane Digital Memory Bank reads, "One of the most grievous losses after Katrina was the family collection of photographs. The London Ave. levee breach let in an awful collection of yuck which obliterated all photos, amazingly except for Polaroids. I found this one of my son stuck in the buckled wood flooring of mama and daddy's house. We all cried because in 2002 at 24 he died of an asthma attack. Losing all his photos was like losing him again, until God led us to this lone survivor. Amen." (From Kathleen DesHotel, "Online Image Contribution, Hurricane Digital Memory Bank." Hurricane Digital Memory Bank, object 1853, February 18, 2006, 1:07 a.m., http://www.hurricanearchive.org/object/1853.)

The photograph reproduced in figure 7 led one visitor to the database to post her own story of similar loss. Flooding in the same Gentilly neighborhood had destroyed her home and all of her mementos regarding her deceased son. The women have never met, but their parallel stories unfolded only blocks away from one another's homes. The second entry turns on the fact that not one item memorializing her deceased son survived the flooding.[23]

For those not directly affected by the hurricanes, digital technology has allowed observers to document the losses of others and then share their work via the memory bank. It is striking how thoughtfully one amateur documentarian represented a Mississippi couple's story without photographing them or sacrificing their dignity. The caption to the image in figure 8 reads:

Fig. 8. Bill Sullivan, "Online Image Contribution, Hurricane Digital Memory Bank," object 2166.

I will never forget this day at the American Red Cross shelter in Citronelle, Alabama. An elderly couple that was staying at the shelter went to their home to see the damage. They returned with a small box of jewerly and these photos on the cot, that was all that was left of the couple's home. The poor couple couldn't even remember the name of their insurance company.[24]

Collaboration Needed

One theme expressed by New Orleans academics and other locals has been the lack of the positive, collaborative relationships one finds in the dirty work of house gutting and house raising. Unlike the thousands of church and student groups that reach out to locals, gauge their needs, and travel to the city to work side by side with them, too many academics and cultural

workers maintain their individualism and even compete among themselves. I asked one biologist how much support he had received from researchers outside the area. None, he replied. He had been so busy rebuilding his life and home that he had had no time to write grant proposals and
had received no offers of collaboration from colleagues outside New Orleans. His experience underscores a somewhat obvious corollary: those
professionals affected by Katrina least directly, meaning those who did not
lose their homes, spend more time writing about, analyzing, documenting,
and ultimately benefiting from the tragedy. The theme of excluding locals
from the troughs in our own backyards is found in a variety of professions.

The producers of a New Orleans documentary that aired on public
television's *American Experience* provide an excellent example. The production originated with the grand premise of featuring the pre-Katrina New
Orleans story with a few breaks from the historical narrative during which
viewers could enjoy short visits with colorful representative figures. This
conceit had been well received when employed in earlier productions regarding notable American cities, so it would be adapted to their New Orleans project. When it is assumed from the outset that two hours of New
Orleans history will be boring, the production is flawed. The production
process itself remained closed to talented local documentary producers.
When one of the New York City producers complained to me about a hur-
ried production schedule and a tight budget, it irked me to think of one of
New Orleans' best documentary producers who remained exiled in Ohio
more than a year after Katrina. The New Yorkers apparently never considered saving time and money by hiring local talent or helping a fellow filmmaker return home. New Orleans has long attracted producers with national reputations and budgets to match, making it even more difficult to
complete projects in one's own community. The same New Orleans independent producer devastated by the flood had earlier castigated the
Louisiana state government for having donated one million dollars to Ken
Burns's *Jazz* when local independent filmmakers were struggling for funding.[25] When *American Experience* came to town, more than one local producer received overtures suggesting that he or she might be hired to help
capture the colorful interludes, but even that role was handed to a staff
member.

Grousing without some notion of how things might be rectified is not
helpful. Collaboration might include outside producers working with local
independent filmmakers long familiar with the city. Instead of merely

watching the documentaries created by local producers and lifting their ideas, the circle of creativity could be broadened to include local producers. The exiled filmmaker and his family have returned to their flooded Gentilly neighborhood, where he has spent many months editing for-hire jobs in his FEMA trailer. Great documentaries are being produced along with the bad, but even the best ones could be improved by widening the circle to include local independent producers in the production process. Ironically, well-funded documentary and television news producers regularly loan cameras to children and others to capture their perspectives.[26]

Some may dismiss these criticisms as coming from one who simply disdains outsiders, but it's the competitive and noncooperative outsiders and insiders I target. A compassionate and insightful journalist such as the *New Yorker*'s Dan Baum advances his career while maintaining a holistic sense of his research topic and the people in the city he writes about. Many of the Common Ground volunteers, dedicated Vietnamese college graduates, and others contribute much good to the area's recovery. Alan Gutierrez, a relative newcomer to the city, is not simply a blogger. He offered training and assistance on behalf of New Orleans and its residents via several online projects.[27] The "voluntourism" organized by universities and religious groups exemplifies how outsiders can collaborate with local homeowners and nonprofits. They have responded to community and individual needs first rather than just showing up to collect data. Unfortunately, too many academics visit the city to build their curriculum vitae instead of building houses.

Even the best intentions can have unforeseen effects. One popular feelgood story covered in many media concerns a musician and piano tuner from Oregon who has dedicated several years of his life to helping New Orleans in memory of his deceased musician son. The father secures and donates musical instruments and tunes pianos for free. He also plans to develop free music camps and hopes to train a couple of New Orleanians to tune and repair pianos.[28] Who could complain about such a situation and the dedication of a compassionate, grieving father who offers so much? How about one of the area's few piano repair and tuning specialists, the father of three kids, who, with his customer base scattered to Houston and Atlanta, is struggling to earn a living and has to compete against free services? Given the positive spin of this story, he and the few others in his trade do not complain, but it does make their rebuilding tougher. Assisting established local tradesmen, or at least contacting their organization to assess their needs, would have helped.

The other couple attending our party just before the flood lost neither jobs nor their apartment, but they opted not to deal with the possibility of evacuating the city every year with a child. They relocated to the West Coast. Their first year of resettlement was rough, and I ended phone conversations with my friend feeling guilty about my family's relatively quick return to normalcy. Following Helen Hill's murder, those conversations now end with a sense of relief on his end.

Helen's murder occurred while we were out of town, so only after returning did we discover its impact on the local and international communities. Many people took their children to the several memorial services and demonstrations against crime. We decided not to mention the murder to our five- and ten-year-old kids, who had just become accustomed to life post-Katrina and the relative permanence of a home. If our daughter asks, and she hasn't yet, we'll tell her that Paul and Helen no longer live in New Orleans. Such explanations are so commonplace that she likely will inquire no further. We will delay the full answer until she is older and better able to handle the truth of violence and how unfair life in New Orleans can be.

NOTES

1. A memorial and archive of Helen Hill's works can be found at www.helen hill.org.

2. The most viable venue for making 2005 hurricane research materials more accessible to both Web surfers and scholars stems from the database project developed in partnership between George Mason University's Center for History and New Media and the University of New Orleans. See the project's Web site, http://www.hurricanearchive.org.

3. I use the term *flood bowl refugee* to evoke the scale of the dislocation that followed the dust bowl crisis of the 1930s. Among the many other issues confronting the nation following Katrina, some groups and media debated the use of the term *refugee* versus *evacuee*. This led Massachusetts and other states to designate hurricane and flood victims transported to their military bases as "guests." Also worth exploring would be such nomenclature as Minnesota's Operation Northern Comfort. Some of these programs devolved into plans to transplant homeless Gulf Coast guests to economically desperate sections of Minnesota. In other words, parts of the state that had been economically crippled by the loss of their native sons and daughters to the Twin Cities and other prosperous areas of the upper Midwest were to be repopulated by people from an economically depressed part of the nation recently traumatized by Katrina.

4. The exception was some of our wedding gifts, which had been tucked into a crawl space beneath the stairs. The saturated walls gave way like wet tissue paper

and provided access to many of these items. Still sheathed in bubble wrap, plates and glasses had to be shucked like oysters stewed in toxic sewage. Future house-guests may want to bring their own plates and glassware.

5. Several months after vacating the rented house, a tornado, rare in New Orleans, ripped apart the second-story bedroom windows and did enough additional damage to warrant a photo of the house in an insurance company ad regarding postdisaster cleanup. Once again, our family's good fortune is quite apparent.

6. See Mary Gehman, "2006 Journal Entries, Mary Gehman," Hurricane Digital Memory Bank, object 28907, June 19, 2007, 12:02 a.m., http://www.hurri canearchive.org/object/28907.

7. One entry to the database captures the anxious concern of a New Orleans resident in Lakeview one year after the flooding. This brief entry depicts the fear and hope found among those who rebuilt their homes and returned to their neighborhoods only to find themselves surrounded by the vacant homes and lots of their former neighbors. See Anonymous, untitled entry, Hurricane Digital Memory Bank, object 11424, September 20, 2006, 9:13 a.m., http://www.hurricanearchive .org/objects/11424.

8. This project's sister database, the 9/11 Digital Archive, was the first electronic archive to be accepted by the Library of Congress. We hope the Hurricane Digital Memory Bank will follow the same path. According to a library press release, "The September 11 Digital Archive and its interactive Web site, 'Contribute Your Story,' was formally accepted into the Library's collections on September 10, 2003, thereby marking the Library's first major digital acquisition of 9/11 materials" (December 15, 2003). The full text is available at http://www.loc.gov/today/pr/ 2003/03-207.html.

9. See http://www.doyouknowwhatitmeans.org. "Do You Know What It Means" is part of the Hurricane Digital Memory Bank. This collection was developed by the chair of the Master of Fine Arts Photography, Video, and Related Media department at the School of Visual Arts in New York in partnership with several New Orleans organizations. Their mission is "to collect the untold stories of the people of New Orleans by chronicling and preserving them in an accessible and public digital archive comprised of collected photographs, videos, family histories, interviews and other artifacts." Their mission statement can be read in full via the following web link: http://www.doyouknowwhatitmeans.org/about.html.

10. "'In the Eye of the Power': The Challenge of Daily Journalism in New Orleans," panel discussion conducted at a conference of the Society for the Anthropology of North America, New Orleans, April 19, 2007.

11. Dave Walker, "On The Air," *Times-Picayune*, August 16, 2006 (review of *When the Levees Broke: A Requiem in 4 Acts*).

12. Ibid.

13. Chris Rose, "Hell and Back: A Chronicler of the Storm Is Crushed by Its Sorrows," *Times-Picayune*, October 22, 2006. The observation was made as part of the columnist's description of his experience with depression owing to his focus on post-Katrina stories.

14. Chris, Rose, "As Not Read by Oprah: What Do You Do When the Most Famous Book Pusher Won't Mention Yours?" *Times-Picayune*, August 29, 2007.

15. Cited in Brian Braiker, "A City Floods and Its Paper Sails," *Newsweek Online*, August 29, 2007, MSNBC.com, http://www.msnbc.msn.com/id/20500938/site/newsweek/page/0/.

16. The *Times-Picayune* uses Proquest Archiver to provide access to news articles two weeks after the date of print publication. For the price structure, see http://pqasb.pqarchiver.com/timespicayune/offers.html. Nola.com is described as an "affiliate" of the *Times-Picayune*.

17. Thinknola.com provides a good entry point into the realm of bloggers and technologists who are using their talents to help rebuild New Orleans. The blogger community's series of Rising Tide conferences are archived at http://think nola.com/wiki/Rising_Tide_Conference. See www.nola.com/forums for the full listing of forum topics.

18. These observations are not intended to ridicule individual arts projects integrating oral history but to highlight the general problem. Those public historians and others with a wealth of experience in conducting oral history interview programs in the affected communities have been relegated to the background. One of the more outspoken of these professionals has argued that as a group they should no longer cooperate when out-of-state disaster specialists and other funded researchers ask for a couple of books or articles that might help them to understand the region.

19. This is especially true when the person has been interviewed as one of the anonymous sources for an article to be published in a relatively obscure academic journal. Often such people were interviewed by local media in other parts of the country.

20. Chuck Jones produced one of the most poignant criticisms of time capsules in the Warner Brothers cartoon that introduced Michigan J. Frog. "One Froggy Evening" depicts the two greatest problems with time capsules: thievery and losing track of their locations. Every organization thinking of investing in a time capsule should view this cartoon.

21. Mary Gehman has provided updates along with her journal entries in a subcollection housed within the New Orleans Writers Collection. Courtney Giarrusso has also updated her collection by submitting photographs and essays. Both writers' work and photographs can be found either by using their last names as search terms in the online archive or by browsing the New Orleans Writers Collection at http://www.hurricanearchive.org/browse/?collection=159.

22. For example, see Jeremy Tuman, untitled entry, Hurricane Digital Memory Bank, object 11514, September 25, 2006, 3:07 p.m., http://www.hurri canearchive.org/object/11514.

23. "Had the levees not breached I would still have my deceased son's books. Photos and family heirlooms are now gone. Grief and anger are not new to me, but this was so completely unnecessary." For the entire essay, see Anonymous, untitled entry, Hurricane Digital Memory Bank, object 2444, August 4, 2006, 4:59 p.m., http://www.hurricanearchive.org/object/2444.

24. Bill Sullivan, "Online Image Contribution, Hurricane Digital Memory Bank," Hurricane Digital Memory Bank, object 2166, April 17, 2006, 9:18 p.m., http://www.hurricanearchive.org/object/2166.

25. "This was no token or in-kind dollop of support, either, but 1 million crisp dollar bills—a medium-sized fortune in the world of independent film. (As usual, we get it backwards—didn't anyone stop to think that perhaps Burns should have paid us a million bucks for the privilege of appropriating our cultural history?)." Steve Tyler, "Way Too Much Money, No Manners at All," letter to the editor, *Times-Picayune*, January 16, 2001, A4.

26. "Soledad O'Brien: Katrina Kids, Spike Lee, and Hope," CNN.com US: Behind the Scenes, February 9, 2007, http://www.cnn.com/2007/US/02/07/soledad.nolacameras/index.html.

27. See http://thinknola.com/ for Gutierrez's community activism portal and http://blogometer.com/ for his blog. Multifaceted assistance efforts provided for individuals and families throughout the Gulf Coast are directed by Common Ground Relief; these include free legal assistance and volunteers to help families in the process of rebuilding their homes. The collective is based in the Lower Ninth Ward, and their various projects are described in detail on their website: http://www.commongroundrelief.org/. A related effort to provide free health care services in New Orleans is the mission of the Common Ground Health Clinic: http://www.commongroundclinic.org/.

28. Nick Miroff, "Fixing the Pianos of New Orleans," May 20, 2006, National Public Radio, http://www.npr.org/templates/story/story.php?storyId=5419893; Darran Simon, "Healed by Harmony: Katrina Became a Clarion Call for an Oregon Musician Devastated by His Son's Death, Summoning Him Here to Give Away Instruments," *Times-Picayune*, June 3, 2007, B1.

Another Evacuation Story

Rebecca Mark

EVACUATION

August 27th
Jeff, Mark, Ben, and I leave early Saturday.

Jeff and Mark live in one house in Uptown, New Orleans.
I live in another house in Uptown, New Orleans. Ben, our son, calls both houses home.

I get gas. I get money.
We leave in a hurry.
I forget to put any money or food on the table for Anne.
I forget to take the pictures of Ben.
I forget to take Maaja's quilt.

I say to eleven-year-old Ben: "Let's leave the cats. I can't do this kitty litter thing again."
"Mom, you know you are going to take the cats."
I take the cats.
Amelia. Bedelia.
Bancha the old.
I take the ancient Sadie dog.

We drive to Beach Colony Resort, Perdido Key, Florida, three and a half hours toward the storm. We gamble.
We have no traffic.

Beach Colony Resort has these flat gray carts we pile with suitcases, dog dishes, cat litter, groceries, and three cats in carriers.

Sadie, the golden retriever, has congestive heart failure and was supposed to die in December of 2004.

Bancha had a brother, Mochi, but he died years ago by jumping off the roof and hitting himself on the New Orleans ironwork.

❧❧

EVACUATION

August 28th
Saturday is a day of elevators and kitties and litter and putting chairs together.

Jeff ordered the chairs from a designer in Toronto, and the designer came with the chairs. Jeff had decided that the condo that he and Mark had owned for a long time needed furniture. On August 26, 2005, he went down to Perdido Key with the interior designer and started putting together furniture. Friday Jeff and the interior designer heard about the storm. They drove home Friday night, helped Mark put up storm shutters, turned around again with all of us Saturday morning, drove to Beach Colony, and started putting furniture together.

We were still expecting to be back in New Orleans the next day. We had packed clothes for two days on the beach.

All that furniture had to be put together with these little screws and little bent-L screwdrivers, and then they turned into big, solid, wood furniture in the condo on the seventh floor overlooking the gulf. We put a lot of furniture together with these little screws. Tables. Beds. Chairs. A life. We are the only people I know—gay, of course—who evacuated with their interior designer.

We go swimming.

We keep watching CNN on a bad television that is in my room. I put together Ben's room—with nice sheets and blankets and bedspreads and a couple of books. I put his three pairs of shorts and two T-shirts in the chest of drawers that we had put together with the little screws. We go to dinner with the interior designer. She finds a flight out to Toronto on Sunday.

I go to bed in exhaustion. I hear Jeff in the other room. We may have to evacuate Perdido Key. No.

We can look out the window of the condo and see Katrina far off coming in and it is a beautiful, thick, dark gray storm at first.

Sunday THEY order a mandatory evacuation of Perdido Key. The monster is pumping his way northwest, but is so enormous it takes in our area. Sunday we evacuate from Perdido Key in all three cars again because Perdido Key, this parking lot, might flood. We take everything. Again. Cats, dogs, kitty litter, food, three cars in a caravan.

꿔꿩

EVACUATION

We drive to Dothan, Alabama, because our big map of Louisiana and Florida only had a small section of Alabama and Dothan is the farthest from the storm.

We are in Dothan for three days. We see everything: museums, exhibits, libraries, city parks, plaques on statues, EVERYTHING.

We eat at the Hibachi place next door three times.

I have dinner at the club with my Pa's first cousin Bess and her husband, a Buddhist who happens to live in Dothan—who knew—Alabama, Bess in her eighties, and her husband planted a blueberry farm in Dothan but then turned it into an airfield. Her father helped build one of the first synagogues in New Orleans before he moved to Australia. I am trying to be polite. I am trying to remember how to use a knife and fork.

On Monday the levees break. We watch CNN and eat Hampton Inn rolls and juice at little tables. We watch our neighborhoods go under water. There are many people from New Orleans at this Hampton Inn in Dothan, Alabama.

We listen to stories of family members left in houses that are now under water.

We watch one television set on CNN in the lobby and one in the room, but Ben is too upset to watch. My relatives in Alexandria and Seattle and Los Angeles see more than I do. I watch the Food Channel with Ben. Iron Chef.

The day of the storm the trees in the back of the hotel, three hundred miles from the eye, bend deep.

We leave on Wednesday.
On the way out of town, we spend time with the cousins, thank them for their offer of living in a trailer on their property. Ben nearly kills Bess's husband in a golf cart driving to see the blueberry field turned airport.

The levees have broken. Bodies are floating.

My heart is lying in the water.

I search CNN for Anne's face—for all our faces.

We are in three cars: Mark, Jeff, and Rebecca. They are all silver, and we drive almost as if there was a fine line between us of eleven years of loving, arguing, second-guessing, joking, blazing through the adventure of raising Ben, our son.

Amelia. Amelia. Come on Kitty. Come here Kitty.

❧❧

EVACUATION

Hana calls from L.A. while I sit finishing a poem at the car wash in Pensacola.

She says "You must write."
I am.
No. You must record.
She says it with direction. Emphatically.
Small stories are the most important now.
She says historical moment.
She says now. Write.

She is for me an Israeli soldier.
I slip into a past I don't know.
I think of the designated survivor—the white-haired man from Lodz.

I am wandering around Pensacola, looking.
I don't know what I am looking for.

Coffee shop or a shotgun house?
I don't drink coffee.

Hana was born on a train in Poland.
    Her parents liberated from the Nazis.

❧❧

EVACUATION

We return to Perdido Key on Wednesday.

Before we leave, a good church lady comes up to Mark in the parking lot of the Hampton Inn and says: I would like to give someone a home—a nice Christian family—not any of those homosexuals.

And so back to Perdido Key. Some dog peed in the elevator, and it smelled. It wasn't Sadie, but she could never quite make it to the dog walk and the storms blew the sand. A lady out in the flying sand spoke in a monotone. I lost three homes in one day she said.

I imagined the bodies of Kalamu and Jim's SAC [Students at the Center] students floating face-down in the water. I flick back and forth, CNN CNBC, falling asleep and then jerking awake to see if I missed something. Searching for faces. Where is Anne?

I try to read, but the black marks of typewritten words look like floating bodies.

We attach ourselves to computers. Lifelines. We spend hours looking at the weather, the maps, the latest reports, WWL, NOLA.COM, odd flood maps that make it look like water is everywhere. Ben and I say good-bye to things. I mourn the pictures, and the quilt. He mourns his books. We go to Barnes and Noble, and he tries to replace them all in one day.

Searching for e-mails from lost ones. Getting abandoned cell phone calls.

Ben pulls up a cement buoy.

We are swimming in the water that swept away the houses of Biloxi and Pass Christian and Bay Saint Louis that broke loose the boats that carried away the cement buoys.

Swimming in grief waters.

We spend hours with our heads under water watching schools of fish.

Gone, thousands of homes, simply gone.

Did Jeff get blood poisoning because of the water? He had cuts on his legs. We don't listen to him when he says I am cold. I am shivering. So get out from under the air-conditioning unit. We are all shivering.

I took two days off and drove to Tuscaloosa for a conference on Emmett Till. Miles of driving to hear about a dead African American boy killed by racism floating face-down in the Tallahatchie.
Jeff and Mark have a dog. His name is Flash.
Flash is two, acts like a puppy, and we all call him Spike—Jeff and Mark's dog before—Flash, and then we all say,

Spike is dead.
 How can there be a Bedelia without an Amelia?

🌾🌾

EVACUATION

Jeff and Mark go to the hospital. No one pays any attention to them. Too many huddled masses. They go back the next day. Jeff has red streaks going up his legs. He nearly dies—he says he didn't, I say he did—in a small hospital in Foley, Alabama. We will wake up.

Ben has been talking about the evacuation as if it were a book we are writing. He thinks the chapter with Daddy Jeff in the hospital is far too long.

We decide to send Ben to a school called the Creative Learning Academy. It is fabulous, an amazing creative gem in the middle of nowhere. I am ashamed of my evacuation car.

Anne? Where is Anne? She had a new pacemaker put in ten days before the storm. I speak to her on Friday, and she sounds like she is going to evacuate. I cannot reach her. How could she survive?

Mark is called back to work at a cobbled together LSU Medical Center in Baton Rouge. Talk of doctors living in trailers, on boats. We struggle to find a home, a school, a life in Baton Rouge, but there is no room at the inn. Thank god. Thank god.

The calls start coming in from friends all over the country. Hundreds of trees fell on Sue Jo and Myra's house.

The Jews call, They understand, have lived it all, fear is in their voices, they call me and my family at all hours, terrified, convinced until they hear my voice that I am in the Convention Center or wandering the roads alone or on a train to some unknown destination. Harriet, Hana, and Emily watch over me with a fierce much-needed love.

Brenda waits patiently for the second date that was supposed to occur on September first.

Jeff is in the hospital. The roads in Pensacola go on forever. There are no friends at the end of the roads. Kathy comes to help me gut the house the third weekend in September. Rita hits New Orleans. Kathy helps us drive to Virginia instead. Jeff follows. Mark lives with Granny and Papa in Baton Rouge and tries to help dis-

placed people. Ben goes to his evacuation school, Burgundy Farm, for free. We live in a beautiful house. The Jewish Endowment takes care of us. I spend months with my ninety-year-old father, some of the last months of his life. I spend Rosh Hashana at a strange synagogue. Ben learns Hebrew at Beth Israel where my friends from childhood studied for their Bat and Bar Mitzvahs. The days are short. In October my brother Andy and I travel to New Orleans and gut my house.

Amelia escapes out of the back of my parents' house while we are gone. Gut.

❧

EVACUATION

It is cold in Alexandria, Virginia in October.
Amelia. Amelia. Here Kitty Kitty Kitty. It's Mommy. Ben and I make flyers of her face on a piece of paper; I remember I have a colored photo of her on the computer that Mark brought up from the house his first trip back. We make two hundred copies. I spend one morning of many putting flyers in the mailboxes of the houses behind Martha's Circle where the Thorpe Estate used to be, where my brother Charlie got arrested in the sixties with his long Jewish Afro and hippy pants with the purple stripe for loitering. The flyers say Lost Cat. Evacuated from Katrina. Cat lost in Hollin Hills.
I spread our evacuation all over the neighborhood.
I run between houses because I have so little time.
I run because I can.
I run because I have so much adrenaline pumping through my body.
I could have run ten marathons. I ran and ran and ran and have never stopped.

❧

EVACUATION

Epilogue

In the community of beautiful Japanese-style houses the trees gathered their tentacle branches and ate my Amelia as fiercely as they gathered me in their arms and kept me sane. We drove home on December 23 in time for Christmas with Granny and Papa in Baton Rouge. As Ben and I sped through Slidell and New Orleans East I made sure that we listened to WWOZ blare their silly Christmas songs, and I cried silently in the front seat so that Ben would not grow up too fast as we passed mile after mile of darkened silence where communities used to stand.

SECTION 2

❀❀

New Beginnings

Amy Koritz

THINKING ABOUT WHAT GOT DONE in the arts and culture sector of New Orleans in the year following the storm, I am reminded of one of the principles of open space—a meeting facilitation technique—which asserts "whoever shows up are the right people." Distressingly few of these were university faculty members or administrators in the arts and humanities disciplines. Individuals and small nonprofit organizations frequently got the most done with the fewest resources. They moved quickly to reestablish networks, actively invited participation by newcomers, and put programs on the ground in response to a fast, but well-informed, analysis of needs and opportunities. While people located in universities often established partnerships, formal and informal, with these programs, their driving force came from elsewhere.

Carol Bebelle was one of the most articulate advocates for the arts and culture to emerge after the storm. As cofounder and director of the Ashé Cultural Arts Center in New Orleans' Central City neighborhood, she had for many years brought visibility to African and African American cultural practices. In the fall of 2005, she began opening Ashé to community groups and others that needed meeting space, making Ashé a hub for recovery activity. After being appointed to a committee of the Mayor's Bring New Orleans Back Commission (the first attempt at recovery planning by local government), Carol became a highly visible spokesperson for the centrality of the arts to the city's revitalization. Unlike similarly positioned leaders who focused on infusing resources into large cultural institutions and tourism, she from the start attempted to give voice to the needs and contributions of traditional culture bearers and individual artists. Efforts of Grace, Ashé's legal home, became the fiscal agent for numerous small projects and startup organizations. Carol herself generated a sense of warmth and possibility in the midst of crisis that gave those around her hope and strength. Moreover, the focus and vision she brought to the table gave confidence to funders who were worried about the capacity of New Orleans organizations to implement and administer large-scale initiatives. With an infusion of support from the Ford Foundation, she was able to purchase Ashé's building, securing its tenure in a neighborhood desperately in need of stability. Other foundations also stepped forward, allowing Ashé's role in the community to expand far beyond its prestorm capacity. Carol Bebelle's contribution to this volume had its origin in a speech, and while not doing justice to the power of her personal presence, it exemplifies her gift for naming injustice while refusing victimhood and for honoring the past while staying focused on the future.

One of the projects Carol Bebelle assisted was Mat Schwarzman's educational theater troupe for high school students, Creative Forces. Mat has been active in educational reform efforts incorporating the arts, and particularly theater, since I first met him at meetings of the Douglass Coalition, a loose group of community activists organized around supporting one of the city's many failing high schools. We worked together in 2003 organizing the National Convergence of Artists, Educators, and Organizers, an event that served as my introduction to a rich and extensive network of community-based artists and educators. Deeply committed to the belief that creativity is a capacity we all share, though one too often squelched by or relinquished to mass media and the elite arts, he has spent his career looking for ways to incite and support the potential of youth to engage the world through the arts. Through the Crossroads Project, Mat has sought to communicate the insights gained from his experience and that of other community-based artists. Through Creative Forces, he is putting this experience to use in improving math and science education for New Orleans youth. While he has worked closely with university professors, particularly at Xavier University, Mat partners strategically with higher education, being careful to ensure that its interests and limitations do not define the agenda of his work.

A cautious but welcoming approach to higher education likewise characterized the efforts of D. Hamilton Simons-Jones and Kyshun Webster to fill a desperate need for youth programs in the summer of 2006. At the time, Kyshun was both special assistant to the president for community programs at Xavier University and executive director of Operation REACH, a nonprofit organization he founded as a student at Xavier. Hamilton was the director of community service at Tulane University. Neither one holds a university position any longer. I have known Hamilton since he was an undergraduate at Tulane in the late 1990s. As president of CACTUS (Community Action Caucus of Tulane University Students) and then a member of the Student Affairs staff, he had developed broad and deep relationships with community organizations and public schools in the city. These relationships enabled him to have an immediate impact once the university reopened. He organized service projects for Tulane and other college students and helped Carol Bebelle start the Mardi Gras Service Corps as a mechanism for integrating the city's dual need for tourism dollars and volunteers. He and Kyshun Webster took on the urgent challenge of providing programs for middle school children returning to the city that summer not because they had a plan or funding or infrastructure but because they saw a need. Kyshun had years of experience in youth programming, a PhD in education, and a position at Xavier University that enabled him to leverage some of the university's resources to meet this need. The two together deployed a national network of contacts in higher education and experience in fund-raising to recruit sponsors and college students to support and staff a summer camp. Since then, Operation REACH has been awarded a multi-million-dollar grant to replicate this program.

The new beginnings described in this section illustrate responses to changed conditions that did more than provide shelter and safety; they built on the knowledge and experience of their leaders to address circumstances both new to the city (the dearth of summer camps) and long standing (poor education in math and science) in ways that leveraged the emergency in the service of a better future. In the same manner, the response of Hispanic-serving nonprofit organizations to the influx of Latino workers has begun to prepare the city for a browner future. Elizabeth Fussell's research documents how the pre-Katrina Hispanic population of New Orleans reacted to this changing demographic. As mostly Mexican workers converged on the city to clean up and rebuild its physical landscape, organizations such as the Hispanic Apostolate of the Archdiocese of New Orleans braced for new demands on their services. A demographer by training, Beth watched carefully as the city began to repopulate, looking for any data available that could help her understand the likely impact of Hispanic migration on the city. In describing how an existing Hispanic population responded to these newcomers, she has laid the groundwork for understanding what will be a long and perhaps contentious story. The ambivalence of local governments to an increasing Hispanic population with the capacity to upset long-standing racial politics has been made repeatedly evident. Beth's essay makes clear how crucial the advocacy of an established Hispanic population will be in protecting a vulnerable group of immigrant workers from injustice and exploitation.

Of all the new beginnings enabled or exacted by Katrina and its aftermath, this last may end up having the greatest impact on the culture of the city. Already as much Caribbean as American, New Orleans now has a plethora of taco trucks serving lunch to customers raised on gumbo and jambalaya. Every beginning has a past, however, and the legacies of New Orleans' rich cultural traditions and failing institutions can be traced in each of the selections in this section. Each also exemplifies an ability to combine urgency with analysis and analysis with action. This combination of knowledge—both practical and theoretical—with a bias toward action characterized the most effective responses to the chaos and devastation of New Orleans. Perhaps there is a lesson for higher education here. Or, if not a lesson, perhaps a moment of clarifying insight about the ways in which civic engagement can and cannot happen in universities.

The Vision Has Its Time

CULTURE AND CIVIC ENGAGEMENT IN
POSTDISASTER NEW ORLEANS

Carol Bebelle

Write the vision down plainly on tablets for the vision has
its time, presses on to fulfillment and will not disappoint. If
it delays wait for it for it will surely come.

—Habakuk 2:2

Katrina, or, the Federal Flood

IN 2005, THE AMERICAN PHENOMENON of postdisaster living was created by
Hurricane Katrina. Shifting in status from category 4 to a category 5, Katrina hit the Gulf of Mexico and caused catastrophic disaster all along the
Gulf Coast. In New Orleans, the hurricane was a near miss. It had been re-
duced in velocity to a category 4. It stalled in the gulf near the mouth of the
Mississippi River, then miraculously veered east, averting the perfect formula for a maximum destructive hurricane hit to New Orleans.

We had avoided the catastrophic storm, but we were not so lucky in escaping the incompetence of the U.S. Army Corps of Engineers, the federal
agency responsible for the poorly constructed and inadequate levee system. Depending on the source referenced, five-eighths to seven-eighths of
the city of New Orleans was flooded in the unprecedented occurrence of,
the shutdown of, and near destruction of an American city. Adding insult

to injury, the federal government then took six days—nearly a week—to organize a supposedly effective rescue response for American citizens in New Orleans trapped in a flood caused by federal negligence.

Ironically, propaganda has it that Katrina was the culprit. The clever use of the Katrina prefix on almost everything related to the disaster makes it hard for everyday folk to hold on to the fact that it was, indeed, a federal flood that accomplished the vast destruction in New Orleans. The Corps' intentional unwillingness to accept responsibility laid the foundation for the inhumane, callous, and unjust way in which New Orleans has been handled in the wake of this tragic event. Blaming the victim has become high sport, and New Orleans is the game.

Culture, Front and Center

Americans were glued to their television sets in horror as people died and human dignity was compromised. But they also witnessed the activation of civic engagement. While New Orleanians, herded like cattle to evacuation centers and other cities, were trying to get their bearings and, more importantly, trying to regain control of their lives, an unprecedented volunteer response began to form. Government may have been lethargic in its response, but the American people were not. Starting with religious institutions of every kind, Americans were stepping up, front and center, to help their fellow citizens.

The American landscape is a stage on which life dramas have taken place throughout our history. This disaster, however, was the worst in the annals of American history in its scale and impact. This federal flood played out in a drama of epic proportions, and the influence, theme, character, and persona of racism were given unrestricted permission to improvise everywhere.

Unfortunately, a culture exists in America that supports racism, both institutional racism and individual racist behavior. The combination of these was visible in individual behaviors. What regard and respect were given to the humanity of one person over the other? What urgency was given to taking care of business for one kind of person versus another? How did institutions attend to the needs of people of color? What considerations existed for them? What prejudgments existed? How willing were these institutions to flex, expand, or otherwise adapt to give people of color a compassionate and humanitarian quality of service? How determined was the commitment to help them?

When we look at how people survived initially after the disaster, while the government was running in circles, getting nowhere fast, and trying to figure out what it was going to do, we saw individuals stepping up to, and sometimes stepping away from, their negative values and feelings toward the people who needed help in order to answer the call of humanity. These legions were not always organized to provide this type of relief service, but they accepted the mission and responsibility of having to do it. As a part of accepting this responsibility, the notion of *not* being successful became an unacceptable outcome. And so, with their deep commitment, they succeeded, checking their personal prejudices in inspiring human displays of kindness all over the American landscape. Individuals, families, friendship circles, businesses, and organizations beat a path to the Gulf South to give a helping hand and have the backs of their fellow Americans.

The Ashé (**pronounced ah-shay**) Cultural Arts Center (CAC), founded by Douglas Redd and me in 1998 and the place where I currently serve as executive director, is an emerging cultural institution in New Orleans, led by African Americans. We refashioned ourselves to make a greater contribution to the recovery and rebuilding effort in New Orleans. Our mission calls us to combine the intentions of community and economic development with the awesome creative forces of community, culture, and art to revive and reclaim a historically significant corridor of New Orleans' Central City community, Oretha Castle-Haley Boulevard, formerly known as Dryades Street. After Hurricane Katrina, we expanded our reach to support the recovery, revival, and rebuilding of our city and region. One of our adapted programs, our Central City Tour, became a Rebuilding Tour, and we have hosted nearly five thousand volunteers, foundations, corporations, organizations, universities, high schools, and churches on this tour over the last three years.

This role has allowed us not only to see volunteers at work, but also to hear from them about their personal reactions and motivations toward the disaster and New Orleans. Over time, we have accumulated an organic, random sampling of people, not only those who came to help but those who returned to rebuild their city.

In addition to hosting tours, briefings, and orientation meetings for volunteers, funders, and investors. We also host hundreds of meetings of community groups and sponsor dialogues between and among leaders, elected officials, and New Orleans residents about what kind of rebuilding to do and how to do it. It is in this capacity that we have been able to see and hear their passion for justice. Powerful voices, in numbers, are demanding more fairness and consideration for folks who are still working their way back home.

This up-close-and-personal time with thousands of people in intimate samplings has helped us to see the fire of hope burning lively among those who have returned and those who have come to help. In fact, many of those who have come to help have decided to stay for a one-to five-year term to help with the rebuilding.

Many people view this opportunity as a defining moment in their lives. Making a contribution here and now as a resident of New Orleans or a volunteer gives great meaning to their lives on a personal level. Whether they independently sent their holiday money to families in need in New Orleans or asked that gift money for anniversaries and weddings be donated to causes in the city, it is clear that individuals across our nation have been touched by our plight and moved to action.

Families were adopted in the many locations where New Orleanians evacuated. At last count, forty-eight of the fifty states received evacuees. It is interesting and important to note that religious organizations, a spiritual manifestation of culture, were some of the first to come to the aid of displaced New Orleanians. All over the country, temples, churches, synagogues, and congregations stepped up to the plate and walked the walk that their religious principles espoused. Citizens of America lived up to both the value of democracy and the standards of their spiritual beliefs. This is an important observation because if people can rally themselves to cross social barriers, then surely we can motivate and cause institutions to do the same.

Putting Things in Context

It didn't take long for the accumulation of disaster circumstances to combine and contemporize the African Maafa (Atlantic slave trade): the water, the boats, separated families that were herded to places that had no accommodations for human needs, including no water or food. The damage done in reopening those old wounds will be observed for many years to come. But the fallout also accomplished an undeniable validation, dramatically and before the nation, that there really are two faces to America. There is the "them that got face and the them that don't got face." No one can seriously dispute this after the federal flood in New Orleans.

If being right were enough, then we could rest on our victory of exposing to America the existence of racism. This moment of truth serves us best as an opportunity to unite and commit to building a stellar, contemporary, American city. In New Orleans it is possible, with America's help, to create a city of neighborhoods and communities, a city that models to the world the fulfillment of the promise of democracy.

But this opportunity, this possibility, this *vision* is not the current reality. The city is still full of patches of wilderness, it lacks infrastructure, and resources are being withheld ostensibly to assure that there is appropriate accountability. This is the present, the real deal. New Orleanians are frustrated, dispirited, depressed, and losing hope fast. But as dire as this picture is, it is also a fertile ground for cultural healing.

When times are hard, friends and family are away, and our backs are up against the wall, it is the spirit of song, story, memory, image, and creativity that keeps us going. These are pivotal aspects of culture, which, when combined with the spiritual, have the capacity to catapult people through the worst of circumstances. This formula has worked over and over again in human society in the civil rights movement, the Native American resistance movement, and more recently in South Africa, where music is credited with having been a driving force in toppling apartheid. The spirit of culture, song, dance, story, and image creates a spiritual force that energizes and motivates us to endure, move forward, and make it through to the other side.

In a city known around the world for culture that bubbles up from the streets, we need to "catch the spirit"; we need to put the devices of culture to work for us more dramatically. We need to create images of what New Orleans will be so that people can envision something they believe is worth putting forth greater effort for. We must create opportunities for people to gather and draw strength and motivation from each other. We must tell the stories of accomplishment as well as those of difficulty and frustration. We must give ourselves permission to be joyful, to dance, and to understand that this is all fuel for a path leading to better times.

We must also give children a view of adults who are able to emerge through difficulty so that the children can feel they have a future. We must not be afraid to hope or be optimistic out of a fear of being disappointed. Rather, we have to have the courage to dream of better times. We must learn the lesson of the football runner: "If you fail, fail forward reaching for the goal."

Sociologists and psychologists long ago taught us the lesson of the "self-fulfilling prophecy" *if I believe it, I can make it happen.* This works for us both positively and negatively. If we expect things to get better, they do. If we expect them to get worse, they do. We have to raise a legion of cultural cheerleaders who inspire and remind us that we can overcome this tragedy in our lives. This is a hard job, but it is not an impossible one. The active practice of culture in New Orleans gives us a bounty of spirit with which to work.

Volunteers saw the promise of hope and the wonderful opportunity to make a contribution. They realized they were a part of the winning formula for New Orleans. As New Orleanians, we have to find a way to reach this light of hope as well. We have to create prayers, mantras, songs, meditations, visualizations, dances, and stories for spiritual sustenance. We have to continue to lean on each other, trust each other, and be willing to be a blessing to each other. We also have to recognize the need to build our new city with the highest of hopes, standards, and expectations.

The good news is that we are on the way. When we were frustrated and being overlooked, we got roused and angry. We recognized the importance of standing up for ourselves and showing up to represent ourselves. The high level of involvement of residents in the planning processes and town hall meetings is an indication of community organizing at work. The establishment of neighborhood organizations for every neighborhood in New Orleans, and an organizing mechanism for these community groups, is cause for celebration. These are some of the details of how we dream a new city that works for everyone. This is some of the evidence of community engagement in New Orleans at present.

The *New* New Orleans

The new New Orleans is something wonderful to ponder. Imagine all the things we thought were wrong and then fix them. That's the opportunity we have with this rebuilding effort. We need only to have the courage to dream and then to work to make what we dream come true. This is not an easy process, but it is a doable one. Marianne Williamson, a noted author and therapist, stated:

> Our deepest fear is not that we are inadequate. Our deepest fear is that we are powerful beyond measure. It is our light, not our darkness, that most frightens us. We ask ourselves, who am I to be brilliant, gorgeous, talented, and fabulous? Actually, who are you not to be?

This staggering irony of needing to believe in ourselves and each other more than counting on our leaders to produce a decent quality of life for us can be paralyzing. It is certainly not the most recent and accepted view of our individual circumstances in the world.

In this scenario, the job for Ashé CAC is to help call to the forefront the power within. We can encourage people to identify and bring forth a can-do mental attitude and spirit. Using the prism of history, we work to make visible the insight that struggle and a tumultuous existence have been both the cauldron and the womb of fantastic creativity.

New Orleans has been shaped by immigrant communities and the lives of their ancestors, both those who came willingly and those who were snatched up and brought here as labor to help to build New Orleans. Their lives form the foundation of New Orleans and are testimony to the life lessons that struggle and perseverance teach us.

The poor and disenfranchised left their mark on New Orleans. We still have the Irish Channel and, more recently, Little Vietnam. The Haitians and other Caribbean people and the West Africans made indelible contributions to the city's culture and folkways. Even today New Orleans has the reputation of being the most African city in America, affectionately called the uppermost part of the Caribbean. There is a reciprocity and responsibility that should come with being the recipient of such good fortune from "a goose that lays such large and juicy golden eggs."

It is scandalous that Mardi Gras Indians, Second Line Clubs, and the traditional folkways and rituals of this city are now up for grabs by anyone who cares to benefit from them. The culture masters and culture bearers share their gifts generously, sometimes too generously. Their style is warm and giving, and they are authentic and considerate. This includes the thousands of restaurant and hotel workers who provide warmth and special treatment to the millions of visitors to our city. Where are the considerations for them? In New Orleans, we get to know you and like you and then we invite you in closer. If you don't watch it, soon we are calling you "Boo" and you are on your way to being like family.

More than half of what the tourism industry makes from this city derives from the ambiance and allure of New Orleans' authentic neighborhood culture. Yet government and business entities, and many middle- and upper-class residents, don't appreciate these contributions and definitely don't feel a need to invest in, understand or accept the contribution that the workforce and tradition bearers make to their personal lives and prosperity. Therefore, like the federal government's bureaucracy, they fail to invest in the evolution and preservation of the culture and its bearers. Reciprocity is appallingly absent despite the fact that it is in the best interest of the tourism industry, one of the city's leading economic engines. There isn't a place for authentic culture bearers at the distribution table, but often they are a main entrée on the menu.

As a consequence, the culture makers and bearers are left to their own devices to preserve and grow the culture that inspires and supports the robust tourism economy. So imagine this: we have a golden goose, in danger of starving, that is laying big golden eggs for others. It makes you wonder, then, how the goose can create such great fortune when it is on the verge of starving. What could that goose create if it were fed?

Or, better still, imagine hotel and restaurant workers who earn livable salaries, wages and benefits that can keep a family financially stable. Imagine neighborhood studios with Mardi Gras Indians and Second Line Clubs where tourists and our young people get the opportunity to learn from the traditions that have been passed down for generations. Imagine cross-generational events and activities that allow community elders to contribute their wisdom and experience to youth and the community as a whole rather than being afraid to sit on their porches or to interact with young people in their neighborhoods.

As far as education is concerned, we were in trouble *before* the disaster and in deeper trouble now. Our schools are insufficient to meet the needs of our children. Lifelong learning is a necessary life skill, but we can't even teach our youth to learn let alone teach the adults. Before the disaster, we held the distinction of having a 40 percent illiteracy rate. In a democracy where choice is the preeminent freedom, how do we assure choice for people who can't access the information for analysis? This scandal of illiteracy is a huge compromise to the ideal and doctrine of democracy, and yet we tolerate it. Why?

Wouldn't it be wonderful to have small schoolhouses in each neighborhood while the damaged schools are being repaired or rebuilt? This could also be the answer for youth who need alternative environments and styles of learning even after the mainstream schools are restored. Imagine being close to home in a small setting where the community is welcome to help. And there could be computer centers that serve as university distance-learning stations for adults.

Imagine mentoring and tutoring programs that are plentiful in every community and service learning and mentoring programs aimed at exposing young people to diverse work environments. Think about lunchtime at work as an opportunity to eat *and* learn in general equivalency diploma (GED) classes and community college courses on work premises. What if employees were given incentives to attend educational programs? In postdisaster New Orleans, we need to consider intimacy as a critical variable of quality service in education and many other pivotal institutional areas.

In postdisaster New Orleans, our health systems are greatly strained or absent. We have too few hospitals, hospital beds, doctors, nurses, and other health professionals. Mental health services are virtually nonexistent at a time when stress, depression, and emotional breakdowns are on an anticipated and alarming rise. We are constrained by the lack of access to mental health services and in jeopardy of more and more self-destructive behavior and the emotional blowups that often turn violent.

The job market is active, but the cost of both home ownership and renting has skyrocketed. So the jobs may be plentiful, but where are people supposed to live? We are two hundred thousand persons less, and the business landscape suffers mightily from their absence. Couldn't we create vouchers for hotel rooms and rooming houses both to assist folks in the back-and-forth necessary to handle the business of returning home and to serve the needs of displaced New Orleanians who either are employed or would be if they had a place to live?

Our city government is on the verge of bankruptcy! Where is the investment to assure that it won't happen? Are we reorganizing and creating competitive salary scales to entice our city workforce to return and to attract other specialists to help us out of the distress in which we find ourselves? The city cannot operate without a sufficient tax base.

Imagine our most fertile minds solving these problems and meeting the other challenges before us. Imagine us determined to create a better New Orleans, one that offers equal opportunity and a menu of services enviable throughout the world. Imagine a thriving creative and cultural economy. Imagine a startling recovery in the schools. Imagine the institutions for incarceration graduating high school and community college inmates. Imagine jobs being available to the incarcerated when they are released. Imagine our human capacities and resources being used to the maximum. Imagine a contemporary American city morally, socially, and politically meeting the democratic standard of by and for the people with liberty and justice for all.

Suppose we ponder these things and our very thoughts become small fragments of possibility, which, when combined, create reality. Suppose this is the way it works. If this is so, then couldn't focusing on the potential for failure indeed create failure?

Assuring Success

How do we continue to support an engaged community in times like these? Is there a surefire success formula? No, there isn't. But there are several proven strategies for keeping the community's attention. The first rule is obvious: use the efforts that people bring and then deliver on their work. The people have spoken in neighborhood, district and city plans. Implement them. The people must recognize that this is a "chicken or egg" process. Being involved and active generates action and change. The converse is also true: no community pressure, no change. "Power concedes nothing without a demand. It never has and it never will."

For individuals, the process is more spiritual and emotional. We must frame our day with possibility. We can't look at the shape we are in every day and just *wish* that things were different. We must create our daily to-do lists; they are the fuel for our engines. When we complete our lists, we will see progress in our personal lives, and that progress will make us feel better. Feeling better will energize us, and our combined energy will sustain the activism. Our lists will also better prepare us to seek and receive help from engaged fellow Americans who are still looking for ways to help us out of our crisis.

One of the most important aspects of culture is its ability to adapt to people's needs; isolate certain desires, needs, and feelings; and immortalize them in ritual. In this period of redevelopment for our city, an important role for Ashé CAC is to assist in the development of new cultural rituals, to adapt old ones, and to allow the community to influence and participate in the conversion processes. It is important for creativity to be given its freest rein in all neighborhoods in order to demonstrate what is possible and doable in destroyed and damaged neighborhoods. Seeing is believing.

The Ashé CAC should be committed to collecting resources and fueling artists and tradition bearers in their efforts to reestablish their homes and create ripple effects of creative energy to support fellow New Orleanians as they attempt to return to their neighborhoods and communities.

We should be producing and presenting an active schedule of cultural, community, and art activities and events that allow people to come together to refuel their spirits and be inspired by the success of returning evacuees. We should be listening to members of the community and immortalizing their thoughts, insights, and feelings in art. And we should be encouraging them to discover their own creative talents. Creativity is sorely needed in our efforts to rebuild our neighborhoods and heal our souls after this great tragedy.

It takes a lot of cultural energy to convert depression, despair and frustration into positive energy, and we must call forth cultural traditions that can be useful during this very trying time. Dancing, drumming, visual art, theater, poetry, music, filmmaking, and writing are all ways to help people process their experiences, generate strategies, and enliven their spirits. This is a time when we should be full of culture and creativity.

We should be redoubling our efforts to reach our youth and work to support teachers in their efforts to inspire young people to pursue an education. We should demonstrate our deep and abiding belief in the power of culture and creativity, and we should be creating and manipulating culture so that it can effectively fill its rightful role: revisioning, rethinking, and healing our community. The Ashé CAC fully embraces its role as an advocate for the community, the culture, and the right of people to be creative.

We are so steeped in the left-brain region of analysis: plans, facts, figures, projections. Well, it may sound great and it may make us feel like we are getting things done, but the irony is that with the best formula in the world the thing that makes the formula, the strategy, the plan a reality is the activists, the "somebodies," who are willing to become emboldened with the spirit of determination to get things done. When it gets hard, not putting it down and keeping on with it is where the spiritual fortitude comes in. Culture is the pathway to that resource and energy.

Spiritual fortitude and character are usually formed by families and inspired as ideals kick into play. It's the cultural and spiritual connections, the values our family demonstrated and taught us, that determine our ability to struggle, to live with disappointment, to find peace and joy in the worst of circumstances, and to imagine our way through hard times so that we can see our way through the dream into a new reality.

The Ashé CAC has positioned itself on the cultural and creative landscape of New Orleans. If we had our way, we'd help mamas learn lullabies again so they could take the fear out of, and the edge off, their children's days, so they could sleep at night restfully and wake up in the morning without having to carry adult fears and worries. We'd find ways for men to learn to be sweet to their women again. We'd help to find ways to direct and assist teachers, once again, to discover the joy of opening a door to knowledge to someone and watch them explode and leap. We'd help elders regain their rightful place of respect and love in the community. We'd bring people together to hear music and ideas that help them make it through this difficult time.

Something's gone terribly wrong. And we keep jumping over it and around it and not getting to it. There is tension between young people and elders. It's the tension of the young people becoming their own individual selves and not being told what to do by others and the adults in their lives wanting to be sure that the young don't make costly mistakes. This is a natural tension. However, there is another tension at work in the community that is insidiously bad. It's the tension caused by young people living lawless lives that are unnaturally short because they can't count on the adults to create a world that has more to offer them. We must do something to reverse this trend.

We see the need for young people to succeed. They need encouragement and validation. We need to look at their art and their lifestyles to reinforce and validate them. They have evolved a mature, almost cynical view of life. This is due, in great part, to our failure to create a life for them that has more promise. Poor schools, no work skills, and no legitimate access to resources lead to frustration, depression, and desperate, lawless behavior.

Artists and tradition bearers are ready to use their creative spirits as healing balm in every place that needs it. They would practice their brand of trash-to-treasure conversion on neighborhoods, schools, people, and spirits. This community of artists and tradition bearers can see the brand new day, the new possibilities. This vision makes us hopeful and spirit filled. We would gladly infect the whole community given the chance.

Our greatest challenge in this rebuilding phase is the challenge of imagination, faith, and spirit. Armed with vision and committed action, we can, and we will, succeed.

How to Raise an Army
(of Creative Young People)

Mat Schwarzman, with illustrator Keith Knight

> So which of your spectators
> Should you then follow, actors?
> I would suggest
> The discontented.
> —Poet/Educator/Activist Bertolt Brecht

PROLOGUE: This is a report from the cultural battlefields of New Orleans written in July 2007 and then updated approximately one year later. By the time this reaches you, our circumstances will have changed again, perhaps many times over, so we need to talk quickly. No conclusions are possible yet, but a few of my comrades and I can share some of our thoughts and experiences in-progress . . .

July 2007

My name is Mat Schwarzman, and I am the founder of CREATIVE FORCES, an educational theater ensemble made up of New Orleans high school students and mentored by a team of adult teaching artists and schoolteachers. It's been almost two years since Hurricane Katrina touched our shores and set off a wave of destructive events unprecedented in our nation's history. Creative Forces' four-year mission, begun this month, is to help rebuild our city's broken education system by introducing more creativity into the curriculum. Currently, we number eleven (six teenagers and five adults), but we plan for many more to join us. As with any campaign, we have allies, a strategic timetable, a core group of inspired believers, and a long-term vision of success. Our enemies are the fixed and limiting attitudes that we as New Orleanians carry to school, home, play, and work and the negative assumptions we carry around about our neighbors and public systems, especially schools. Ideas, however intangible, are the most powerful things in the world.

The strategies and visions contained in this report came from our group and have been filtered through my personal perspective. I was raised far from here in suburban New Jersey, and I have been living in New Orleans only since 2001, but it did not take me long to realize what everyone here already knew: the failed school system and the failed levees are only the latest in a very long series of staggering public systems failures that dates back decades. Without going into the specific reasons behind these events, suffice it to say that we adults have become so accustomed to the failing public schools, collapsing roads, unreliable mass transit, and multi-generational unemployment that we have a standard sarcastic phrase to describe the situation: "Close enough for jazz."[1] Translation: when it comes to New Orleans, substandard is all we're ever going to get.

The situation is so bad that it is sometimes hilarious. For example, for the last several months Mr. Sidney D. Torres IV has become a great local celebrity. For many, he is outshining elected officials, athletes, and even Hollywood actors (the new locals Brad Pitt and Angelina Jolie) in popularity. Why? Because last year his company got a contract to collect New Orleans' trash, and he took the radical step of actually doing his job *better* than it had been done before. Many of our streets are the cleanest they have been in anyone's memory, and the sanitation workers are taking a lot of pride in their work. Health violations are down, and every day people are walking around in places they never used to and are *not* seeing trash. Mr. Torres told our local newspaper that he has been overwhelmed by a flood of cards, media attention, and personal thanks from a populace both astonished and grateful.

New Orleanians have become so accustomed to smelling and seeing garbage that we have forgotten what it is like to have clean streets. It is the same with the school system. If it were possible to remind people, even in little ways, that learning *can* be joyful, interesting, and relevant, then perhaps over time students, parents, teachers, administrators, leaders, and the people as a whole would decide to organize ourselves and ensure that nothing less is allowed.

I love New Orleans and the things that make us so special, but I am convinced we have to somehow flip our entire paradigm so that nothing less than excellence will be close enough for jazz.[2] I understand that in the current context this may sound trite. Our people are facing enormous *political*, *economic*, and *physical* battles in the streets and boardrooms of the city that will decide the breadth and depth of the rebuilding process. But to the extent that we as democratic citizens will only get what we believe we deserve we are also in a long-term *cultural* battle to win over our own hearts and minds and demand a world-class education system.

Young people are the logical catalyst for this change. They have the most to gain from it. Plus, this kind of broad-based cultural transformation requires long-term changes in everyday habits and behaviors over an extended period of time, and generally speaking young people are better equipped for this. Young people with a vision for change will also be well positioned to develop alternatives and advocate for them over the long haul. It seems obvious: New Orleans must tap the power of our teenagers as creative resources and leaders.

> But how to get this going? How now
> To show the knotting and casting of fate's net?
> And that it has been knotted and cast by men?
> The first thing you have to learn
> Is the art of *observation*.
> —Bertolt Brecht

Our Strategy

We are Creative Forces, an ensemble of teen peer educators and adult mentors, and our four-year mission is to infuse more creativity into education. We conduct original music theater workshops and perform plays in schools, in community centers, and for educational groups throughout New Orleans and beyond. We use our state and national curriculum standards, but our goal is to convey a larger message: high schools *must* do much more than teaching to the tests. For our children to succeed as adults and citizens in our community of the future, it is vital that they can not only understand information but can master and manipulate it through

Fig. 9. The Creative Forces logo was created by Young Aspirations/Young Artists and Big TaDa Productions.

creativity. Our motto expresses this concept as an equation: Information + Imagination = Knowledge.

As an ensemble of actors, singers, musicians, poets, dancers, and storytellers, we know that the tools of the theater are extremely effective in developing creativity and communicating vital information. Since our very beginnings, human beings have sung, danced, spoken, and played instruments with one another in order to interpret, remember, and convey what is most important to us. We can use theater skills to help our peers think, learn, and interact more effectively.

Because we believe that in the theater it is always better to demonstrate than explain, Creative Forces' young people are the objects as well as the subjects of change. Our educational workshops are co-facilitated by teens and adults, and our plays feature students as writers, performers, and protagonists. Luther Gray, a master African drummer, educator, and founding member of the Creative Forces faculty, puts it this way.

It's going to take at least ten years to rebuild New Orleans, and that is probably optimistic. That makes it these young people we are working with now who have the most at stake in the outcome. They need to be talking to each other much more than we adults need to be talking at them.

The stakes are astronomical. If young people have an investment in the future of the city, they will help protect it. If they are shut out again, like they were before Katrina, they are going to tear the city apart.

Early on we talked about creating a philosophy, a higher aesthetic purpose for our work together than just helping their peers understand the tests better. What emotional effect do they/we want to have? *Healing* was what we decided upon—first ourselves and then others. We want to help our young people, and our people in general, become whole again.

Currently, we focus on two academic areas, *science* and *math*. Our reasons:

1. A lot of science and math subject matter can be made more interesting using drama, dance, poetry, and music.

2. Well-paid science and math workers of the future will require creativity and imagination in order to succeed.

3. Incorporation of the arts into science and math learning is at the forefront of twenty-first-century educational research.

Recent studies by the National Science Board and the American Academy for the Advancement of Science suggest that science instruction in American public schools compares poorly with science instruction internationally; and that most science curricula for American schoolchildren fail to meet the most basic criteria necessary to engage students and encourage learning. These include: (a) providing a sense of purpose, (b) taking into account student ideas and experiences, and (c) engaging students in relevant phenomena. Infusing the creative arts into science and math curricula can address each of these concerns.

A biology professor at Xavier University of Louisiana, Dr. Barbara Green, was the first scientist to consult with us in developing our musical theater pieces. Although Dr. Green was not very experienced at integrating "theater" into her teaching as such, as a twelve-year teaching veteran she had learned a lot about what interested her students.

> Long before I was approached by Creative Forces, I had learned to use storytelling in my teaching. I found students not only became more engaged in what I was teaching, they were better able to generalize the in-

formation when I made them apply it in real life situations. Without calling it "theater," I had naturally gravitated towards it as a learning device. I just called it "case study."

The connection may not be obvious, but once you realize it, it is very powerful: Biology is the observation and study of the processes of life, and so is Theater.

We began piloting the program with a group of Creative Forces peer educators at the New Orleans Charter Science and Math High School a few months ago, drawing on the traditional model of a touring repertory theater company. Full membership will be at fifteen members in the troupe, and individuals are admitted based on an audition and interview. Each peer educator has to "multitask" as needed while focusing on particular areas of performance, management, or writing. Peer educators are paid a stipend, receive professional development support, and get to travel around the city, region, and country to perform and present. Parents and family members are involved as chaperones, guest lecturers, advocates, and co-evaluators. The group is set to perform for hundreds—and one day thousands—of children and teens after school and during the summer each year.

The U.S. Army says it is the place for young people to "be all that you can be." Creative Forces also allows teenagers to become part of a cohesive, highly trained group of individuals dedicated to a higher purpose, in this case the reform of New Orleans' educational system. We offer some of the same kinds of benefits as the military (pay, travel, and professional development) while pointing ourselves in a very different philosophical direction. As we declare twice a year when we induct and graduate peer educators, "Knowledge and beauty, peace and justice, are the most powerful forces in the universe."

We are still a very new group, and given the unstable situation in schools and community organizations throughout New Orleans today much has yet to be finalized, but we are moving forward with ambition, hope, and faith things will work out. We are setting up a kind of "touring circuit" of after-school and summer programs at schools, churches, and organizations. We are also talking and beginning to work with a small group of our colleagues to see if we can spread our approaches and resources to other community sites and schools throughout the city so that we can reach many more peer educators and young audiences each year.

From the beginning, we realized that the *processes* of art, as well as its products, could be useful to us as educators, particularly when it comes to teaching math. Inspired by the groundbreaking work of the Algebra Project in Cambridge, Massachusetts, and an inventive physical science teacher at Science and Math High School named Margo London, the ensemble has begun to experiment with the use of African drums to teach physical science equations. As Ms. London, now another member of Creative Forces adult leadership team, opines:

> I know, for me personally, my love of music and dance and my love of science are completely connected to one another. I recognize that in our society there is this perceived split, but that doesn't mean it has to be there. In actuality, being an artist is very similar to being a scientist, and when I can step back, I realize both are essentially about the same thing: patterns.
>
> To say it in a fancier way, by linking the physical sensation of playing drums with the cognitive process of manipulating math equations, I believe we can help students—many of whom are highly physical, kinesthetic learners—better understand and remember what they need to learn.

We knew from the beginning that documenting our program thoroughly was going to be important. For the Creative Forces program to have a broad effect, we will have to pass on what we learn to others in other places. We hired video producer Matthew Rosenbeck to act as our chronicler.

> When I document Creative Forces, I always have multiple audiences in my mind. First, I am gathering data on the students and the program for our evaluators. Second, I am gathering key moments to pass on our approaches to other teachers and teaching artists. And, third, because I personally find their life stories so inspiring and compelling, I want to produce a documentary about the young people for a general audience. It might sound a little complicated and multilayered to accomplish, but it is the reality of life in New Orleans today.

First Recruits

At a recent Creative Forces workshop, five of the founding members of the ensemble had a chance to share their thoughts about themselves, the program, and the state of public education in New Orleans.

Roque Caston (Writer, Actor, Class of 2009): "The number one thing I do, every day of the year, is write, but in Creative Forces I've done a lot more. I act, I sing, I do some writing, too, whatever needs to be done. In one of our plays I portray three very different roles: a goofy doctor, a good friend, and a highly disciplined basketball coach. At first, this was hard and I wanted to quit, because I really just want to write, but they needed someone to step up and it turned out I kind of enjoyed it."

Rose Gilliam (Singer, Actor, Company Manager, Class of 2010): "In New Orleans, students are not encouraged when they know the answers, but when we went to another city the kids were encouraging and they applaud the other students. I was shocked. I asked one little girl 'What makes you all study so hard?' And she told me 'We want to do something with our lives.' And I wondered why there aren't any kids in New Orleans like that."

Donnanice Newman (Writer, Performer, Class of 2008): "I live in New Orleans East, and my family is one of only three living in our entire subdivision. Think about what it's like coming home to a ghost town every night and waking up there again every morning, and you'll have a taste of what life is like for me right now. That's why I participate in Creative Forces. I'm not only giving hope to other children, I'm giving hope to myself."

Will Powell Jr. (Composer, Musician, Actor, Class of 2009): "Creative Forces for me has been this kind of beautiful unfolding puzzle that keeps growing and changing every day. At first, it was just this after school program I would go to, none of us really knew each other. One day I was sitting at the piano and someone asked me how I felt that day, so I just start playing something. Then this girl sitting next to me, who turns out to be Brandy, she says she's got a poem she wrote that might go along with my music, and she reaches into her bag and starts singing with me. It was her song (entitled 'Do I Have the Right?') that really got us thinking about the role we wanted to play in the program as leaders."

Brandy Thomas (Singer, Songwriter, Class of 2007): "I sing because it makes me a better person. Before, nothing seemed to fit, but when I sing everything comes together and I see the role I was meant to play in this world. The music I write is supposed to speak to people at a higher level. I don't write just to send 'a message.' If you are interested in what I am talking about, you will get something from it. It may not be the

"I act, I sing, I do some writing too, whatever needs to be done. At first, this was hard & I wanted to quit, because I really just want to write, but they needed someone to step up & it turned out I kind of enjoyed it."

ROQUE

"In New Orleans, students are not encouraged when they know the answers, but when we went to another city, the kids were encouraging & they applaud the other students. I was shocked. I asked one little girl "What makes you all study so hard?" And she told me "We want to do something with our lives." And I wondered why there aren't any kids in New Orleans like that."

Rose

"I sing because it makes me a better person. Before, nothing seemed to fit, but when I sing, everything comes together & I see the role I was meant to play in this world."

BRANDY

Fig. 10–12. Illustrations and lettering by Keith Knight.

same thing as I meant when I wrote it, and it may not be the same thing as the person sitting next to you, but you will get a feeling from it that you can use."

Key Allies

Beyond the teen members and adult mentors of Creative Forces, we are developing a network of allies who contribute their expertise, resources, and wisdom to enable the ensemble to function effectively. They help us develop and refine our curriculum and plays, provide needed program facilities and staff time, collaborate with us on projects, and act as community sponsors.

Staffas Broussard (Professor, University of New Orleans, and Creative Forces "Math Officer"): "The standard math and science curriculum focuses almost exclusively on lower order types of thinking—formulas and facts—not how to put those formulas and facts together in the context of life. There's almost nothing in the curriculum that helps students develop higher order skills, to prioritize or make judgments. But I can think of a hundred ways to make a performance that requires you—either as artist or as audience—to make decisions and judgments based on an understanding of core curriculum material."

Carol Bebelle (Ashé Cultural Arts Center, Creative Forces Community Partner): "It's about solving problems. If we have learned nothing else from the aftermath of Katrina, we know that life can throw a lot at you all at one time, and your ability to respond in a creative, positive, and determined way—even when things seem to be at their worst—is an important key to life. What I envision is a group of young people who, whatever particular song or poem or monologue they may be performing, are underneath it all teaching their peers about this ancient art of problem solving."

Jane Wholey (Kids Rethink New Orleans Schools): "Two years after Katrina, only half of our schools are up and running. It's time for students to claim their rightful role in restructuring the school system. Decision makers can learn so much from children; they are experts on the schools in this city."

Our Arsenal

In order to move hearts and minds, we are building a repertoire of proven Creative Forces educational workshops and plays. This is both the material that we will perform and the legacy we will pass on to others. We use the "CRAFT" (Contact, Research, Action, Feedback, Teaching) methodology and a graphic textbook entitled the *Beginner's Guide to Community-Based Arts* to guide our creative process.

We received our first two assignments from Creative Forces science officers Dr. Green and Ms. London a few months ago. We were to help students learn: (a) in physical science, the "speed equation" (speed equals distance divided by time); and (b) in biology, the workings of the pulmonary system. All of us will admit that at first we were stumped. We knew how important the information was, but how could we use music and theater to help students really sit up and *care?*

Six months later we are happy to report the creation of our first two educational music and theater pieces: the *Drum Time* workshop and *Lifelines*, a play. It took more than one hundred hours of collaborative brainstorming, research, rehearsal, test performances and feedback to refine these first two pieces, but we did it, and we are on a roll. Thanks to our initial tryout performances, we have requests to tour to more than a dozen middle school classrooms and youth programs around the city and to travel to conferences and gatherings of educators and young people across the region and country.

Drum Time: A forty-minute interactive curriculum that uses African hand drums to teach twenty-five to thirty middle school students both the formula for calculating speed and the role of culture in transmitting vital information. Led by a team of five peer educators and one adult mentor, the main element of the workshop is a series of speed trials in which students race by playing drums and then use the speed equation (speed equals distance over time) to determine the winners. We also teach students an indigenous New Orleans rhythm and dance, the Bamboula, as we lead them in an infectious chanting of the speed equation. We have found the workshop to be a deceptively simple and effective way to engage students who are otherwise unengaged.

Lifelines: A forty-minute curriculum for twenty-five to thirty middle school students led by five peer educators that uses a short play with music and sound to teach about the pulmonary system, specifically asthma. Based on the life of one of the members of Creative Forces, the play has three scenes: first, when the protagonist is a child and learns about her asthma for the first time; second, when she becomes a teenager and rebels against those who want to educate her about her asthma; and, third, the night she almost has to die in order to come to grips with her life as an adult asthmatic. In a short period of time, the play can spark lots of questions, dialogue, and research assignments about the pulmonary system. The Creative Forces peer educators return to follow up with the students over the next few days.

Our Next Moves

Your task, actors, is to be
Explorers and teachers of the art of dealing with people.
Knowing their nature and demonstrating it you teach them
To deal with themselves. You teach them the great art
Of living together.

—Bertolt Brecht

July 2007

In the few short days it has taken for me to write this report, many more losses have taken place in the community. In one day's newspaper alone, Dillard University, already one of the city's most flood-damaged universities, is being investigated by the accreditation commission. The killer of a beloved local musician and youth mentor is going free because a group of teen witnesses is too frightened to testify, despite the fact that the shooting was witnessed by dozens of people. Post-Katrina public school data are already suggesting that a new "separate but equal" segregated reality is taking shape in the different New Orleans public school systems. Make no mistake about it, a war is going on in New Orleans, a war of attrition, and the winners will inherit the city.

We, the members of Creative Forces, will draw on our creativity, our artistic skills, our anger, our frustration and, as artists have done since time began, channel and transform them into something useful and beautiful.

Wish us luck, reader. Stay tuned.

EPILOGUE: *April 2008. It is almost a year since I wrote that report. Much has changed, and much has remained the same. Chaos and duplicity still reign in many quarters, but it seems inevitable now that New Orleans will rise again and perhaps be better for the experience, at least in some important ways. The question now is, how long will it take and who will be able to last long enough to benefit?*

We, the teens and adults of Creative Forces, have hung on together: striving, working, improving, expanding, and reaching hundreds of children in New Orleans with valuable information and (if I do say so myself) inspiration through our "edu-taining" performances and workshops. The prospects for the future of the program are highly positive.

Meanwhile, the culture wars of New Orleans continue. In the paper today, there is a wide-ranging discussion about three recent corruption scandals involving local legislators, district attorneys, and judges, and Mr. Sidney D. Torres IV, owner of SDT Waste and Debris Services, is referred to as a likely candidate for the city's highest office.

END

To stay in touch, visit www.xroadsproject.org.

Creative Forces is a joint project of the National Performance Network and the Crossroads Project for Art, Learning, and Community. Major support is provided by the Ford Foundation.

CRAFT Methodology: Drawing on the fields of art, education, and community organizing, the Crossroads Project has established a basic framework for implementing and evaluating community-based arts activities.

> CONTACT: *Cultivate trust, mutual understanding, and commitment as a foundation for your creative partnership.*
> RESEARCH: *Gather information about the people, places, and issues you are working with.*
> ACTION: *Produce a new work of art that benefits the community.*
> FEEDBACK: *Spark reflection, dialogue, and organizing to spread the impact of the new work.*
> TEACHING: *Pass on skills to sustain the impact.*

NOTES

The epigraphs are from Bertolt Brecht, "Speech to Danish Working-Class Actors on the Art of Observation," in *Bertolt Brecht Poems, 1913–1956*, edited by John Willett and Ralph Manheim (London: Eyre Methuen, 1976), 233–38.

1. As an important aside, I should mention that I hear the expression used by white New Orleanians and black New Orleanians about equally.

2. And how did jazz, one of the most elegant and grounded musical systems on earth, become associated with carelessness, anyway?

Thanks to Keith Knight, Bill Cleveland, the Crossroads Project advisers, and the folks at New Village Press for their ongoing partnerships. Thanks also to the staff, peer educators, partners, and families of Creative Forces that were not mentioned. And special thanks to creative counselor Mimi Zarsky. All these people contributed to the content of this essay.

The Gulfsouth Youth Action Corps

THE STORY OF A LOCAL CBO'S RESPONSE TO RESTORING YOUTH PROGRAMS IN NEW ORLEANS AFTER KATRINA AND RITA

Kyshun Webster and D. Hamilton Simons-Jones

Introduction: Katrina and Rita

HURRICANES KATRINA AND RITA hit New Orleans hard. Eighty percent of the city was flooded by Hurricane Katrina. Hurricane Rita resulted in a second evacuation and second flooding of parts of the city just as New Orleans mayor Ray Nagin began declaring sections of the city safe for residents to return. More than sixteen hundred city residents died from the storms. The city's infrastructure was devastated. More than a million people were displaced, scattered around the country, many separated from their families. National and international journalists fetched these stories of survival and catastrophe off of rooftops and out of shelters, hospitals, and even grocery stores for more than a month following Katrina. The images aired and printed in the national media, however, revealed just the beginning of the disaster. The storms not only destroyed housing, facilities, and human lives, but they also tore apart community networks, leaving a dramatic void in services for young people.

The Impact on Youth and Youth Services

Many families with children began returning to the city as schools slowly reopened by early January of 2006. With a second wave of families expected to return as schools let out for the summer, concerns emerged regarding the restoration of youth services and opportunities for the summer. The New Orleans Recreation Department (NORD), the normal sponsor of summer youth programs for tens of thousands of children, had incurred major damage to the majority of its facilities while surviving a 90 percent reduction in its staffing capacity. Local public funds for youth services were eliminated in the financial straits the storms created. Money set aside for youth programs was nonexistent. Likewise, across the Gulf Coast region, parks and recreation facilities were not spared from this wrath. The National Recreation and Park Association released a report stating that the state, county, and local parks, sports fields, hiking and biking trails, waterways, historical and cultural sites, and recreational facilities faced major restoration, reconstruction, or replacement. While communities continued to assess the damage and address the longer term challenges of reconstruction, they were faced with attempting to meet the immediate ongoing needs of their communities. The ravished infrastructure of these public services posed a crisis for returning youth.

Once vibrant playgrounds and recreation facilities for youths and families were converted to shelters. Playing fields, home to multiple youth sports leagues and camp activities, now housed Federal Emergency Management Agency (FEMA) trailers. Grassy ball fields were covered with gravel and lined with FEMA trailers, mere feet apart, in an effort to provide a temporary fix to the housing crisis the hurricanes had created. Both inside and outside of the declared disaster areas, parks and recreation centers literally became *home* to many displaced families seeking shelter. Overnight, public parks and recreation agencies in nearby cities absorbed hundreds of children and families into their existing facilities, sports team rosters, and recreation programs.

In its report, the National Recreation and Park Association pointed out the importance of the infrastructure that recreational outlets provide for community. First, seniors, adults, youths, families, and persons with disabilities frequently rely on these programs as their essential needs are served by the staffs of parks and recreational programs. Second, psychological researchers have found that positive social support programs offered in parks and recreation settings greatly enhance individuals' and communities' ability to recover from trauma. The healing aspects of nature through access to parks can help improve individual and community support for the recovery effort.

Operation REACH, Inc., Takes on the Restoration of Youth Programs

Recognizing this need, the community-based organization (CBO) Operation REACH, Inc., with naive ambition, put together a proposal to bring relief to the local recreation department and restore summer youth services in New Orleans. Operation REACH was founded in 1998 by Kyshun Webster, who was an undergraduate student at Xavier University of Louisiana at the time. The nonprofit organization is dedicated to providing access to high-quality educational opportunities for youths and their families through a variety of community-based programs. Begun as the Home for Homework program in New Orleans' Saint Bernard Housing Development, in which college students provided academic support for youths and their parents in a homelike environment, the program grew to operate in multiple sites around the city.

By 2005, Operation REACH had developed a reputation for providing high-quality, innovative, educational programs to children around New Orleans. The organization came to be known for its community-based approach, its ability to develop public-private partnerships, and its focus on youth leadership development. Since 2000, it had built a strong working relationship with local colleges and universities, as well as NORD, to provide quality programs outside of school time.

In the spring of 2006, while the shortage of programs outside school time continued and local colleges and universities began to reopen their campuses to students, more than ten thousand college students from around the country descended on New Orleans for their spring breaks. The majority gutted flooded homes around the city, helping families get past the massive physical and emotional first step of removing all their belongings and gutting the house down to the studs. For many people, these college students were providing an incredible service, allowing families to see past the devastation to the possibility of returning and rebuilding. The students worked with neighborhood organizations to survey the basics of each neighborhood: who had returned, who was living in FEMA trailers, where piles of debris remained, and what businesses, schools, and bus routes had returned if any. Many slept on church floors, in empty community centers, and in extra dormitory rooms at the local colleges and universities. As Operation REACH staff members spoke with college students and those who worked alongside them, they found them overwhelmingly excited about coming back to New Orleans for the summer. The students, however, expressed an interest in working with more than just bricks and mortar. They wanted to work with people, especially children.

Despite losing its New Orleans headquarters to the storm and the fact that its staff members had evacuated to four separate states across the South, Operation REACH proposed to provide summer camps for middle school students through a strategy that would minimize the costs to NORD by employing volunteer counselors. Building on a record of providing quality youth programs and developing community-focused leadership in local college students, the organization sought to expand the base to include college students from across the country for the summer. In a relatively short period of time, funding was secured, a program skeleton developed, and plans made for 25 idealistic college students and 360 youths to collaborate in operating a summer camp for middle school students across three sites in New Orleans. Thus, the Gulfsouth Youth Action Corps (GYAC) was born. The corps would follow the model of many traditional youth service corps but with a special focus on restoring youth programs after a major disaster. It was launched to take full advantage of the large number of civic-minded college students who came to the region immediately after the storm as a means of meeting the critical need for youth services in New Orleans.

Operation REACH sought relationships with national, local, and city agencies to bring together a public-private partnership to serve children in New Orleans after the storms. The recreation department agreed to make facilities that were not damaged (approximately three) available for the Gulfsouth Youth Action Camps. Universities, private foundations, and other relief organizations joined in to help the organization assist NORD. Local agencies and foundations such as the Institute of Mental Hygiene and the United Way joined national relief organizations such as Save the Children and Mercy Corps to provide funding for the inaugural program. Local universities such as Xavier University of Louisiana and Tulane University agreed to assist with recruiting and screening local college students as well as providing housing for college students from across the country and abroad who would serve as GYAC members. The Phillips Brooks House Association at Harvard University, the Lang Center at Swarthmore College, and the University of Minnesota allocated individual fellowships for their students to commit to a summer of service with GYAC. National experts affiliated with these prestigious institutions and agencies, including the National Youth Leadership Council (NYLC) served as trainers for the intensive one-week training program required for corps members in June.

These national experts also served the program throughout the summer by acting as coaches and mentors to corps member cohorts.

Developing the GYAC Curriculum

In a city that did not have the capacity to service its youth, this public-private partnership came together under dire circumstances to provide them with an outlet to increase their resiliency as they coped with catastrophic stress. Research shows that in times of natural disaster the most vulnerable are children and the elderly. Disaster experts note that as resources become strained communities focus on immediate priorities. However, they assert, reductions in essential services for children often have long-term implications for those children and the families and communities in which they live. Consequently, the lack of youth programs during out of school hours has been identified as a major risk factor for youth associated with violent crime according to the National Institute of Out-of-School Time (NOIST). Complicating matters further, New Orleans children had experienced "catastrophic stress," defined as severe stress brought on by unexpected events such as the serious illness of a child or family member, natural disasters, or abuse. According to mental health experts, the child experiencing such a crisis is often too overwhelmed to use basic resources to deal with pressure and fear. In an article published immediately after the storm entitled "Children as Victims of Hurricane Katrina," Dr. Judith Myers-Wall, a national expert on teaching children to cope with major disasters, suggested implementing programs that do the following.

- Help children use creative outlets such as art and music to express their feelings
- Help children and youth find a course of action
- Help older children learn about current events so they will know a lot about the situation
- Take action and get involved in something

The GYAC was informed and inspired by the work of Dr. Myers-Wall. Two international child advocacy agencies, the United Nations International Children's Fund (UNICEF) and Save the Children, concurred in their reports on the crisis along the Gulf Coast. While it is essential to ensure that adequate food, water, medicine, sanitation, and shelter are avail-

able for everyone affected by the hurricanes, it is also imperative to miti-
gate the impact of the disaster on children. They suggest getting children
back to a normal routine through recreational activities and enrollment in
school. According to these international relief agencies, evidence has
shown that in times of disaster getting children back to a learning environment is one of the most effective ways to help them feel safe, cope with
trauma, and begin their emotional healing.

Taking Dr. Myers-Wall's recommendations into account, Operation
REACH searched for innovative approaches to developing this "postdisaster" camp for youth who had suffered the trauma of their entire world being uprooted, shaken up, and destroyed by the hurricanes and their aftermath. While most Americans experienced the trauma from their television
sets, some of the youth whom Operation REACH staff knew would attend
the camps had more dramatic experiences as they waded through the waters, stood on rooftops, leaped from helicopters, and swam for their lives
while watching others drown in the rushing waters. After this set of lived
experiences, many youth in "refugee" communities still went without a
change of clothes and food for days and continued to be isolated from
friends, separated from families, and truant from school for months. Many
youth found few outlets for their voices or experiences as they were initially severely downplayed while adults grieved over "more substantive material losses." The challenge of restoring youth services in New Orleans
was great given the trauma of the youth experience of Katrina. Not having
the space to grieve like the adults and being disconnected from peer groups
left a vacuum, and youth could not embrace each other's suffering as a normal part of their coping and resiliency mechanisms.

At the outset, Operation REACH staff knew that the Gulfsouth Youth
Action Camps had to make room in the program design for youth to liber-
ate their repressed emotions, discuss unaddressed questions about their experiences, and debrief unfolding events in their lives. Moreover, many
youth who were returning for the first time after their evacuation in the
summer of 2006 would experience firsthand the shock of a dramatically
changed physical, social, and cultural environment. They would have to
quickly assimilate to what many called the "new New Orleans." Thus, the
program design had to create opportunities for youth to phenomenologi-
cally get reacquainted with their city. To do this, Operation REACH staff
selected critical pedagogy and service learning as the instructional techniques for the camp. Courses were intended to be fun yet intellectually

stimulating. They would provoke repressed conversations and agitate youth to action while providing a therapeutic outlet for young people to begin their healing.

The Curriculum: Critical Pedagogy And Service Learning

The Gulfsouth Summer Youth Action Camps' curriculum and activities were developed through the spring of 2006 over a series of conference calls and Internet communications. A national network of college students and volunteer educational experts from around the country gave input to provide a powerful learning experience for both the campers and the college students who volunteered. Traditional disciplines were transformed into intriguing, highly interactive, real world learning experiences with emphasis placed on these disciplines as instruments of social change. The curriculum promoted analytic reasoning, self-expression, and social consciousness through project-based learning. Reading, writing, and analytic reasoning were infused into all course offerings to address the learning regression that had taken place because many of the middle school student campers were unable to return to school following the hurricanes. In addition, campers were exposed to an array of thematic field trips and meaningful community service projects and courses with a provocative social justice bent on media, health, visual arts, and community organizing.

Operation REACH. staff believed these courses would create opportunities for appreciative inquiry into topics consequential to the posthurricane environments in which the staff and students lived. Undergirding each course was a set of critical thinking skills intended to bring about awareness and stimulate youth becoming more civically engaged. Independent program evaluations showed that using critical pedagogy in instruction seemed to increase political and social awareness among youth ages nine to thirteen, especially regarding their newly sophisticated analysis of their hurricane experiences. As a direct outgrowth of the critical media service-learning courses, a film documentary was produced entitled *Children of New Orleans: Still Weathering the Storm.* This professionally produced documentary was developed by the campers in partnership with a volunteer Florida-based film company. The critical media course taught campers how to use the medium of film to tell their stories of Katrina. As youth, they were a yet to be heard segment of the diaspora whose voices the mainstream media had not amplified. In addition to having the opportunity to have their voices heard and stories told, the youth also learned technical skills by using advanced computer software to edit their compelling accounts of the storm and their most introspective moments.

Service learning was another component of the camp's guiding pedagogy. Service learning has been shown to provide powerful opportunities for youth to reflect critically and constructively on their world and to develop skills for facilitating meaningful social change.[1] Youth were given opportunities to engage in community work as part of their camp experience. Students at the Cutoff Recreation Center were involved in a community beautification project that included preparing and planting decorative plants around the perimeter of the community center. Students at the Watson Memorial Teaching Ministries site were engaged in developing a community garden on land under a freeway crossing. These activities were more intensely covered in the Community Action Capstone course. Despite minor logistical issues, campers reported positive outcomes for the service activities.

Impact of the Curriculum on Youth: Promoting Healthy Dialogue

Focus group conversations conducted by an independent evaluation team revealed that youth thought the service projects helped them to learn some important things about community service. They reported that they learned about the value of service to others. They most frequently described community service as "helping to clean up the community" or "helping to fix things." One respondent talked about a change in attitude, saying, "At first I didn't know and didn't care, but later [I] realized it [is a way] to make New Orleans better and a way to help around the community." Developing this ethic of service and change in attitude was one of the ultimate intentions of the service learning program.

Based on Operation REACH's history of youth leadership development, the staff determined that it made the most sense to adapt the teaching methodology from critical pedagogy. Critical pedagogy naturally lends itself to creating evocative democratic learning environments. Hence, the Gulfsouth Summer Youth Action Course was designed to be heavily dialogic for the youth, allowing them to have their turn to voice their thoughts, opinions, and experiences "at the mic." In focus group debriefings, a team of independent program evaluators asked youth about this instructional innovation and whether the dialogic process helped them deal with issues related to the hurricanes. The results were as follows.

- About a third of the participants thought they had talked about it the right amount and seemed to have found it therapeutic.
- They thought it was good to talk about the problems they encountered and that it helped get "stuff off your mind."
- Almost half complained that there was too much talk about Katrina and it was an uncomfortable subject for them. Some said it upset them. One young man said it was "too sad to talk about it" because his grandmother and cousin had died. He added, "I don't want to talk about it. I want to move on."
- Another girl had a terrible experience at the [Ernest N. Morial] Convention Center, and she didn't know how to approach dealing with the aftermath.
- Youth did talk about what made life stressful and uncomfortable. Several mentioned stressful situations such as being separated from their parents (e.g., living in Texas without their parents) and missing friends.
- Seeing the city in ruins and disrepair caused feelings of frustration, especially because of the slow response.
- They mentioned uncomfortable environments in other places such as dealing with unfriendly people or violent classmates in Texas.
- They struggled with reconciling the death of friends, not knowing how to address these hurtful situations.

Clearly, Katrina remained a touchy subject. While the camp helped to alleviate some of the issues related to the disaster, the evaluations showed that the subject needed to be addressed more delicately, noting that not all experiences and reactions were the same.

Some youth were more specific about the ways in which the camp supported them.

- It reconnected them with friends and relatives and provided an opportunity to make new friends. One youth said, "I hadn't seen my cousins and my friends in one place since the storm . . . and it allowed me to make new friends."
- All the youth felt that the counselors went out of their way to assist the students, in some cases pulling them aside and counseling them one-on-one. They described this as being similar to a minitherapy

session, and they appreciated the time. Of the counselors, one student said, "They won't let nothin' get you down."

- Others felt the discussions about Katrina were helpful and therapeutic. Besides this, they felt the opportunity to have fun and return to a somewhat normal life gave them hope and a feeling that they would be OK. One student said, "Seeing everybody doin' better" made everyone feel better.

While several of the participants were still dealing with the effects of post-Katrina trauma, good relationships with the college student counselors and the proximity of friends at the camp helped many cope with the situation. Thus, evaluators concluded that the goal of having the camp play a therapeutic role in the lives of the youth was achieved. For a camp that was put together in less than three months in an environment severely hampered by the city's ongoing recovery from a catastrophic storm and with a small budget and staff of relatively inexperienced volunteer college students, the overall assessment was that things had worked remarkably well. Participants liked the camp experience, enjoyed several of the classes and the recreational activities (especially the swimming), and had an opportunity to have a relatively stable, socially satisfying experience. Given all the trauma and turmoil caused by the hurricanes and the ensuing disruption during the year, the camp allowed the youth and the college counselors to develop relationships and enjoy each other. These relationships and the positive time spent together appear to have been the most meaningful parts of the camp experience.

Impact on College Students: The College Student Service Experience

In coordinating the experiences of both the corps members and the middle school campers, Operation REACH staff recognized the importance of reciprocity in the service experience. They would create opportunities for both groups to learn and serve in the community together. College students who traveled from afar to be a part of the inaugural year of the Gulf-south corps and camps had a rare opportunity to interact with a group of middle school youth in a community still recovering from a grave natural disaster. In exit interviews, the volunteer camp counselors were asked, "How will you bring GYAC back with you to your own community? How will your work this summer inform the work that you do in the coming months?" In general, counselors expressed a commitment to tell friends and family about life in post-Katrina New Orleans and to lead awareness campaigns back on their campuses. They had begun to see themselves as ambassadors for the region. Some also expressed a desire to engage in community service in their home communities.

The college student counselors also developed personally and professionally. Some indicated that they had developed a greater understanding of youth, the challenges they face, and the ways in which they deal with these challenges. Half said they had a greater awareness of young people's resiliency and how they cope with trauma and disruption. They also learned how to develop strong relationships with youth. Given that this program operated in such a devastated environment, corps members reported that they had developed a greater ability to "roll with the punches" and deal with crises. They learned patience in dealing with challenges and developed a greater ability to reflect in crisis settings. Corps members also learned to be more flexible. Some said they had learned to lead under stressful situations. They also said the experience made them appreciate more what they had at home. A few counselors described feeling that New Orleans was a second home and its problems were their problems. Several expressed a desire to return at some point and continue helping out.

Counselors were also asked about the overall impact of the Gulfsouth Youth Action Camp. Their responses were fairly consistent with the exit interview data. Some of the strongest effects were on their personal development and relationships with peers. They reported that they had developed a better understanding of teaching, with more than 70 percent saying that they had acquired a more "sophisticated understanding of teaching." Similarly, approximately 70 percent said they had developed a much better understanding of human services, education, and youth development. As for a better understanding of themselves, more than 70 percent indicated that this was a major outcome of the experience.

Developing interpersonal relationships proved to be the highlight of the camp experience for the college students. Almost 90 percent of the counselors rated developing relationships with their fellow counselors as a great outcome, and more than 94 percent said they found the relationships they had developed with the youth to be outstanding. Clearly, the strongest impact in the camp experience was the relationships developed between the campers and their counselors. When the college students were asked to reflect on "the most significant impact of this program on you as a human being," they said,

"I realized that this is something I love to do."

- More specifically, they said, "[I love] waking up in the morning excited about teaching and working with the kids and realizing 'this is where I am supposed to be.'"
- They talked about how rewarding youth work is and especially loving to see the campers grow. They enjoyed the deep relationships with campers and the feeling they had an impact on them. They were overwhelmed by the kids' enthusiasm and creativity and realized that "this work matters." They felt the kids trusted them and felt the power of having had an effect on others.
- Eight people thought they would go into teaching or youth work. Several had a new focus on public interest careers other than teaching and youth work and expressed a desire to work with low-income families, even connecting a career in art with social justice issues.
- Eight shared that they were interested in becoming a youth worker or educator. Two said that they had initially been interested in academia but now wanted to become youth workers. Two others not only wanted to work with youth but wanted to pursue graduate degrees and start nonprofits or charter schools.
- Five others shared a desire to pursue public interest careers other than teaching and youth work. One planned to become a doctor and as a result of the summer wanted to work with low-income populations. Another found herself less interested in youth work but more interested in social work, perhaps with other women. Another was unsure of her abilities as a teacher but was very intrigued with education policy. A fifth person in this subset was pre-law and had been very concerned about making a sizable salary. Now she was less concerned about money and interested in dealing with people recovering from crises.

"I have a deeper understanding of service."

- They realized how much life experiences affect people and how challenging teaching can be. They were able to get beyond the notion of service as charity, no longer pitying others but seeing service as a human responsibility. They also learned more about how nonprofit organizations work.

- They learned how difficult it is to run a program that includes service activities, that there are no quick fixes to problems, and that it is difficult to communicate the notion of service to others.

- They said they learned some of the pros and cons of volunteerism, especially "teaching with" as opposed to "teaching to." They also saw service as a way to build relationships and better understand youth. One counselor said, "I don't feel like the kids need anything . . . [because service] isn't something you 'give'; [there was] greater faith in solidarity rather than charity as you became aware of kids' autonomy and resilience. There is an importance to learning from the people you serve, the importance of homegrown service."

"I have a greater awareness of identity, especially as it relates to race, class, and culture."

- They felt they had achieved a better understanding of their identity in encountering local traditions as outsiders. Experiences of diversity, including being around vegans for the first time, being in a multiracial environment for the first time, becoming aware of their own whiteness (for some), and feeling like an outsider, all made a difference in who they were.

- For others, getting comfortable with their blackness or socioeconomic privilege, or achieving a greater understanding of how to fit into black culture as someone who is white, changed their understanding of racial and community issues.

- They learned how race plays into the picture. Counselors had a better sense of how race affects government policies and a greater understanding of the assumptions that come with whiteness and blackness. They also learned what it means to be a racial outsider.

- Some learned about the role class plays in dealing with social barriers, especially ones that are rooted in racial issues.

"I developed people skills."

- Several counselors mentioned that they were now better able to work with youth, function as coworkers, and act as managers. The experience gave them real world opportunities to hone their people skills.

"I have more self-confidence and a greater sense of responsibility."

- Like the youth, the counselors felt a greater sense of self-confidence at the end of the program. They became more self-assured as they worked effectively with youth and peers. Also their impact on the youth and the program gave them a stronger sense of responsibility; they saw themselves as actual agents of change for the young people and the community.

"I have a greater degree of patience in dealing with challenges."

- Given the number of frustrations with the overall camp, ranging from challenges and snafus related to communication and management to maintaining the control and direction of all the campers, the corps members learned to develop more patience and understanding. "Challenges can either drive you nuts," one said, "or they can help you to become more tolerant of things when they don't go right."

"I realized my inability to deal with the stress of the program."

- Several counselors who faced the stresses of the program on a day-to-day basis realized that the experience had tested their tolerance for stress. Many felt stressed at times because of all the things they had to do and because of their lack of control over situations. But they felt the camp experience had better prepared them to deal with stress in the future.

Conclusion: Lessons from GYAC

The summer camps have continued for three years, and the Gulfsouth Youth Action Corps has since been sought out by the Corporation for National and Community Sservice as a national model to be replicated throughout the Gulf South. In large part due to the extraordinary commitment of the volunteer college staff, the patience and persistence of the youth participants, and the efforts of the management team to secure funding for the program, a camp was conducted that was both fun and intellectually stimulating. The program and the experience of Operation REACH staff can teach us several lessons about civic engagement in the wake of a disaster.

Crisis gives way to innovation and new uses and combinations of community resources. While Operation REACH built the GYAC program on a successful formula and solid track record, the postdisaster environment required innovation. The program tapped the energy, idealism, and enthusiasm of college students from around the country to serve as counselors to address the lack of staffing capacity in the local recreation department. In addition, the camp drew on a combination of local, national, and international funds, resources, and expertise, including international disaster relief organizations, local and national foundations, state and local governments, and universities and youth-focused organizations around the country.

Service learning and critical pedagogy are keys to restoring normalcy and efficacy not just for youth after a disaster but also for volunteers responding to a disaster. The curriculum, pedagogy, and values of the camp created an environment in which young people were encouraged to lead, act, reflect, and make their voices heard in relating their experiences and feelings about their communities. This democratic learning environment not only empowered young people by giving them a sense of self-confidence and self-efficacy, but it also proved to be therapeutic for them in coping with catastrophic stress. As a result of coordinated research efforts by Joy D. Osofsky, Howard J. Osofsky, and William W. Harris to understand the impact of Hurricanes Katrina and Rita on Gulf Coast youth, over two thousand young people have been observed through interviews with mental health professionals. Consistently, the research found, older youth worried about themselves, their future, their friends, their parents, and other family members. High school seniors worried about their senior year experiences. Symptomatic of their grief over losing friends and social connections, overwhelmingly this population postponed college pursuits and the completion of prerequisite examinations such as the ACT and SAT. Despite their stress, the Osfofskys and Harris observed from their research with this population that, profoundly, "students sufficiently symptomatic to qualify for mental health services frequently described their first concern as 'how can I rebuild my community?'"[2]

Feedback from the participants in the GYAC indicated that, while the program model may have been effective, one needs to balance the amount of sensitive content introduced. In postdisaster settings, greater attention needs to be paid to the presentation and amount of sensitive content in the curriculum. A number of studies report that civic engagement creates resiliency and promotes prosocial behaviors. Post-Katrina, a number of service-oriented organizations debuted for the purpose of engaging youth in the recovery of the region. These models provide forums in which youth can come together around common issues, reflect and divulge collective concerns, and engage in positive visioning. As noted, youth impacted by disasters do not necessarily want to be passive spectators and/or recipients of services. Hence, following disasters more intentional programming should be designed with youth and by youth to address their ambitions for the redevelopment of their communities.

In the face of a major disaster, strong results can be achieved through partnerships between international or national organizations and local ones. In the immediate aftermath of Hurricanes Katrina and Rita, while the New Orleans community—from individual families to local businesses—struggled to regain its footing, organizations from around the country were raising millions of dollars for relief, research, and programming to impact those who were affected by the hurricanes with few, if any, local connections on the ground in New Orleans. The world opened its consciousness, hearts and pocketbooks to New Orleans and New Orleanians, but there were few local guides. While national organizations were able to provide support to local New Orleans offices and affiliates, local community-based organizations (CBOs) faced a full recovery on their own. The families and households of staff, as well as the programs and infrastructure to continue their missions for their communities, were all in need of assistance.

Operation REACH's Gulfsouth Youth Action Corps is an example of what is possible when national and international organizations seek to support the recovery and rebuilding of a region through local partners who know the landscape and its needs and opportunities. The Operation REACH staff had to overcome incredible personal and professional obstacles, including the relocation of their own children, families, offices, and programs; the devastation of their homes and offices; and the loss of some of their programs and funding in the aftermath of Katrina and Rita. The success of the GYAC, as well as the mere fact that it was put together in such a short period of time, is due to the commitment of the dedicated local staff and the depth of such local, national, and international partnerships.

NOTES

1. J. Claus and C. Ogden, eds., *Service Learning for Youth Empowerment and Social Change* (New York: Peter Lang Publishing, 2001).

2. Joy D. Osofsky, Howard J. Osofsky, and William W. Harris, "Katrina's Children: Social Policy Considerations for Children in Disasters," *Social Policy Report* 21, no. 1 (2007): 6. The journal is published by the Society for Research in Child Development.

Welcoming the Newcomers

CIVIC ENGAGEMENT AMONG
PRE-KATRINA LATINOS

Elizabeth Fussell

EVEN AS NEW ORLEANS' POPULATION has diminished overall, the absolute number of Latinos has increased as a result of the intense and sudden demand for construction workers to repair and rebuild the city.[1] The new visibility of Latinos in New Orleans has sparked the civic spirit of many pre-Katrina Latinos as they seek to assist and assimilate the new arrivals. Although the pre- and post-Katrina Latinos differ in their national origins, social class, and degree of assimilation into U.S. society, their common status in the United States as a panethnic group and immigrants nevertheless unites them. This essay explores how New Orleans' pre-Katrina Latinos responded to the arrival of untold numbers of Latino immigrant workers in the post-Katrina environment. It is informed by forty-six oral history interviews with pre-Katrina Latinos who were interviewed because of their affiliation with Spanish-speaking social institutions, in other words, those at the front of the receiving line for the newcomer Latinos.

Newcomers and Established Latinos in New Orleans

Since its founding in 1719 as the port of entry to the Louisiana territory, New Orleans has blended the cultures of Latin and Anglo-America through the circulation of people and goods from throughout North America, the Gulf of Mexico, and the Caribbean Basin. Trade patterns of the twentieth century shaped the mix of Latin American immigrants residing in the city today. Central Americans, particularly Hondurans, came to New Orleans in exceptionally large numbers because of the New Orleans–based multinational companies that owned plantations in Central America and shipping lines to distribute these commodities.[2] Until the 1990s, New Orleans had the largest Honduran population in the United States, but there were also significant numbers of Costa Ricans, Cubans, Guatemalans, Mexicans, and Nicaraguans that accumulated gradually.[3] In contrast, the sudden and intense demand for labor brought on by the destruction of Hurricane Katrina brought a large wave of immigrants. This latest immigrant influx is also diverse in its national origins and includes Brazilians, Guatemalans, Nicaraguans, and Salvadorans, but it is dominated by Mexicans and Hondurans, most of whom are recent arrivals to the United States with skills in construction and limited language ability.[4]

The new migrant flow into New Orleans resembles the rapid influx of Latinos in new destinations that has occurred all over the southern United States since the 1990s, although it had largely bypassed the stagnant economy in Louisiana. Georgia, North and South Carolina, Tennessee, and Kentucky all experienced a more than 30 percent increase in their foreign-born populations between 2000 and 2005; in contrast, during this same period growth in the foreign-born population of Louisiana was only 6 percent.[5] Since Hurricane Katrina hit on August 29, 2005, Louisiana has joined the list of new migrant destinations. These destinations are often dominated by Mexican immigrants due to the simple fact that one of every three foreign-born residents in the United States today is from Mexico.[6] Furthermore, of the twelve million unauthorized immigrants in the United States, 56 percent are estimated to be Mexican and about 22 percent are from the rest of Latin America, primarily Central America.[7] Thus, it is commonly assumed that Mexican and other Latino workers are undocumented migrants or "illegals."

A T-shirt sold in many New Orleans tourist shops reads "FEMA: Find Every Mexican Available." This racist quip reflects the immediate post-Katrina reality. When the Department of Labor allowed employers in the Gulf Coast region affected by Hurricane Katrina to hire without asking about employees' eligibility for work, it effectively sent this message to the government subcontractors and others that were cleaning up and rebuilding.[8] Not surprisingly, many Mexican and Central American construction workers arrived in the city in the months following Katrina, and they continued to arrive two years later. Exactly how many Latino migrants have come to New Orleans is unknown.

In the months after Hurricane Katrina, it was evident to anybody in New Orleans that Latino workers were on the front lines of the cleanup effort while most of the city's residents were still displaced.[9] The recovery economy has brought a steady stream of Latinos, but demand for such work has been spatially and temporally uneven so that shifts in demand have corresponded to a shifting number of laborers. As rebuilding progress has slowed and wages have dropped, the growth in the number of Latinos in the city appears to be leveling off, though not declining. These trends suggest that point estimates of the Latino population are quickly outdated, but it is clear that the Hispanic population has grown considerably. In 2005 before the hurricane, 3.1 and 8.1 percent of the populations of Orleans and Jefferson Parishes was Latino, respectively.[10] The first population estimate to include a measure of race and ethnicity after the hurricane occurred in August 2006 and estimated the Latino populations of these parishes to be 9.6 and 9.7 percent, respectively, an increase in both relative and absolute size.[11] These newcomers had special needs related to their status as relatively new immigrants and the exploitative conditions of the disaster zone and the recovery economy.

Assistance to Newcomers

The organizations best positioned to serve the needs of the newcomer Latinos were those that were already serving New Orleans' Spanish-speaking population. However, the newcomers' needs challenged the resources of these organizations because of the area's state of emergency and the sheer size of the newcomer population. The large number of newcomers and their weak or nonexistent ties to established Latinos made outreach the most urgent and difficult task. With few Spanish-speaking residents in the city, and those who were there having their own crises to manage, it was difficult to attract new workers into Latino-oriented social service organizations. Furthermore, there were few outreach workers with knowledge of the problems many of these newcomers faced—including employer abuse and lack of access to health care and housing, as well as problems with law and immigration enforcement—and therefore many organizations required special training and assistance from national groups. The Latino community was thus challenged first to recognize and understand the problems of the newcomers and then to organize themselves to respond appropriately.

The Hispanic Apostolate of the Archdiocese of New Orleans was in the best position to respond, although, like all other social service agencies in New Orleans, it was crippled by the devastation of Katrina. Martin Gutierrez has been the apostolate's executive director since 1997. He came to New Orleans as a child in 1979 when his parents fled Nicaragua after the Sandinista revolution. He anticipated the changes that would occur after the hurricane.

> I remember being at the hotel and having to deal with the fact that I had to decrease my budget soon after the hurricane . . . [since] the archdiocese depend[ed] on the donations from the people. . . . But I remember writing to my superiors at the archdiocese and telling them, "Don't think that our Hispanic population is going to decrease. Do not cut my budget that much because instead of a decrease in the population we will have an increase." And I knew that from past experiences looking at what happened in other parts of the U.S. You know, who went to New York after 9/11? You know, you ask anybody who was around the Pentagon after 9/11, who rebuilt the Pentagon or who repaired it? And just from traveling throughout the country, in every major city, we're going through a lot of construction, you would see a lot of Hispanics. So I thought, you know, once I knew what happened here in New Orleans, I knew that there would be a wave, a huge influx of Latinos. . . . I really had no idea how many would come. I never thought that it would be this many.

The Hispanic Apostolate received a grant from Catholic Charities, and Gutierrez expanded his staff from nine to thirty-five, adding programs on workers' rights and psychological counseling to their usual work on immigration, English-language learning, health, education, and emergency assistance. The partnership of the Hispanic Apostolate and Catholic Charities built on their pre-Katrina organization and has continued to provide the most comprehensive response to the newcomers. Gutierrez says that before Katrina they served five thousand people per year and now they serve twenty thousand, a fourfold increase.[12]

Some churches responded more spontaneously to the needs of the community. Pastor Jesus Gonzalez of Monte de los Olivos Lutheran

Church in Kenner, Louisiana, had evacuated to Texas. He was born there and grew up speaking Spanish in a largely Mexican American neighborhood; he calls himself a "Tex-Mex." The Lutheran Church brought him to New Orleans in 1998 to serve the Latino community. After Katrina, one of his parishioners called him, saying, "Pastor, I don't have a place to stay; you've got electricity in the church." So Gonzalez told him how to get into the church. Many of Gonzalez's parishioners lived in the nearby Redwood apartment complex—a federally subsidized housing project in Kenner that was home to many low-income Latinos in the New Orleans area. It had been rendered uninhabitable by the hurricane, so some of the former residents came to live in the church. When Gonzalez returned from Texas in October, he found twenty people living there. He called the Lutheran authorities to ask for cots and other supplies, and he has continued to provide shelter, food, and comfort to local residents, newcomer Latinos, and Lutheran volunteers. Gonzalez describes the development of his post-Katrina ministry.

> So as time went along . . . I got a little more organized, okay? If you stay here, you had to go to church. You had to go to Bible class. If you don't know any English, you've got to go to English classes because basically in the evenings there was nothing to do. There were just like people just walking around, and then they started drinking. I said, "No, you can't drink here." "Well, we don't have nothing else to do." "Well, we'll find something to do." Then on Friday nights we'd have movie nights; me and my wife, we would make popcorn or whatever. We would make a movie. And then Saturdays it was a clinic. We had a clinic from California, Common Grounds, where every Saturday they were here. And, of course, my wife was out of work. . . . And I don't have a paycheck, so we couldn't—I don't know what we're going to do. However, money was trickling in, not from our paycheck but just people giving, giving, and giving. Then I told her one day, "Well, why don't you cook?" And so I remember she made Mexican food and . . . we put the signs out and at eleven we had a line from here all the way to the street.

Monte de los Olivos Lutheran church continues to host Latino workers and church volunteers, and it offers English classes and clinics and, of course, church services.

The most critical need of the newcomers is also their reason for being in New Orleans. They come for employment and therefore need protection from employer abuse. Immigration lawyers, labor organizers, social justice groups, students, churches, and even the Mexican government have responded to this need. The Student Hurricane Network interviewed 706 workers between January and April 2006 and found that newcomer migrants were especially subject to wage theft and nonpayment, inadequate housing, occupational health and safety violations, and police and immigration harassment.[13] This and other reports documenting abuse were useful for mobilizing legal actions on behalf of the migrant workers, mostly for wage claims. Eva San Martin, who migrated from Honduras as a child and became an outreach worker with Catholic Charities and the Hispanic Apostolate after the storm, notes that wage claims are often the first of many needs.

> Once you meet the workers and process their wage claims, you come across . . . other needs. They need medical care. Lots of them get traffic tickets. Lots of them were getting arrested for driving without legal presence. And so [I] ended up [being] an interpreter in traffic court or medical interpreter [and] giving them rides. I also distribute safety gear because that's another problem that we came across in wage claims, that many of the contractors not only steal their wages but don't provide safety equipment.

Employment problems are rooted, however, in a deeper national problem: workers' undocumented legal status. A study of reconstruction workers in March 2006 found that nearly half of the workforce employed in construction in New Orleans was Latino and more than half of those workers were undocumented.[14] The undocumented workers in the study received lower wages and were more likely to experience wage theft or less pay than expected compared to the native-born and documented foreign workers. Furthermore, they were less likely to receive safety equipment from their employers and less likely to be aware of health risks in their work environment. This unequal treatment on the basis of legal status is the root of the problem for many undocumented newcomer migrants since they often believe they have no legal recourse and therefore they tolerate these abusive practices. Documented newcomer Latino migrants may also suffer discrimination because they are assumed to be "illegal."

For Mexican migrants who want to report employer abuse or are in deportation proceedings, their national consulate is one of their best advocates. The consulate has been extremely active in post-Katrina New Orleans in spite of the fact that it had closed its New Orleans offices in 2001 due to budgetary constraints and demographic shifts of Mexicans to other parts of the southern United States. Lisa Marie Ponce de Leon, a Mexican American who worked as a volunteer for the Mexican consulate prior to the hurricane and continues to do outreach and advocacy work, describes how she connected with the migrants who arrived after the hurricane.

> I worked closely with the Mexican consulate in Houston to keep them up-to-date with abuse cases, emergency cases, and contact with the ICE [Immigration and Customs Enforcement] when they picked up people and called the protection department within the consulate. I handed out information and business cards with the phone numbers of the consulate in Houston at [day labor pickup sites such as] Lee Circle when they were piling up there. I told [the day laborers], you know, just don't go with anybody without getting the phone number and name of company, name of person who picked you up, make sure that they pay you, so, you know, if they don't pay you, we know how to get in touch with them.

In this way, she serves as a critical contact person for Mexican nationals and the Houston-based Mexican consulate.

Carlos García Delgado, the director of protective services at the Mexican consulate in Houston, has worked to reestablish the consulate in New Orleans. He describes how the consulate advocates for its nationals in New Orleans.

> We know that a lot of workers have moved here, and they have been cheated—there is no other word that I can use. And this situation has only worsened in the past months. Since Katrina, there is a whole new ball game here in New Orleans. And nobody really knows what New Orleans will look like five years down the road. What we know . . . is that Mexicans are here and that they're going to be here for at least five years or something like that. . . . It's very hard to try to help them without having a permanent representation here in New Orleans. [They need] . . . passports, consular IDs, powers of attorney, birth certificates, all the stuff that the Mexican consulate does. It is very difficult for them to travel back to Houston. Some of them cannot do so, and those who do are risking many things.

Consular officials have made three visits to New Orleans since the hurricane, mostly to issue passports and *matriculas consulares*. These consular identity cards allow Mexicans to gain access to financial services, and they provide secure identification to the police if they are stopped for any reason.[15] Without this, the police commonly take them into custody, where they are likely to be turned over to the ICE. Although the Mexican consulate is hardly a local civic organization, the Mexicans in New Orleans were able to mobilize a very powerful advocate to work on their behalf.

Immigration law clinics and other legal advocates have worked on behalf of the newcomer immigrants, but often these groups come from outside New Orleans. Two high-profile cases illustrate this point. The Southern Poverty Law Center successfully represented a group of 175 migrant workers who cleaned up after the hurricane in a suit for unpaid wages filed against the Belfor USA Group.[16] The Southern Poverty Law Center, the National Immigration Law Center, and the Louisiana Justice Institute represented the Alliance of Guestworkers for Dignity, an organization of H2B visa holders recruited by a New Orleans hotelier, for protection under the federal Fair Labor Standards Act.[17] These national organizations brought resources to the newcomers that were not available through local organizations run by and serving New Orleans' Latino community.

Latino Political Participation

New Orleans' Latino population has had little representation in local government because it is a relatively small proportion of the electorate, because Latinos have a relatively low rate of naturalization and enfranchisement, and because of the low esteem in which politicians are held in their origin countries. Many pre-Katrina Latinos came from countries where the political process had been corrupted with patronage, violence, and civil war, so they lacked political experience and civic sentiment. Instead they channeled their energies into religious organizations and national-origin social groups. But it is becoming evident to many that this will not be sufficient for dealing with post-Katrina New Orleans.

The lack of political participation and leadership is widely noted by pre-Katrina Latinos. Brenda Murphy, who migrated from Honduras in 1996 when she married a Mexican man living in New Orleans, was the founder and editor of a struggling bilingual sports newspaper, *Jambalaya Deportiva*, prior to Katrina. In October 2005, when Murphy saw the growth of Latinos in New Orleans, she expanded the mission of her newspaper to include local and international news and sports. Murphy reported on topics salient to the Latino community: the losses suffered by pre-Katrina Latinos, the problems they had gaining access to assistance from FEMA and the Red Cross, conditions among the Latino day laborers, and the May 1, 2006, march that demonstrated the labor power of undocumented workers in cities throughout the country. She uses the turnout for the 2006 demonstration in New Orleans as an example.

> We have a lot of [pre-Katrina] Hispanics . . . in New Orleans. They [are] afraid for everybody, for everything. We [are] supposed to have leaders—Hispanic leaders . . . When I made the march, believe me, nobody—any supposed Hispanic leader in the city—said "I'm here and support your activity.". . . The workers are the heroes in the big [May 1] march.

Murphy believes the pre-Katrina Latinos are politically passive and won't organize on their own behalf while the newcomers will.

Civic engagement among pre-Katrina Latinos was often channeled into social organizations and businesses serving the Spanish-speaking population. Ernesto Schweikert, a Guatemalan migrant whose long-standing family ties to New Orleans brought him there in 1970 as a student, is the owner-manager of *Radio Tropical*, one of two Spanish-language local radio stations. Schweikert played a key role in disseminating news to the Latino community during and after Katrina. He waited until the last minute to evacuate so that he could connect those who needed transportation with those who could provide it. After the hurricane passed, he returned to New Orleans with an electric generator so his radio station could continue broadcasting and relay information about Central Americans who were affected by Hurricane Katrina to their families and friends through linkages with thirty-five radio stations throughout Central America. Since Katrina, the radio station has continued to serve the evolving needs of the community and caters increasingly to the newcomers, playing less tropical, Caribbean music and more Mexican music. Schweikert explains the lack of organization in the community.

> What the Hispanic community in New Orleans needs is to really organize ourselves, sort things out and really make a good effort to help the

bulk of the people here. Because, after Katrina, with the influx of this many Hispanics here, most of them are just arriving to this country within the past two or three years. So they don't have the knowledge. In this country, you have to learn a lot of things in order to get the opportunities. . . . For instance, me, I feel blessed the way I came into this country because my parents helped me out. But, even myself, I did not know that school loans existed. Had I known that school loans existed, I would have . . . taken a loan [and] go[ne] to Tulane. . . . So there are many big things that this country has to offer that a lot of people don't know about. This is why the Hispanic community in New Orleans needs leaders. We need to get together and really make a good effort, including the Chamber of Commerce, the Hispanic Apostolate, the other institutions like the Guatemala Club, the Honduran Foundation Club. . . . And we have the media to help them. But we need to make sure that if we get all this help that the money is going back to the people that we are representing.

Schweikert looks to the businesses and social clubs to provide this assistance, reflecting what has in fact occurred.

Darlene Kattan, whose father migrated to New Orleans from Honduras as a child, became executive director of the Hispanic Chamber of Commerce of Louisiana in March 2006 after the hurricane. She describes the changed mission of the HCCL after the storm.

[P]re-Katrina, the mission of the Hispanic Chamber of Commerce of Louisiana was to promote trade between Latin America and New Orleans. . . . After Katrina, trade became secondary. Survival was the primary key here. And we realized with everything that happened that there were more urgent needs, like food and shelter and clothing. And so we were contacted by the United States Hispanic Chamber of Commerce Foundation in Washington, DC. They were in contact with us very shortly after the storm, saying that they wanted to do something immediately to help, and they were going to give us twenty thousand dollars to help do something for the Hispanic community. So we thought about it, and we realized that . . . in order for this area to rebuild it would be necessary to have a literate, assimilated, and trained workforce. And so we needed to be able to provide services to accomplish that end.

The HCCL opened the Hispanic Business Resource and Technology Center in Kenner, Jefferson Parish. The center offers English as a second language (ESL) classes, citizenship classes for those eligible for naturalization, and business classes. It has also partnered with Catholic Charities Hispanic Outreach to provide a space for its legal, health, and counseling programs. This center serves both the established, pre-Katrina Latinos and the post-Katrina newcomers, but its focus is clearly on socially and economically assimilating Latino immigrants into New Orleans so it tends to appeal more to those who are already settled or intend to settle in the area.

Established Latinos often offer assistance to the newcomers with the hope that it will encourage them to assimilate. Oscar Avila, a prominent member of the Honduran community, arrived in New Orleans with his wife in 1984 to study and pursue greater opportunities. He carefully voices this sentiment.

> Most of the [newcomer] Hispanics come basically from Houston. . . . The Hispanic community in Houston is different than the Hispanic community in New Orleans. . . . It's like we are more integrated into the American way without leaving our culture behind. We still have a big festival in October, El Mensaje, and we still have our parties and . . . we want to show the world that this is our culture and we're very proud. But we live the American way. We stick to the language [English]. You're going to see many Hispanics doing interesting jobs all over at every level. And we still have the low-income Hispanic, but even they have a certain pattern of behavior. . . . I'm not saying we want them [the newcomers] to leave. I just want them to adjust to the way we do things here as a community. We don't want to import any manners, especially bad manners, from anywhere. . . . We have a way to do things here. I wish they could do it that way. But I know this is a new town for them. . . . I mean they might feel lost in the different environment. I feel we should embrace them and say, okay, you're welcome here but let me show you how we live so you learn how we live. We don't want [you] to live like you live back in Houston. We want you to live like we do in New Orleans. We will see, I guess, when this situation in New Orleans is sort of coming down to normal. We'll see who will stay. If there is a big majority of Hispanics, that's what I'm afraid of, to lose the way we used to live pre-Katrina.

Many of New Orleans' pre-Katrina Latinos say that New Orleans is the only place they could live in the United States because it feels so similar to their Central American homes. Like all New Orleanians, they are wondering whether things will return to "normal" as the city rebuilds. They recognize that assimilating the newcomers is critical for the city's cultural recovery.

Whether the newcomers will simply participate in the physical rebuilding of the city or will become part of the social structure of the new New Orleans is still an open question. The tension between providing assistance to newcomers and hoping that they will assimilate was evident at a public meeting of the City of New Orleans Human Relations Commission whose agenda was to hear the concerns of the Latino community. This meeting was held in June 2007, and forty to fifty members of the Hispanic community turned out for the event.

The newcomer Latinos and their advocates were concerned with workers' rights, police harassment, and other social justice issues. They see New Orleans' issues in a national context, where comprehensive immigration reform is high on the political agenda in Congress and localities across the country. They spoke to the basic rights of immigrants but were less concerned with assimilating into New Orleans or anywhere in the United States. In contrast, the pre-Katrina Latinos voiced their desire for the incorporation and assimilation of the newcomers. These concerns ranged from offering ESL courses to ensuring that they would have access to health care, housing, and transportation. For many pre-Katrina Latinos, the incorporation of the newcomers promises to increase their own political and social prominence in the rebuilding of New Orleans by increasing the size of the Latino community and laying claim to the heroic efforts and sacrifices of this group.

Civic Engagement among Established Latinos

The stories related here reflect the fact that to a greater or lesser degree New Orleans' established Latinos have put down roots in the United States, although they maintain strong ties to their origin countries. Their migration experiences allowed them to maintain this dual loyalty. Typically, established Latinos' entry into the United States did not involve a clandestine trip over the border, breaking laws, or avoiding detection. Often they entered seeking refuge from countries undergoing revolutions and civil wars where legal disorder reigned. Or they arrived as sponsored family members of those already legally in the United States. Many have naturalized, although some maintain citizenship in their origin country. Their warm reception has allowed them to be politically active, although many refrain from politics because of their experiences in their origin countries or because they do not feel truly part of the U.S. political system. The political uncertainty in post-Katrina New Orleans changed that by showing them what they had at stake in the city, what might be lost, and what might be gained.

Lucas Diaz, a Dominican who immigrated to New Orleans with his family as a child, had not been involved in any social service organization before Katrina. He described his newfound desire for civic engagement this way.

> Most Latinos—except for the militant-type Latinos that work with worker rights or the activist types—are very conservative in nature because of their cultural upbringing, and so was I. But I gravitate toward wanting to help more people. . . . I'm now . . . learning about becoming civically engaged as a thirty-seven-year-old person. . . . So right now the idea of coming up with some kind of equitable immigration plan that makes sense is most important. But then beyond that is . . . being a voice in discussions [about] how to create equitable and thriving communities. . . . If you let the market do its thing, then you can always have a conglomerate of bigwigs that just make decisions for the betterment of not the community but for themselves. And you get what happened in the nineteenth century in the industrial age where . . . the Rockefellers and the Fords [made millions] off of the backs of these poor people— you know, the Irish and the Italians and the Slovaks. . . . And so that's the free market? I believe in the government having to check business. I think the government plays a role . . . and the citizens should keep the government and business true. So if there's no discussion . . . and one is not civically engaged to say, "Well, what about this group? And how are you considering this group as you plan this?" So that's what I'm getting into now.

Whether other pre-Katrina Latinos are similarly motivated by the realization that they have a lot at stake in New Orleans' future is an open question. These interviews identified two main barriers to their civic engagement: their mostly negative experiences with politics in their origin countries and their partial integration into the U.S. political system. These barriers were lowered somewhat when the arrival of the Latino newcomers gave pre-Katrina Latinos an opportunity to assist the newcomers who were helping rebuild New Orleans. Mayor Ray Nagin's statement in October

2005 that he didn't want New Orleans to be "overrun by Mexicans" made them realize how little political clout they had in the city and perhaps motivated them further still.[18] Hurricane Katrina catalyzed pre-Katrina Latinos' civic engagement by making them realize how deeply their roots had grown in New Orleans' swampy soil and that they therefore had a stake in how the city recovered from the hurricane. The newcomer migrants' participation in rebuilding and their social incorporation give the pre-Katrina Latinos greater leverage for participating in the rebuilding of New Orleans' civil society after Katrina.

NOTES

1. Louisiana Department of Health and Hospitals, "Louisiana Health and Population Survey: Expanded Preliminary Results, Orleans Parish," October 6, 2006, http://popest.org.

2. Luis Emilio Henao, *The Hispanics in Louisiana* (New Orleans: Latin American Apostolate, 1982).

3. Norman Wellington Painter, "The Assimilation of Latin Americans in New Orleans, Louisiana," PhD diss., Tulane University, 1949; Henao, *The Hispanics in Louisiana*; Mary Karen Bracken, "Restructuring the Boundaries: Hispanics in New Orleans, 1960–1990," PhD diss., University of New Mexico, 1992.

4. Elizabeth Fussell, "Post-Katrina New Orleans as a New Migrant Destination," paper presented at the Population Association of America annual meetings, New York, March 2007.

5. Pew Hispanic Center, "A Statistical Portrait of Hispanics at Mid-Decade," table 11: "Change in Foreign-Born Population by State, 2000 and 2005," http://pewhispanic.org/docs.

6. Elizabeth Grieco, "The Foreign Born from Mexico in the United States," Migration Information Source, Migration Policy Institute. October 1, 2003, http://migrationinformation.org, accessed October 26, 2006; Jeffrey S. Passel, "Mexican Immigration to the U.S.: The Latest Estimates," Migration Information Source, Migration Policy Institute, March 1, 2004, http://migrationinformation.org.

7. Jeffrey S. Passel, "The Size and Characteristics of the Unauthorized Migrant Population in the U.S.: Estimates Based on the March 2005 Current Population Survey," Pew Hispanic Center report, March 7, 2006, http://pewhispanic.org, accessed October 18, 2006.

8. U.S. Department of Labor, "Guidance on the Suspension of the Davis-Bacon and Related Acts in Areas Impacted by Hurricane Katrina," September 5, 2005.

9. Gregory Rodriguez, "La Nueva Orleans: Latino Immigrants, Many of Them Here Illegally, Will Rebuild the Gulf Coast—or Stay There," *Los Angeles*

Times, Opinion Page, September 25, 2005, http://www.latimes.com/news/printedi tion/opinion/la-op-latino25sep.

10. U.S. Bureau of the Census, "American Community Survey, General Characteristics, Orleans Parish and Jefferson Parish, 2005," http://factfinder.census .gov/.

11. Louisiana Department of Health and Hospitals, "Louisiana Health and Population Survey: Expanded Preliminary Results, Orleans Parish, October 6, 2006," http://popest.org; Elizabeth Fussell, "Latino/a Immigrants in Post-Katrina New Orleans: A Research Report," *World on the Move* 13, no. 2 (2006): 2–4.

12. Maria Morales and Lena Hansen, "A Hispanic Renaissance in New Orleans," *People en Español*, September 2007, 20, http://www.peopleenespanol.com.

13. Judith Browne-Dianis, Jennifer Lai, Marielena Hincapie, and Saket Soni, "And Injustice for All: Workers' Lives in the Reconstruction of New Orleans," 2006, http://www.neworleansworkerjustice.org/en/doc/workersreport.pdf, accessed June 20, 2007.

14. Laurel E Fletcher, Phuong Pham, Eric Stover, and Patrick Vinck, "Rebuilding after Katrina: A Population-Based Study of Labor and Human Rights in New Orleans," Vol. 2 (2006): http://www.payson.tulane.edu/katrina/katrina_re port_final.pdf.

15. Monica W. Varsanyi, "Documenting Undocumented Migrants: The *Matriculas Consulares* as Neoliberal Local Membership," *Geopolitics* 12 (2007): 299–319; Instituto de los Mexicanos en el Exterior, "Matricula Consular de Alta Seguridad," *Mexicanos en el Exterior* 1, no. 10 (2004): 1–4, http://www.ime.gob.mx/ noticias/boletines_tematicos/bol10.doc.

16. Leslie Eaton, "Migrant Workers to Get Overtime for Storm Cleanup, Ending Suit," *New York Times*, September 8, 2006.

17. Julia Cass, "Guest Workers Sue New Orleans Hotel Chain; Immigrants Say Decatur Group Failed to Deliver on Promised Employment," *Washington Post*. August 17, 2006.

An H2B visa is a visa for a temporary non-agricultural worker in occupations for which there is a recurring seasonal, intermittent, or one-time need. These are not highly skilled occupations. The employer must establish that there is no domestic labor force available. Employers request a fixed number of visas and recruit the workers from abroad. The Department of Labor is responsible for oversight of the work conditions of H2B visa workers.

18. Arian Campo-Flores, "A New Spice in the Gumbo: Will Latino Day Laborers Locating in New Orleans Change Its Complexion?" *Newsweek*, December 5, 2005.

Interconnections

Amy Koritz

ON A PERSONAL LEVEL, this section tells the story of how I stopped worrying about whether I was still being an English professor. As a young assistant professor, I'd been through the exhilarating years of feminist theory, cultural studies, and transdisciplinary postcolonialism, a time when we all thought that reading and writing differently would have an enormous and immediate impact on the world. Please don't laugh; I was sincere. But it was becoming clear to me, well before disaster struck for real, that a slow, nuanced disaster was creeping up on my relationship with my professional identity. Close reading will only get you so far.

This is not an anti-intellectual or even an anti-academic statement. The point I want to make as we close this volume is that the humanities are fundamentally concerned with interconnection. Canons of literature are one mode for pursuing this goal. There are many others, and the humanities should participate in them all. In order to do so, however, humanists have to be willing to place themselves in uncomfortable situations—in meetings with artists, social service providers, even businesspeople—where no one in the room is sure why you are there, including yourself. I found myself making a career of discomfort in the year following Katrina. While, with one important exception, this made the bureaucratic structures of my university uneasy, I've never seen more possibilities for connecting the academic work of the university with opportunities to build and revitalize community. The pieces included in this section trace, from a perspective not my own, some of the worlds I moved into as my interests and commitments became more centrally responsive to a city in crisis.

Carole Rosenstein was until recently a cultural policy analyst and researcher with the Urban Institute. She came to New Orleans to participate in a conference cosponsored by the Urban Institute and the Louisiana Association for Non-profit Organizations (LANO). Her panel, on which I served as well—along with Carol Bebelle, Don Marshall, and the director of the Contemporary Arts Center, Jay Weigel—focused on bringing cultural sector research to bear on how New Orleans was being rebuilt. This was not supposed to happen, the panel I mean. When, because I showed up at meetings where I did not belong, I was appointed to the local advisory committee for this conference, it quickly became clear that nobody else thought the cultural sector was particularly important. After all, health care, housing, environmental remediation, disaster preparedness, these were the crucial topics, no? Somebody had to be at that table, and in this case it was me, who could say, "Wait a minute, this is New Orleans. How can culture not be crucial to its recovery?" What Carole had to say did not turn out to be what most of the people in the room wanted to hear. Her focus on attending to small, close-to-the-ground cultural organizations and looking for ways to honor and support the value of vernacular cultural traditions and practices was not going to help museums and symphonies or even individual artists in need of galleries and performance space. Her voice was drowned out by calls for special treatment for artists and for further strengthening major players.

There is a rich research project here, which I'll get to sometime, but almost immediately I was called to another meeting I had no business attending. Ron Bechet, an art professor at Xavier University, asked me to join a conversation about a possible arts project in New Orleans that would draw on the ideas of celebrity artists to create a large performance of the pre-Katrina lives of devastated houses in the city. This made little sense to me given the pragmatic attitudes beaten into me by my contact with social service providers, but in my new identity as utter outsider I figured I had nothing to lose by keeping an open mind. The meeting did not go well. But by the end Ron John Barnes, a sculptor from Dillard University; Jan Cohen-Cruz, a theater practitioner from New York University; and I had decided to put something together for the local universities. The story Jan tells in her mixed-genre reflection on creating university projects that partner with community-based artists and cultural organizations expresses the potential, as well as the difficulty, of such work. Without her assertive focus on pulling us together and keeping us productive, *HOME, New Orleans* would not have survived its first year. It has, as of this writing, survived its second and been awarded Ford Foundation funding, which will secure its future for at least two more. Ron, John, and I have just finished teaching Building Community through the Arts, a cross-institutional course on community arts, for the second time. We continue to deepen and broaden our relationships with the neighborhood projects established in *HOME, New Orleans'* first year. Through Jan's new position as the director of Imagining America: Artists and Scholars in Public Life (a consortium of universities interested in furthering public scholarship in the arts, humanities, and design fields), she will bring the possibilities of this kind of endeavor to a national audience.

Without the energy, imagination, and courage of Ron, Jan, and John during this time, I would have been less happy, less productive, and less cognizant of the possibilities of community-directed art in creating strong, sustainable communities. I owe them all my deepest gratitude. Without Don Marshall, the executive director of the Jazz and Heritage Festival Foundation in New Orleans, we would all be in much more trouble than we are. When I began attending community events focused on the arts and culture, Don was the only leader of a major cultural organization in the city who would turn up not only at the high-powered Cultural Economies Summit sponsored by Louisiana's lieutenant governor but also at the Seventh Ward neighborhood festival. His understanding of the full range of the city's culture is extraordinary, but even more so has been his willingness to fund the smallest indigenous expressions of that culture in the same breath as the largest, most influential players. This cross-class, cross-race inclusiveness is rare in New Orleans, which, as he notes in his interview, really has three cultures, three education systems, and three business sectors: white, black, and Creole. Don's commitment to bringing us all together has inspired me with hope during those times when it seemed as though power politics and turf battles were going to scuttle any possibility for real progress in New Orleans.

What the crisis of this disaster and its long, slow aftermath has taught me about civic engagement is that its best hope, the one that genuinely connects the resources of universities with their communities, builds on sustainable partnerships toward shared goals, and develops the strength to withstand the many ways in which institutions shut out engagement and shut down those who seek it out, is interconnection. I mean this on many levels. Not only have the reach and focus of my relationships within New Orleans expanded but so has my awareness of project models, research, and potential partners around the country. This is a good thing not only for me but for the future of civic engagement.

By the way, the one important exception within my university to the general uneasiness my work seemed to provoke has been the Tulane/ Xavier Center for Bioenvironmental Research. Go figure. This group of science- focused researchers immediately saw the relevance of my activities to their interest in sustainable urban ecosystems and understood how integral the arts and culture are to the healthy, vibrant city we all desire.

Cultural Policy and Living Culture in New Orleans after Katrina

Carole Rosenstein

THE FIRST TIME I VISITED NEW ORLEANS, it rained. And rained and rained. I spent that visit feeling ratty, damp from inside out and outside in, sweaty and drenched. But for five soggy hours at the Funky Butt I listened, rapt, to Jason Marsalis (I think it was) play xylophone, sparkly little gumdrops of sound tossed out onto the dirty, puddled sidewalk. On departure day, the clouds cleared. Like a tease. Or maybe more like a hint that things sordid and exquisite intersect somewhere around there, near the corner of Decatur and Iberville, where blue sky broke over the river. Last visit, it was fog—dense and whitish gray, drawn in wispy, shin-high streaks. It was comic book spooky, spooky in a good way, but only when I could manage to push aside the images of bloat and horror. For me, the city always seems to have a dreamy, watery aspect. Out of focus. And it's raucous, too (where I stay). And seedy. And pervasively, now maybe unrelentingly, sad.

If you've been there, I'm not telling you anything you don't know. New Orleans is a place where the fact of dying—not so much of death, but of unremitting decay, degeneration, that particular deterioration that comes with neglect (what comes to my mind is nasty toenails, nursing home feet)—tussles with the counterpoised fact of being alive. Dancing and fucking and eating and falling down drunk, decked out in spangles and carrying a little parasol while you're at it. You can feel the two angels fighting it out in the ether all around, and when they rest there's nowhere more eerily quiet. It's pretty quiet now.

It's not a place, you notice, that makes me think of answering e-mails, paying bills, changing diapers. I'm a visitor to New Orleans, and my visits there are time out of time. I want to fess up to this dewy-eyed lens because this is an essay on policy. And I didn't really want to write a policy essay about New Orleans. I wanted to write something beautiful about New Orleans. Maybe the best I can do, here at the beginning, is to toss a bauble to its dark romance and then go on to say let's resist being seduced by its beauty and sadness. Let's be careful not to let a metaphorical frame of mind—the brown-edged magnolias, the flustered Blanches, the rusting facades of intricate ironwork—keep getting in the way of figuring out what to do and doing it soon. New Orleans holds mysteries. No doubt about it. But New Orleans also challenges us with problems that have real solutions.

Cultural Policy and Community-Based Culture

I was asked to go to New Orleans in the fall of 2006 as part of an Urban Institute team helping to organize a conference on the nonprofit sector's response to rebuilding the city. The conference was to focus on policies affecting housing, children and families, disaster relief, and community health. But a few advocates in New Orleans (including an editor of this volume) demanded that the arts and culture be addressed in that forum, and so, with some trepidation, I went. I was nervous about participating for two reasons. First, the cultural policy issues I was asked to address do not typically carry the same weight and force as those surrounding problems of poverty, housing, education, and health. In just about every forum where I have presented cultural policy analysis on New Orleans, questions—and sometimes impassioned critiques—have been raised about why we should care about the arts and culture when residents are still displaced, children not only don't have schools to go to but are being shot in the street, and hospitals remain closed.

But I also had a second concern. And that had to do with the reaction of my audience that day, an audience made up of museum professionals, arts administrators, and artists. Because what I had to say was that the cultural sector has done a poor job of understanding, prioritizing, and addressing the needs of the community and it is these needs that should form the basis on which cultural policy—like any other type of policy—is created and its effectiveness measured. Why be nervous about saying that? Of course, policies should be created and measured according to the degree to which they serve the public good. Well, the difficulty is that in the cultural sector the public good often seems to have become rather distant from the public. The public and nonprofit sector's relative neglect of the immediate cultural needs of communities can be found in many, many places around the country, but it could be seen starkly in New Orleans after Katrina. So I was going to stand up in front of a gathering of exhausted culture workers who were frantically trying to save their institutions, organizations, and collections and say that that was not the kind of disaster recovery their community needed most.

New Orleans is the birthplace of jazz, often considered the United States' greatest indigenous art form. It also is home to a distinctive architecture and a Creole culture, cuisine, and music found nowhere else. African American cultural traditions born and sustained in New Orleans—second-line dancing, Mardi Gras Indian pageantry, jazz funerals—are respected and beloved around the world. Unlike the cultural assets of some other places, those in New Orleans are rooted firmly in its communities. Rather than its museums and symphony halls, it is the people, neighborhoods, local organizations, and small businesses of New Orleans that make it culturally distinct. Many people who make up these communities are still displaced from their homes. And some may remain in the diaspora for the near term, some close to New Orleans and some farther away. The most pressing cultural policy challenge in New Orleans today is how to preserve the community-based culture and expressions of communities that are tattered and scattered. The hurricanes and their aftermath wrought irreversible change on New Orleans communities. How can some lines of cultural continuity be sustained and conversations about the new cultural look, feel, sounds, and tastes of New Orleans be promoted?

Entrenched attitudes and practices will make it difficult for the cultural sector to meet these challenges. Foremost among these attitudes is a steadfast insistence on seeing large arts institutions as providing the bedrock of cultural life. A growing body of research demonstrates that small, community-based organizations and public-sector cultural venues provide significant and inclusive arts and culture services. A focus on rebuilding and resourcing large arts institutions perpetuates both the marginalization of this vital cohort of small, community-based cultural organizations and the isolation of arts and culture from connections to other arenas of public life. Together these factors create a less equitable, weaker cultural sector, one that can neither meet the needs of the whole community nor effectively advocate for public support. Although a clear understanding of why and how to sustain community-based culture is essential to addressing these gaps, the cultural sector remains remarkably weak on this subject.

Why: Culture and Performative Power

A fundamental of cultural policy in New Orleans post-Katrina must be to articulate the public value of community-based culture. But nowhere are the hazards of New Orleans' dark romance more, well, hazardous than in talking about the city's indigenous artistic and cultural expressions. Poor people create and maintain New Orleans' indigenous forms of jazz and performance: jazz funerals, second lines, Indian gangs. One of the things that makes these expressions so aesthetically, socially, and culturally rich is their multivalence, but an important part of what they are are responses to the sadness and rage that poverty and racism breed. And one of the reasons why these forms are so powerful is that they are created and performed in spite of poverty and racism. These forms assert the power of living in the face of dying, abundance in the face of scarcity, control in the face of disempowerment, pride in the face of disrespect. Of course, the making of such brave assertions is a fundamental ritual trope; asserting human efficacy through ritual action is part of what makes ritual a potent social and cultural form.

To take away the context of deprivation in which indigenous jazz and street performance in New Orleans unfolds is to undermine some of its performative power. We are, sadly, in very little danger that deprivation will disappear any time soon. However, in New Orleans the particular context of deprivation in which indigenous jazz and performance have lived is now displaced along with the people and communities that practice these forms. And this raises a peculiar problem. New Orleans' indigenous jazz and performance genres are performances and traditions not texts, images, or objects; they are aesthetic forms carried in and by people and communities. These people and communities are poor and (mostly) black. You can't have the forms without the people. You can't have the people without their blackness. And thus far we have no systemic programs on the table for getting the people and communities back without getting the poverty, too.

There is intense romance in the image of poor, oppressed folk creating beautiful, communal expressions as a form of resistance. In every other policy area—education, health, housing, public safety—the need and desire to alleviate poverty are clear. But, unfortunately, this is not always the case in cultural policy and practice, where culture and poverty are conceptually bound in several ways. Cultural "authenticity" is associated with images of poor folk: simple, rural, backward, uneducated, marginal, etcetera, etcetera. Also there is a powerful imperative to uncritically respect and cherish the aesthetic and humanistic qualities of poor and marginalized peoples' artistic and cultural expressions. This is ground well covered in some critical anthropology and folklore and even in some emerging development discourse. What is less often recognized is that the romance in the image of poor, oppressed folk creating beautiful, communal expressions as a form of resistance reflects longing not only for authentic, communal, human expression but longing also for a belief in the efficacy of such expressions. The longing for cultural efficacy and the inadequate conceptualization of how cultural efficacy might relate to social and economic justice demand some careful thought.

Arjun Appadurai provides a powerful framework for thinking about the multiple and powerful efficacies of cultural forms in his discussion of the ways in which poor people can use a repertoire of stories, values, and performance genres to create compelling claims in the public sphere. He calls this the "capacity to aspire," by which he means, I think, the capacity to present situated claims in culturally potent terms. Appadurai notes that while culture has "been viewed as a matter of one or another kind of pastness—the keywords here are habit, custom, heritage, tradition," culture also frames orientations toward the future. The capacity to aspire is a facility to connect individual wants and needs to cultural norms about what constitutes "the good life, health, and happiness" and more broadly to belief systems about "life and death, the nature of worldly possessions, the significance of material assets over social relations, the value of peace or warfare." This facility is one he describes in terms of narrative and performance. For example, he writes, "Gandhi's life, his fasting, his abstinence, his bodily comportment, his ascetical style, his crypto-Hindu use of nonviolence and of peaceful resistance were all tremendously successful because they mobilized a local palette of performances and precursors."[1] Individuals and groups institute change by creating powerful stories that explain, persuade, and address their needs and wants in terms of norms and belief systems. This capacity to aspire, and the hope and confidence it generates, thus are directly related to economic growth, poverty reduction, and public action.

It is imperative that the living cultural forms of New Orleans communities be understood in ways informed by this framework. The power of

New Orleans' indigenous performance genres lies in their ability to both express and actively reproduce the will and presence of the people who create and embody them. Because I am not an expert on the cultures of New Orleans, I'll not attempt to interpret the particular and complex meanings and values embodied in those forms. Certainly they have to do with living with the reality of dying, celebrating the fact of life, and putting community at the center of that life, a community created through the process of instantiating these forms with year after year of beading circles, band practice, and crawfish boils. This is the living culture of New Orleans, and every one of the educational, social, political, and economic functions that might be built on it depends on it being vital and robust.

How: Action Steps in Support of Living Culture

There are ways for cultural policy to promote and sustain the living culture of New Orleans, and thus to ensure that the cultural sector post-Katrina can be rebuilt both equitably and to maximize public benefit. Arts and culture can be expansively incorporated into a wide range of public programs from education to health care to human services. Venues that have been shown to be highly inclusive in their arts and culture programming can serve as a focus for rebuilding efforts and resources. And New Orleans' cultural economy can be developed with equitably distributed resources and opportunities for voice from underrepresented members of the cultural community such as community-based organizations and individual artists.

Foster connections between the arts and culture and a broad range of public policy areas such as education, health, social services, and community improvement.
The arts and culture typically are not considered to be very important to core public concerns such as education, community development, health, transportation, and safety. However, research shows that strong connections exist between the arts and culture and the government agencies and nonprofit organizations whose work addresses these issues. Local government agencies outside the arts and culture are essential for the delivery of arts and culture to populations such as youth and seniors through programs sponsored by courts, social service agencies, and police departments.[2] Schools, social service agencies, and community development organizations recognize the power of arts and culture programming to foster community engagement and organizing.[3] Strong connections exist be-

tween cultural heritage activities and nonprofit organizations working in education, human services, community improvement and capacity building, and food, nutrition, and agriculture.[4] By recognizing and fostering these connections, rebuilding plans that focus on delivering resources to agencies and organizations not involved in the arts still can provide support for the development of a strong arts and culture community.

Some effective ways to foster strong, well-resourced connections between artistic and non-arts activities and organizations include the following.

- Creating a concise, coherent, realistic cultural plan that identifies key strengths of the arts and culture and advertises their capacities and benefits to the broader policy community.
- Incorporating specific, targeted cultural policy items into large-scale, cross-sector plans such as the Unified New Orleans Plan.
- Developing a strong, cross-sector advocacy network for the arts and culture that represents all facets of the cultural community.
- Developing and implementing a robust, innovative Percent for Art program for all public building and public works projects.
- Developing opportunities, registries, and employment rosters for local artists who could be employed in programs at non-arts venues.
- Developing opportunities for arts and culture organizations, especially small and mid-sized organizations, to connect with non-arts agencies and organizations.
- Providing funds specifically targeted at establishing and sustaining artistic and non-arts partnerships.

Redevelop well-resourced, inclusive cultural venues such as libraries, parks, schools, public media, and safe street corners.

Urban Institute research has shown that people are much more likely to attend arts and culture events in community venues such as parks, streets, schools, and places of worship than in conventional arts venues such as concert halls and museums. Moreover, community cultural venues tend to include people who are unlikely to participate in conventional arts and culture activities. Twenty-six percent of respondents to an Urban Institute survey said that they attend arts and culture events only in community venues.[5] Other research suggests that this kind of community-grounded participation is prevalent among those typically hardest to reach with arts and culture programs and services: immigrants, African Americans, Hispanics, and people with low levels of education and income.[6] Initiatives seeking to grow vibrant, inclusive arts and culture programs must explicitly and actively engage community venues such as streets, parks, libraries, and schools.

Some effective ways to redevelop strong, well-resourced venues for inclusive, living culture include the following.

- Ensuring that artists and culture bearers have access to public space through open and fair permitting, licensing, and zoning processes and enforcement.
- Establishing an autonomous city commission (such as San Francisco's Entertainment Commission) responsible for decision making about the use of public space for arts and entertainment.
- Building community cultural resource centers for public arts, festivals, cultural heritage, and jazz education (along the lines of San Francisco's city-owned, community-based cultural centers).
- Developing opportunities, registries, and employment rosters for local artists who could be employed in public culture programs.
- Developing opportunities for local culture bearers to participate in public culture through programs in schools, libraries, parks, and public media.
- Developing networks and alliances of professionals in public culture such as park officials, festival producers, programmers in public libraries and schools, and public radio and television producers.
- Rebuilding strong public libraries with comprehensive public arts and culture programming in every neighborhood.
- Reestablishing arts programs in every school, particularly programs with strong connections to community-based traditions such as marching bands in New Orleans.
- Rebuilding public parks and establishing comprehensive, coordinated public arts and culture programming in city and neighborhood parks.

Maintain a balance in cultural economic development between branding and vitality, investment and equity.
Advocates for arts and culture have moved beyond economic impact

studies and, through regional and state initiatives such as the New England Creative Economy and Louisiana: Where Culture Means Business, have begun to fully document arts and culture as an industry through indicators such as audience numbers, workforce size, revenues, and expenditures. They also map powerful connections with other industries such as education, high-tech fields, and tourism. But this emerging perspective has not focused on finding ways to help ensure that the benefits of the cultural economy and the responsibilities for preserving and safeguarding artistic and historic quality are equitably distributed. This undermines the long-term ability of the cultural sector to maintain the authenticity and quality of its cultural products. Not only can stronger ties between communities and economic developers, tourism professionals, and convention planners help ensure that cultural products will retain their value, but research suggests that these ties actually can aid the further integration of underserved communities into market participation and community development.[7]

Some effective ways to ensure that cultural economic development is equitable and contributes to sustaining a vital cultural community include the following.

- Undertaking a comprehensive cultural asset mapping process that can account for the cultural assets of every community, particularly focusing attention on assets that communities identify as most appropriate for inclusion in cultural economy marketing materials and programming.
- Funding and aggressively marketing community-directed, neighborhood-based cultural heritage tourism projects.
- Gathering neighborhood-level data on the economic and community development impacts of cultural economic development.
- Developing and providing neighborhood-based business training and technical assistance opportunities for small cultural enterprises.
- Developing business support and career development services for individual artists.
- Developing community-directed mechanisms for assessing, maintaining, and documenting artistic quality.
- Establishing cooperative studio space for artists in the visual, performing, and literary arts.

- Establishing neighborhood-based incubators for cultural enterprise.
- Establishing arts and cultural management training programs at local colleges and universities focused on key local cultural enterprises such as music, cuisine, and heritage tourism.

Finally: Cultural Longing

When my mother and father got married almost fifty years ago, they honeymooned in Europe for six weeks. Although he'd been in the army in France, this was a big deal for my dad, whose own father was a teamster in the Italian Market in South Philadelphia. The story of what happened when my dad went to tell his Bubby about the trip is famous in my family. I have an image of her standing in the kitchen with a spattered apron on and her bosom barely hidden behind a big bowl of mashed potatoes and schmaltz—because she's always described as vigorously demanding that everyone take more from a big bowl of mashed potatoes and schmaltz—looking askance at young versions of my mom and dad. She delivers her famous line: "What do you want to go there for? We just come from there."

When I was in college and went off on trips to Europe, and when one of those trips was to Germany and Austria, my own grandmother, Theresa Marie Katherine Donato, with the passion of a convert, was appalled that I would even consider going to the place where such evil had been visited on our people, the Jews. Of course, it was impossible to visit there without going to a concentration camp and other memorials of the Holocaust. But what resonated with me about that trip was the food. I found pickles and pretzels, flaky pastries and fatty sausages, things to eat that told me not that this was where my people suffered and were humiliated and murdered but that this is the place where my people are from. And this is simply to say that there are many times to go home and many different ways.

Cultural longing is a powerful force and one that can be enormously productive. People in the diaspora learn to live with the pain and joy of it. I have an image of a future New Orleans where a grandmother will return to Treme or Central City or the Seventh Ward with her grandchildren from Houston or Los Angeles or New York City and the traces of her past will not be marked on the landscape, the ways of life that she knew will have disappeared from the public life in that place. Not that the "culture" will have died. That's not how culture works, of course. It will have been transformed. But will these transformations effectively develop, respect, and incorporate what came before? The work I have done in New Orleans over the past months tells me that a real danger exists that they will not do so. That is the kind of pain and waste that can and should be spared. Good cultural policy guided by sustained community engagement and advocacy can ensure that they are spared and that public resources are well used to aid New Orleans' citizens over the next years and decades in this process of rebuilding, reimaging, and reintegrating what was before with what comes after.

NOTES

1. Arjun Appadurai, "The Capacity to Aspire: Culture and the Terms of Recognition," in *Culture and Public Action*, edited by V. Rao and M. Walton (Palo Alto: Stanford University Press, 2004).

2. Randy Cohen and Margaret Wyszomirski, *National and Local Profiles of Cultural Support* (Washington, DC: Americans for the Arts, 2002).

3. Chris Walker, *Arts and Non-arts Partnerships: Opportunities, Challenges, and Strategies* (Washington, DC: Urban Institute, 2004).

4. Carole Rosenstein, *Cultural Heritage Organizations: Nonprofits That Support Ethnic, Folk, Traditional, and Noncommercial Popular Culture* (Washington, DC: Urban Institute, 2006).

5. Chris Walker with Kay Sherwood, *Participation in Arts and Culture: The Importance of Community Venues* (Washington, DC: Urban Institute, 2003).

6. Carole Rosenstein, *Diversity and Participation in the Arts* (Washington, DC: Urban Institute, 2005).

7. Chris Walker, Maria Jackson, and Carole Rosenstein, *Culture and Commerce: Traditional Arts in Economic Development* (Washington, DC: Urban Institute, 2003). Versions of this essay, or parts of it, have been presented at the State of Louisiana Cultural Economy Initiative Cultural Economy Summit III; the Urban Institute's First Tuesday Policy Convening: Rebuilding a Devastated Arts and Culture Community: How Can New Orleans Recover; the Louisiana Association of Nonprofit Organizations conference Translating Research into Action: Nonprofits and the Renaissance of New Orleans; the 2006 American Political Science Association short course Cultural Industries, Technologies, and Policies; and the 2006 Conference on Social Theory, Politics, and the Arts. Portions of this essay have been published in "New Orleans Arts and Culture," Carol De Vita, ed., *After Katrina: Shared Challenges for Rebuilding* (Washington, DC: Urban Institute, 2007); and "Cultural Treasures of New Orleans," *Material Matters* 55 (July–August 2007), 15–21.

HOME, New Orleans

UNIVERSITY/NEIGHBORHOOD
ARTS COLLABORATIONS

Jan Cohen-Cruz

HOME, New Orleans (HNO) is a neighborhood-based, arts-focused project that incorporates local organizations and residents; local artists, including HNO coinitiator Jan Gilbert of the VESTIGES Project; and students
and faculty members from two historically black universities in New Orleans, Xavier and Dillard, and two predominantly white ones, Tulane in
New Orleans and New York University (NYU), the latter through a visiting professor and two students. Our focus is "home" in its many manifes-
tations: individual dwellings, neighborhoods, and the city itself. Our
grounding is a university course that combines practice and reflection. Our
process emphasizes sustainable ways to use art to contribute to ongoing
neighborhood life. That is, *HOME, New Orleans* responds to local priorities through arts workshops, memorials, youth theater, performance, and
installation art, contributing to revitalizing efforts. Through the arts' capacity to bring people together, we hope to facilitate local bonding and
cross-race, intraneighborhood, and class bridging. Our work is twofold: to
train university students in civic engagement and to engage neighborhood
residents in arts-based projects that modestly contribute to rebuilding
community in New Orleans.

In what follows, Jan Cohen-Cruz, who coinitiated HNO's university
component with Ron Bechet, stitches together reflections with excerpts
from conversations with Bechet, a professor of art at Xavier. Tulane En-

glish professor Amy Koritz and Dillard Art Department chair John Barnes, the other HNO faculty, joined them in one conversation. Cohen-Cruz was a professor at NYU's Tisch School of the Arts; she recently became the new director of Imagining America, based at Syracuse University.

In June 2006, ten months after Katrina, I attended a small gathering in New Orleans of university faculty members who regularly do community arts work with their students. Our host, Ron Bechet, engaged us in conversations about arts departments responding to local crises, brought us to a meeting with about one hundred local artists and a few interested parties from other fields to discuss a role for art in rebuilding community, and showed us around the devastated city. The view on the ground was heartrending. Neighborhoods emptied of inhabitants and basic services with crumbling homes and craterlike potholes bespoke how utterly at the mercy of the storm and levee breaks they were and how little government aid had been forthcoming. Trailers parked alongside a smattering of homes on dark streets indicated that as few as one per every thirty households had returned to some areas. A dearth of reopened hospitals, public transportation vehicles, grocery stores, and businesses made returning wildly challenging even for those with intact dwellings. Seemingly sturdy housing projects remained closed, their low-income, black renters kept out of the city, possibly forever. Was New Orleans going to re-build itself as a different city without the 70 percent African American population that included victims of the most entrenched poverty but also many of the carriers of the city's celebrated culture?

Coincidentally, a few days after I got home I heard from Richard Schechner, a former professor of mine who forty years previously had gone to graduate school and then taught in New Orleans and been part of the Free Southern Theater. He had also recently been in New Orleans, at the invitation of local artist Jan Gilbert, and now imagined a project he called HOME: New Orleans, *which would con-sist of installations and theater snippets in front of and inside ruined houses, briefly bringing back to life a range of memories before the houses were bulldozed or re-paired, turned into condos, or otherwise irrevocably changed. He wanted Gilbert to coordinate an artist component and me to head up a university component. He saw the project on a very large scale, necessitating many artists and students, moving from neighborhood to neighborhood, and culminating in a giant parade to the Su-perdome to exorcize the bad spirits that remained after the ordeal many people had suffered before being evacuated in the immediate aftermath of the storm.*

I wanted to do something in New Orleans. I had never witnessed my govern-ment less responsive to a domestic disaster, and it simply was not okay. I also won-dered if the level of need in New Orleans would cause people to take art interested in social engagement as well as aesthetics more seriously. Art with content and in venues at a distance from everyday life is the conventional norm against which community-based art frequently needs to justify itself. Would Katrina challenge those limits? Would it catalyze a crisis of meaning among artists like the one I had witnessed in the immediate aftermath of 9/11? In the conservatory-type atmosphere of my own work place, NYU's Tisch School of the Arts, my political theater classes overflowed. My office and those of my colleagues were sites of continuous, heartfelt conversations with each other and students alike about what kind of art mattered, if any, in a world seemingly bent on fratricide if not self-extermination. Under such circumstances, how could one not question one's priorities?

As an outsider I would not presume to head up HNO, but I e-mailed the proposal to Bechet and asked if he would take that role. He asked if I would come down and work with him, and I said yes. Ron and I committed ourselves to the project with the understanding that it might change significantly in response to what people wanted in the various neighborhoods. And so we embarked upon "Home."

How was Katrina a catalyst for *HOME,*
New Orleans and your participation in it?

RON: Katrina was definitely a catalyst for me doing HNO. I was chomping at the bit in Houston, where we had evacuated, wondering what we could do. The Xavier Art Department was already heavily involved in community arts. We always talk about the arts rejuvenating community and giving back; this was a fantastic time to actually put it into action. I thought we should use the arts to heal, to bring people together, and to figure out what was valuable and who we were now as New Orleanians.

I also wanted to teach students how to bring people together, especially through the arts. A lot of Xavier students want to be doctors, and you ask them why and they say, "To help people." But then they're forever talking about grades. How to get students to look at a bigger picture, get beyond themselves? We're bombarded by the media and the American dream to strive more for what you gain individually through material wealth than what you gain for the community through knowledge. I'm trying to figure out what I can do to teach students not just about craft but also about substance. I want college students to understand they come from someplace and they need to go back to someplace and think about where they fit in and why they are learning. Training alone is too closed.

AMY: When I first got back to Tulane after evacuating from Katrina there were memos that we were all going to help rebuild New Orleans. I figured that the details of how would follow. But they didn't. I saw no effort to learn what people were doing and how Tulane might have an impact. At that point I thought I'd either just sit in my office and cry or find a way to do something as an individual. It was imperative that I stop being a traditional English teacher to the extent I even was and that I become more engaged in the community. So when Ron called me during the summer and invited me to that late August HNO meeting, I was already thinking about centralizing civic engagement in my work as a teacher and scholar. HNO made perfect sense. My major motivation was teaching a course with people who shared my agenda.

JOHN: Katrina was definitely my catalyst. Before the storm I didn't have a serious interest in community-based work. I thought there were compromises I'd have to make. I tend to be pure in my methodology in making artwork. So I had an insular attitude. I saw myself as someone who lives in New Orleans but is more of a global than local citizen. I didn't have a problem with that perspective until after the storm.

In fall 2006, we laid the groundwork for four neighborhood projects. I remember a Central City meeting on a street corner because no nearby cafés or restaurants had reopened and our local partner, Ashé, was hosting a drumming circle making sustained conversation there impossible. Here are brief descriptions of the projects and the neighborhoods in which they are situated.

Central City

Visual artist and Dillard professor John Barnes is working with students, the Ashé Cultural Arts Center, and the Central City Economic Opportunity Center (EOC) to create a mixed media quilt/installation-cum-legacy of the community pre-Katrina. Visual artist Jeffery Cook is offering insight into the found-object collection process and art making in community settings through workshops at the EOC. The content of the quilt is being developed through story circles and conversations with the senior citizens who use the center. Ashé is a well-established African American cultural organization. Its beautiful gift shop features traditional African as well as contemporary African American handicrafts, art, and clothing. Some people criticize Ashé for not reflecting the neighborhood; nobody goes around in African robes. I'm told that its audience was initially mostly people of color who are into art and African culture but is now quite diverse racially. Even before Katrina, Central City was the site of one of five Main Street projects in New Orleans that intended to revitalize formerly bustling neighborhoods that had for some time been economically depressed. Hopeful signs of rebuilding include Café Reconcile, a place for a tasty, low cost lunch, which was set up to train low-income people in cooking, serving, and other restaurant jobs. It features such dishes as catfish, fried chicken, red beans and rice, barbecue, cornbread, and collards.

Lakeview

Former Lakeview residents—visual artist Jan Gilbert, theater artists Kathy Randels and Andrew Larimer, and writer Jan Villarrubia—are creating a bus tour through this white, formerly well-to-do neighborhood, one of the worst hit by the levee breaks near Lake Pontchartrain. It will commemorate Lakeview life: citizens, stories, and sites. The first stop is the Lakeview Baptist Church. Kathy Randels's father came out of retirement to lead the twenty-five or so congregants remaining when the former minister left, believing the neighborhood would never come back after the storm. Based on story circles she conducted with church members, Kathy, who is a well-known local performance artist, is using theater to connect the congregants' religious faith to the process of neighborhood reconstruction and revival. Teachers and students from the Metairie Park Country Day School are conducting oral histories with and making portraits of neighborhood residents, which will be displayed at the church. Site-specific installations and performances are taking place at some of the artists' former homes (as imagined in the original proposal). To conclude, audiences will partake of an intergenerational meal and musical performance at the lakefront site of the much beloved Bruning's Restaurant, of which all that remains is the concrete foundation. Beacons of Hope, a network of post-Katrina rebuilding centers located in people's garages, is incorporating the project in its efforts to encourage people to return.

Lower Ninth Ward

Xavier University visual artist and professor Ron Bechet, neighborhood sculptor Rashida Ferdinand, and a group of students are collaborating with the Neighborhood Empowerment Network Association (NENA) Center and the Martin Luther King Elementary School. They plan to establish a healing center as part of NENA that will include the use of clay to provide an opportunity for people to think, evaluate, and participate in something pleasurable, building cups rather than houses. The first step was supporting the NENA Center through university technological proficiency. Next the group organized a clay workshop at the King School in its temporary uptown home. In fall 2007, King moved back to the Ninth Ward after the school was repaired and the kids' houses re-

built. Then people of different ages who use the NENA Center came together with the kids in workshops, using the skills that they're learning and developing together to create a memorial or monument commemorating and reflecting their community.

Seventh Ward

Dancer Stephanie McKee, Ed Buckner of the Porch Cultural Organization (the neighborhood sponsoring organization), and I have started a theater program for neighborhood youth. When I arrived in January 2007, the Porch leadership wanted a workshop for local teens using the problem-solving techniques of theater innovator Augusto Boal. What they got was a theater and education project for fifteen children age five to fourteen. The reason for the shift is instructive. On the one hand, very few teenagers wanted to join. Moreover, Boal's techniques work best when there are likely to be participants with experience in solving the problems at hand, and no one here has dealt with a catastrophe on the scale of Katrina. Given that community art is finally about working with whoever is in the room, we took an asset-based approach, creating pieces based on positive initiatives that already exist in the neighborhood in order to offer the kids something of meaning with potential continuity. We address problems that existed pre-Katrina such as the low level of reading among youth and the paucity of positive activities for them. We began by recruiting students and securing a space in which to hold the workshop until the Porch's own building was renovated. With the help of Troi Bechet of Neighborhood Housing Services, we got use of nearby Saint Anna's Church.

There is also a fifth HNO component, the Bridging Group, led by Amy Koritz, associate director for community and culture at the Tulane/Xavier Center for Bioenvironmental Research, with Xavier's community arts coordinator Shawn Vantree and e/Prime executive producer Kevin McCaffrey. They look for cross-project connections and help with overall documentation and publicity, although each team documents and publicizes itself as well.

As we were getting the neighborhood projects going, faculty and students from the four schools met once a week at alternating universities for two-and-a-half hours through the course Rebuilding Community through the Arts. We laid out the theoretical groundwork for the practice, shared ongoing challenges and successes, and planned, in teams, for the neighborhood work. There is enormous energy around rebuilding in New Orleans, and the scale is such that people hear about even our very modest efforts. This is quite unlike New York City, where nothing I do gets this much traction.

How were university students organized into neighborhood teams and what did they contribute?

RON: We placed the students according to their availability with a maximum intracollege mix in each neighborhood team. We probably should also have prioritized a skill mix so students could have taken on different roles at the sites. Everybody doesn't have to do everything.

JAN: At NYU my community work is mostly with drama and other arts majors who all have art skills to apply to the community. Going cross-school like we're doing and incorporating different student skills may be even better because the real world needs are multidisciplinary themselves.

RON: Yes. For example, Donisha, a Xavier medical student, could easily talk about nutrition or provide information about health to use in artwork. Conversely students from the health field would see that more people might understand their data if they were communicated through the arts rather than through a technical document. The students who are not artists—I have one art minor but no art majors in the Ninth Ward—are more excited about the actual doing of the clay than the ceramicist, Rashida Ferdinand, who's cofacilitating. The development of the craft is built in through doing it with the people that they're working with. Is it the craft or is it the communication that's more significant in the outcome of this particular project?

JAN: I think it's a balance. If I didn't have Jack, a student who's so strong and comfortable facilitating theater, our Seventh Ward workshop would have been a lot harder to do. He's been more like a partner than an assistant. All the university students and the kids get along great, a real lovefest, and those relationships are essential but they happen through the work. Another student, Rachael, has brought invaluable visual art skills. We need students who are proactive and use whatever their skills are. But I count on at least one or two having the skills in which the workshop is based.

RON: Yes, that's true for us, too. The center had been trying to solve certain computer issues for a couple of weeks, and Patrick went in and fixed them right away.

Then there's the value of racial diversity. I was talking to Donisha about her experiences in the Lakeview team [a white community site]. She's an assertive individual and has been very good for them.

JAN: She's the only person of color in that group?

RON: And Takako, who's Japanese. The topic of race came up and she [Donisha] said, "Why does everybody look at me when they start talking about race? What is your experience with black people?" She noticed how frightened some Lakeview residents were of people of color at the bus stops. Attitudes about working-class people, fear because of the way that they're dressed, and how insulting that is . . .

The three Tulane students working with us in the Ninth Ward are white. So we've been able to deal with a lot of things that we wouldn't even have been able to talk about. Actually working in a largely black neighborhood effects internal change.

JAN: Given that the students come from such different schools, experiencing commonalities, like the desire to get beyond the university into the community, as well as the differences, collaborating across race and class, is invaluable.

How has the integration of students and faculty from the four universities worked?

RON: The most significant part for me is that students from these universities are able to interact with each other. Even that they got to know each other's names and called each other is important.

JAN: Yes, which is especially rare given that two of the universities are predominantly black and two are predominantly white.

RON: It's a big step that they're going to each other's campuses. They had no clue where the other colleges even were, much less . . .

JAN: Right, much less having ever stepped foot on them.

AMY: But the students didn't all make a big enough effort to get to the other institutions.

RON: True. Still, the level of engagement in class conversations deepened by the second half of the semester. We subtly started to address issues of class and race. When Jan's colleague, Rosemary Quinn, from NYU visited with eight students and shared the work they are doing against gentrification in their neighborhood, some of our students felt that was hypocritical since they contribute to it by renting apartments there. One asked Jack [an NYU student spending the entire semester at Xavier], "When you're done here are you just going to go back and do your own thing?" And other students said, "What are we all going to do?" It got students really thinking about their own class privilege.

JAN: It's good the conversation took place, though it was naive for the New Orleans students to see the NYU students as more hypocritical than they are. Even when we put our energies towards what we care about, we still have contradictions. The percentage of the resources we use in the U.S. compared to the part of the land mass that we occupy is grossly unfair, but I don't see anyone in the class moving to another country. Reflection is part of demystifying civic engagement—seeing we might at the same time be implicated in a social problem and want to help solve it.

RON: I was encouraged that the students began to bring in their personal concerns. A couple of Xavier students talked about their recent Stomp Show, a student dance competition, which a dean shut down because he thought the moves were too sexual. The students felt hurt and powerless and still do. It led to thinking about how they could use art around their own issues, here.

JAN: That's what the NYU students were trying to do with the antigentrification project. They worked with a housing activist and made a pamphlet about how students can be more responsible renters. They performed short scenes about housing around campus and got students who were thinking about moving off campus to come to a panel with the housing activist and an NYU housing administrator on the subject.

RON: A lot of our students were very taken by the gentrification scenes those NYU students performed. Some said they felt like they were in the same situation here. It raises a question about the *university's* long-term responsibility to the community, in our case to Gert Town [the low-income black neighborhood in which Xavier is situated]. As they try and develop Gert Town, what do we professors and administrators do to sustain those projects?

JAN: We have to find ways to pass the torch from one student group to another.

AMY: Even if they don't realize it now, the students learned a hell of a lot from each other and became comfortable working together, which will serve them well when they graduate and are, I hope, working in more diverse environments. Given how segregated our universities are, getting them to work together across racial lines, on shared projects, can make an enormous difference in breaking down stereotypes. The bridging we wanted in the neighborhoods took place in class with the people from the different institutions.

JAN: The projects in each neighborhood had to be in place before we could bridge them. I think that bridging will happen as the project continues.

AMY: A downside of bringing the students from various universities together is I haven't gotten to know them well. We've had to spend so much time planning among ourselves that I've only really gotten to know the students in my little team. And attendance is so spotty I didn't even get to know all of them. And the time it takes to do the planning. I can't just sit alone in my office and find thirty minutes here or there. We have to get to one place, fit into each other's schedules, and discuss so many components of the project, we often get to planning the class last. Probably all of us have done much more for this course than any of our institutions are willing to recognize.

RON: The cons are primarily logistic. Another thing that's been difficult—I don't know if it's a pro or con yet—has been working across the arts and humanities. There are different uses of time in different kinds of classrooms, balancing amounts of reading and writing with practice.

JOHN: It's been great working with senior faculty from other schools, as a junior faculty who seeks mentorship. You all have given me tips on raising money, navigating campus governance, which to some degree I've avoided, stayed in my zone, only surfaced when I had to. You've also opened my eyes to what's important to university administrations, how you can make them interested.

RON: HNO has shifted *our* relationship, John, from you being a younger emerging artist to being a partner. I like that. I want to continue this partnership with you. And our schools, which have so much in common, have a way to develop a relationship at the same time.

JOHN: It's good for our universities to have that formal relationship. The mix of students can inspire each other; it might even have been healthy to have a more competitive spirit among the teams to energize students. When all the students aren't equally motivated, you have to create an atmosphere to get them to respond. You can also reward the ones who set a high standard for everyone to strive for.

Just living in New Orleans post-Katrina is instructive. It reminded me how the immediate aftermath of 9/11 presented an opportunity for people in the United States to understand the vulnerability with which so many people around the globe live. Every once in a while I got a taste of danger in New Orleans. I woke up early one morning after a tornado and the electricity was out. My first thought was so petty—how would I get my coffee? I felt isolated and worried about my two NYU students in the Xavier dorms, where they were living for the semester. Reaching them by cell phone, I learned they were locked down, also without electricity, and no one was telling them anything. I found out that the administration was just keeping them all safe while they cleared up fallen electrical wires. Soon they were able to leave the dorms, and we went to a neighborhood with electricity for a good brunch.

Like anthropological fieldwork, spending time with the people with whom one is engaging civically in their everyday environments sheds invaluable light on their lives. Only by going to one of the kids' houses who had not turned in her permission slip the day we were taking them on a field trip to a bayou did I find out that her mother did not always come home, leaving her fifteen-year-old sister in charge. Civic engagement through the arts goes beyond an after school workshop, where one is simply teaching kids a little craft, to this more holistic approach to their lives, to connect those particulars to a larger societal picture.

Such an approach makes possible the reciprocity at the heart of most successful projects. Civic engagement goes both ways, including both what I learn about other realms of human experience and what they learn about me and whatever craft I've been lucky enough to acquire. And we both learn from the initially surprising relationships we develop. These experiences replace the most insidious kinds of racism we all have absorbed with the joy of finding kindred spirits where we did not expect them. My partner in the Seventh Ward, Ed Buckner, who grew up in a housing project, not only cared as much about kids as anyone I've ever known but also was totally intrigued by theater, hungrily absorbing any new technique I tried out on them and always wanting me to push the kids farther.

How does HNO function as civic engagement and what are the curricular implications?

RON: Our emphasis on civic engagement brings up the question, "Is this a university project or a community project? Where's the community's voice in all of this?"

JAN: Maybe such work is better housed in a center that university people are partners in but that is located on neutral ground. Whoever controls the space and the budget controls the project whether they mean to be equitable or not.

RON: Another important part of the exchange is those people who have been on the ground for many years: community scholars. Maybe we can pay community scholars to work in these kinds of classes at the university.

JAN: It's great for students to recognize that not all education is formal both in terms of where we find expertise, like you raise, Ron, and [in terms of] the nature of learning. In civic engagement much of the learning is embodied, through the senses in real time, unlike the more condensed learning of a lecture hall.

AMY: Art as a mode of civic engagement can give students a sense of purpose in community. But non–art majors, with whom I've worked almost exclusively, run into issues of competence. I'm in an English department, and in another course I assigned students to Science and Math High School. They started a spoken word club to connect with the students there. They researched poetry slams even though they had never heard of them before; neither I nor the group of students who picked it up knew how to do them. But slams connected them with the high schoolers, and my students learned a lot doing it. From that we built a program, got funding, and brought in a spoken word artist who now teaches a spoken word class with me. But my current students say they don't know how to help the high schoolers because they don't know how to do spoken word. Students in the other class hadn't raised that concern, I think, because the other class was *about* civic engagement, not spoken word. Anything they did was an occasion for civic engagement, shifting their views on excellence and competence. It was more about knowing how to interact with people from different backgrounds. It wasn't an occasion to teach students to do spoken word but how to interact with communities in ways that were mutually beneficial.

JOHN: My mentor, John Outerbridge, forfeited his art for community. I didn't understand then his not making time for the studio, but now I see you can get so involved with these relationships that they can become your whole focus. Especially when you see results, it's probably impossible to walk away. Our students are getting that in incremental stages. You see a transformation every time they go out into the community. They understand that their presence in the neighborhoods is valuable, even just in getting them out of their isolated world. They learn to cautiously and respectfully engage. There are not a lot of opportunities for students to be humble during their college years, and this is definitely a humbling experience.

JAN: Civic engagement is enhanced when we see the relationship between our specific project and a larger issue. Dan Etheridge said that as much as he wants the community garden in the Seventh Ward to flourish, it's got to be about something larger, part of policy, not just one isolated garden. That garden alone doesn't build the case that people need relationships to nature and fresh food. But once a lot of people get their hands dirty in a garden, they might think about the wetlands and the landscape; it grows into larger issues. That's what we're trying to do with our neighborhood projects, get them strong individually and connect them to something bigger.

RON: Yes, I agree. All politics are local, and that's the case with the artist, too. Something bigger begins by making the connection to you right then and there. That's why the arts are so valuable in civic engagement, spreading into advocacy for the larger problem. As Dan also said, art can make very complicated issues very personal.

JAN: In the Seventh Ward, the people who started the Porch Cultural Organization provide our workshop with the bigger frame, improving that community without gentrifying it. New experiences can set the kids on another path, opening possibilities that serve them in deep ways, not things that just get them in trouble and that are not ultimately satisfying. I've heard there's a drug problem in the Seventh Ward. I don't know how extensive it is.

RON: Willie [Birch, the Porch cofounder] knows some of the local young men who deal drugs and believes that they don't have other opportunities. That is the only way they know. It provides them with money but also [serves] other needs like a sense of belonging.

JAN: Right. And while some of them could get work at McDonald's, they're not willing to take the lowest rung on the job ladder.

RON: Yes, and it's a matter of replacing some of those other needs, not just monetary, with ones that the larger community values.

JAN: To be sensitive to issues like this that come up on site, we need to think about what constitutes a civic engagement curriculum. Service learning is criticized for failing to teach civic skills such as learning to express one's own point of view and working to achieve common goals. Art making offers a ready vehicle for both these skills.

AMY: The students need confidence that they're still in college even as they do practical work in communities.

JAN: [Roadside Theatre director] Dudley Cocke, [community cultural development specialist] Arlene Goldbard, and I are working on a learning model with three elements: hands-on community engagement, disciplinary training, and study of principles and theory. Students also need to understand policies governing the issue their work addresses. In the Seventh Ward, for example, what mechanisms exist to support residents buying their own homes and staying in the neighborhood?

RON: Our students didn't have enough time to stew in the principles and issues which actually make the doing more meaningful.

JAN: We have so much to cover for one session per week. The teams need to meet and just getting everyone one place is chaotic, but still it's worth it. Then the students are on all different levels; what's necessary for one student is boring and repetitive for another. Maybe if students chose one prerequisite from an array of courses they might be better prepared for the hands-on component.

RON: Yes, since we have three different universities with three different curricula. And over time we hope to involve interested professors from other departments as well; there's someone from communications and music at Xavier who told me they want to come in. Students from different fields will offer different skills and perspectives.

JAN: They'll all need training in community facilitation skills: teaching a workshop is, of course, different from practicing skills yourself . . . learning how to work with the particular age group . . . adapting one's specific skills to the workshop goals.

How does HNO compare to service-learning projects you've encountered?

AMY: HNO is in line with how I approach service learning, which is different from many approaches you find in the literature and that are dominant at my institution—faculty and student centered. An abnormal psych professor, for example, will tell the office about his research interest in x and request a placement for his students in, say, a hospital wing for brain-damaged people to observe the effects. I'm sure it's beneficial to the hospital, but, whereas in that case the motivation of the placement is almost entirely controlled by the pedagogical content demands of the class, I'm for a balance between community need/opportunity and discipline-based material. To the degree that the discipline base is driving the placement, it's not reciprocal with the community, nor is it quite civic engagement. It's just using another site for your teaching goals. I thought there was no way I could teach a canonical English class—one organized by history, genre, or theme—that would support civic engagement. So I decided to focus on civic engagement itself as the center of the class and find literature that would feed in. HNO is much more like that. I know what to say to students at predictable points such as when it feels to them like there's not enough structure. It is very difficult to align the time frame and rhythm of the semester with the community work. No matter what you say, students expect a beginning, middle, and end to the work. I say no, you're just taking a chunk out of something bigger or different from what you imagine.

JAN: Unlike most of their university education, students are not at the center of civic engagement. They have to think of the community constituents equally.

RON: Unlike most service learning, we as faculty are engaged in placement. Our projects don't happen out of an office.

AMY: Yes, adding a level of work for us. We have to reinvent our relationships with the service-learning people on our campuses. One of the obstacles is that even when students understand the experiential aspect they don't necessarily understand the serious research they need to do around the issues they are working on in the community. When they are not well thought out, these programs create experiences for students without adding value to the communities. I've been interested in some of the models at University of Pennsylvania. The director of their Center for Community Partnerships, Ira Harkavy, starts from developing community-based programs and then feeds university resources into those rather than starting with university needs.

RON: Service learning is also about the continuing education of *faculty*. That's crucial in HNO. It's broadening our vision, our understanding of what teaching and learning are. We are mentoring each other.

JAN: Yes, we're actually meshing what we do together through team teaching and planning. I have to stop and think more about what I do.

RON: HNO has also necessitated different ways of interacting with students. It varies with the class, but usually we have a teacher up front. With HNO, the class is also in the neighborhoods and the learning is multisensory. The informal time we spend with students, driving to and from the sites, and when we're presumably just waiting for something to happen, is a different kind of teaching.

JAN: Right. And the colearning as we figure out together how to shape the work in each of our neighborhood projects. It's not like a class that we fully prepare before we enter the room. We have a plan, but how we carry it out changes in the process. The students see that as important as knowledge is; it's constantly adapting to circumstances. And they are adapting right alongside us.

RON: Exactly. And, I think, too, we're learning that it's okay—we know this, but in practice we don't always—it's okay for things to go wrong.

Each of the neighborhood projects offers its own pleasures. The membership of the governing council of our Seventh Ward partner, the Porch, is diverse. Willie Birch is a well-known visual artist whose focus has long been black life. Helen Regis is a cultural anthropologist who works on vernacular New Orleans culture. Mr. Hubert is a retiree interested in neighborhood initiatives that provide physical activity. Miss Carrie taught in the local schools for many years. Ed Buckner worked as a machinist, lost four fingers in an accident, and is now a baker who delivers pies from his truck. He lives in a house with his wife and three kids. He coached football for many years and was initially hired to recruit the kids and get them to and from our workshop in the back of his truck. But rather quickly he became fascinated with theater and began acting to help anchor our scenes. He is now assistant directing as well.

The entire Seventh Ward is not as united around community development as are Porch members. When the Porch began operating in January 2006, neighborhood turnout was good, with about fifty people at each meeting, but over time the numbers have dwindled. Helen thinks they don't see enough getting accomplished, and until the Porch's community center building is renovated meetings and other activities take place at an assortment of venues. Moreover, the neighborhood, poor to begin with, is in even further disarray. The Seventh Ward was not badly hit by Katrina, being on relatively high ground. But even modest damage is beyond the means of many landlords. So houses further deteriorate and are abandoned. Rents have gone up in the smaller stock of houses that are habitable, a secondary effect of the storm that has resulted in the continued exodus of people from the city.

Helen, who is white, observes overt institutional racism specific to post-Katrina life. For example, the Porch neighborhood, which is majority poor and black, was still not getting its trash picked up in the spring of 2006 while neighboring Marigny, especially the white middle-class section, was getting service twice a week. Helen called the responsible city agency often, certain that someone could fix the problem, in the way middle-class people, especially whites, are used to seeing problems addressed. Helen would walk the neighborhood with her cell phone and make calls: "Come to the corner of Pauger and Urquart and pick up a big pile of trash." Neighbors would call out, "Good, you tell 'em," but did not think their calling would have the same success.

Helen lives in and contributes actively to the neighborhood and has good relations with most of the residents. But some people resent middle-class white people moving there. A teenager said to her, "One day we gonna buy our house back." It seems that his grandmother rented the house years earlier and moved out before Helen bought it. She says that how she feels as a middle-class white person in the neighborhood depends on the day. She doesn't like the gunshots she hears and commented on teenage drug sellers cutting though her backyard as they are chased by police. "You unnerstan," one smiled to her as he jumped her fence.

The Porch members make for fabulous partners in a university-based civic en-gagement project because they are united around improving the neighborhood, not around homogeneity of race, class, or education level. Reminiscent of early settlement house founders such as Jane Addams, they live in the neighborhoods to which they contribute and thus gain from improvements along with other residents.

Wanting to bring people together was one of the big goals for the project, as was helping rebuild communities. How did we do, and what could we be doing better?

RON: We are almost at the point of bringing people from the different neighborhood projects together, particularly those dealing with common issues. The kids in the Seventh and the Ninth Wards may find much to talk about given their shared interest in identity and community. Sometimes finding that common point, as simple as it seems, is the most difficult part. Even though we know in our hearts that coming together is very important.

JAN: True. Willie says that people try to get him to bring the Porch community into things they want to do, like yoga. He responded, "Why do you want me to do yoga, I have my own thing." It's not for us to mandate what people should come together to do. We need to approach community building as an inquiry: "What would you like?"

RON: Which is crucial. Initially I thought people from different communities would see what each other is doing and that would lead to a healthy competition: "Wow, look what they did. We can do the same or we can do better." I grew up with sports, where there's definitely a winner and a loser, but even if you win you know that you could've been the loser. As you develop your skill, you know that you have better odds of winning. That kind of competition can be an ego booster. Young people's egos are often based on things that aren't real, so to have their egos boosted based on what they can actually do . . . and doing other things together, maybe as simple as music sharing or a dance competition, where you have a younger and an older partner.

JAN: So having structured a bridging team into *HOME, New Orleans*, that's the kind of activity it can organize, now that all the projects are up and running.

JOHN: Our Central City team made a solid partner out of the Economic Opportunity Center, and art was a catalyst for that. But we're not rebuild-ing community yet. Naively I imagined the project being more easily promoted throughout the neighborhood; people would just hold hands and do it. If that were so, they could just rebuild their connections through making the quilt. But I think we're building opportunities for people to connect. People don't really know each other, so it's not *re*building, partly because people haven't come back, partly because people are pretty segregated. Ed Blakely [New Orleans director of the recovery effort] has made insightful comments about cultural domination in this city: if whites or blacks are planning something from a policy standpoint, one side or the other takes over. There are community, cultural, behavioral, and personal habits that make it difficult to meet a lot of goals under the conditions of a partly destroyed city. The bad habits get expanded upon, like the tendency for an insular point of view. Even before the storm, it was common not to know people even a block over. HNO being racially integrated is valuable even in itself.

Change is imminent. In August '07 the FEMA trailers must all be returned to the government. That will be a big factor in who will be able to stay here. The real work can't happen until we know who's staying and what newcomers are helping reshape the city. Then we can build new connections through the arts.

RON: It's a slow building process. Being seen and just saying hi is a big step. It's really important to make that contact; even if it feels like nothing's happening, it is. Maybe it's a southern thing. What we're doing with these projects takes a lot of contact.

JOHN: You don't glow in the dark as much when you really spend time in the neighborhood. You're not in the spotlight anymore, like you don't belong there, even if you're just hanging out.

RON: We do a lot of that at the NENA Center, and then we're there if something concrete does come up. Like someone came in and didn't know how to work the computer and our students were there to show them.

In the Seventh Ward, our first show, Local Heroes, *was a rousing success. It accompanied the postering project Porch member artists Willie Birch and Ron Bechet conducted about local heroes. First Ron and his Xavier printmaking class created images of ten black New Orleanians who contributed in a variety of ways to local life. Then, early one morning in February (Black History Month), they hung copies of each one on every block. Two weeks later we performed our play, which identified and brought the ten people to life. Nearly fifty people attended, half of them community folks. Not all the kids had family members there. One ten year old said to me softly, as the audience was gathering, "I don't know anyone here." I*

asked if she would like to meet people, and she said yes, so we went around intro-
ducing ourselves and shaking everyone's hands. We began the show by inviting
people to join our warm-up circle, or watch around us if they preferred, to see the
sort of thing we'd been doing with the kids. Ranging in age from five to seventy-
five, and diverse in race, class, and neighborhood, everyone was happy to connect
with each other. Then we did the show followed by a barbecue.

When I left New Orleans, a young, white, local theater director (and one of my
former NYU students), Andrew Larimer, joined the Seventh Ward workshop
leadership team. Larimer imagines a youth theater festival presenting the work of
our kids, who are all black, with white theater youth groups with which he is fa-
miliar. McKee looks forward to developing leadership skills with the older partici-
pants and involving students' parents. Troi Bechet of Neighborhood Housing Ser-
vices, another Porch partner, is pursuing city youth jobs money so the older kids in
our group can be paid to assist a theater workshop in the Porch's summer camp.
Touring the plays has also been discussed. Emerging is a little theater troupe that
is able to present a positive and varied view of the Seventh Ward.

Do you plan to continue HNO? If so, what do you want to do differently during the next phase?

AMY: Of course, I intend to continue. It's an incredibly powerful concept on many levels. The biggest issue for me is what, if any, level of institutional support am I going to get for doing this? My chair, administrators, dean, have no idea how time consuming it is. They assume I should just volunteer my time on top of everything else I'm doing rather than see it as integral to what we are supposed to be doing as educators. This approach is not viable. A faculty member said to me, "I'm interested in doing something about civic engagement, but that's what my third book is going to be about and I'm on my first." From an institutional perspective, they are probably right; this kind of work won't get them there. So the reward structure at institutions has to change for faculty to be able to do HNO.

RON: Yes, we have opportunities for release time, but it's competitive with scientists and everyone else. I didn't even apply for it. Junior faculty shouldn't do this, I hate to say it, unless it is their research. It will be detrimental to their advancement.

JOHN: I definitely need some money to be able to do it again.

JAN: So each of us is just getting credit for HNO as one of our courses.

JOHN: Right. And on top of that we come from institutions with completely different compensation systems. At historically black colleges, it's a given that you'll get 30 percent lower salary than [at] predominantly white ones with similar degrees.

RON: Right. But I can't imagine doing the typical thing my professors did: go to class and do their personal work separately. That I wouldn't include my students in what I do. Training in visual arts is important, but I'm also committed to students understanding more possibilities of what they can do with their training.

AMY: We need money but also support from upper-level administration. You need to sort of be anointed.

RON: Would our institutions have allowed us to do this without Katrina?

AMY: They think I'm a loose cannon anyway . . . so you get this kind of exemption . . . but Katrina and the rhetoric of partnership made it easier for them to accept it as worthwhile. It has shifted attitudes somewhat. It might shift the culture of the students eventually, though hasn't yet.

RON: Our department has been pushing to get out of the box. Even though what we do with civic engagement and community partnerships fits Xavier's mission: "educating leaders toward a more just and humane society."

JAN: NYU describes itself as "a private university in the public interest." That doesn't go as far as Xavier, but it does suggest the value of *something* beyond self-interest.

AMY: What bothered me most post-Katrina was the gap between my experience as an employee of my institution and its rhetoric.

RON: Our president is fairly conscious of outside communities and is very active himself. That's why we are able to do some of the things we do. The history in our department has been toward community arts. In the late fifties, one of our students, Victor Labat, used to sit on neighborhood kids' porches and talk with them. And the Sisters encouraged that. [Xavier is a Catholic school.] They even had an arts center at the time working with [the] community around the school.

AMY: I don't think Tulane has a history of civic engagement. It's been serving the white elite of the city, even though it does house Cactus, one of the oldest student-run community service organizations in the United States.

JAN: There are, of course, different traditions—the "noblesse oblige" to give charity to the poor is one and social justice is another—those who see the problem with the social structure making it incumbent on all of us to work for equity.

AMY: I don't want to devalue charity. If you have a lot it's better to give something than not. But there's also that saying, "If you've come to help me, I don't want you there. But if you see your liberation as bound up with mine we can work together." That means an attitudinal shift. These different underlying philosophies are significant in how you approach, understand, and measure the success of the work.

JOHN: I like the principles of the class, the texts, and the large group of students meeting. I wish it were easier. Maybe if class met on the weekend and at neutral sites, in the neighborhoods where we are working with no problem with parking. The universities enforce barriers, attitudes that are part of the academic indoctrination process, and create a false impression of their individual greatness. When the students come into class together they realize they have more in common than they think.

RON: I'd love to have it run in the spring again. We can't do it every semester. Maybe we could have a theory class in the fall which they basically apply in the spring.

JAN: Maybe each of you can teach your own theory courses at your own schools and bring students from the three schools together for the course in the spring.

RON: Maybe do a few seminars with the students from all three schools over the fall semester. One might be a panel in a quasi-debate format, presenting and defending their ideas.

JAN: But can we get enough students to commit to a two-semester sequence consisting of two different but connected courses? Students have such a smorgasbord of possibilities. We'd have to design a really rigorous recruitment plan.

RON: Service-learning offices can help us with a strategy for students who are interested in community service and how academics can address policy issues.

JAN: We could work more closely with other teachers who do public scholarship.

RON: And pitch HNO not just to humanities students but also to science students.

JOHN: The lion's share of the work is done—the mechanics are in place, the partnerships are established. In Central City next time, the old man we met on the porch could be one of our guides through the neighborhood. It'll take us a couple more excursions to know who's there, but once we do it'll be easier to carry out the project.

RON: Most students want to know that they're going into a successful situation before it begins and what to expect. So we could get testimonials from students who have gone through it. And do shorter sessions: once a week all together to discuss readings and a second time each week in the teams to troubleshoot our own projects using class ideas.

JAN: Are you worried about the logistics of students meeting twice a week in class and then a third time a week to do the internship?

RON: No. They're meeting a lot this semester. I'm really impressed.

JAN: I offer students extra credit because it's so many hours.

RON: We're looking again at our minor, community arts management—

JAN: To make it community arts more broadly?

RON: Right, and rethinking the courses that fulfill that minor.

JAN: We require an internship in our minor in applied theater at NYU.

RON: Which makes a lot of sense. Another issue for me is keeping students motivated. The story circles boosted student involvement every time we did them. They're wonderful opportunities for sharing.

AMY: We also need to work more on understanding each other's processes. I don't have a sense of what processes artists go through to make their work. I read things and write things. I know that process. So this is another issue in our collaboration.

RON: On the artist end, we know about the doing but need to know more about what's out there that students need to read.

JOHN: Post-Katrina is so busy, with layers of challenge in New Orleans now. It's very difficult to coordinate things. Still, the young people in Central City, who are descending into chaos, got something good from seeing us come in and vice versa, hearing each other's points of view. It's been a great cross-cultural exchange.

Students are used to being in positions with power, but they had limited control of this environment. It's healthy to be vulnerable like that from time to time. It breaks students out of their shell and introduces them to a larger world. That's going to lack even more as college education becomes even more expensive, more class based. You're gonna see very few students exposed to people who aren't in their same category, which creates people who make policies like no child left behind . . . they haven't seen the recipients of those policies . . . that's who we see in the neighborhoods. I wonder if any of the students will independently seek other situations like this. In spite of some of the reasons students took the class—thought they were gonna get on a bus and gut houses, hand out T-shirts, polish their egos—its becoming a badge of ego to "spend spring break in NOLA" kind of thing. A lot of our conversations brought them beyond themselves.

RON: Now that we're at the end of the semester and the students are getting it, I think it just takes a certain amount of time. Like a basketball team, we had to play together for a while. Makes me think some of the problems we thought we were having we weren't. Practice reinforced the theory and vice versa; we didn't think the theory was getting through, but I think we actually were on the right path.

JAN: So where are you now about how the arts can help rebuild?

RON: The effect of one person on another person, which I experience with the children at King School. I've been working with one young man doing a self-portrait and talking about how to, first of all. That was so important to him, to get it right. I asked what that meant. He said he wants everyone to see him the right way. Each week we talked about this right way thing and his identity. I told him any way he does it is his right way. He's finally coming around to seeing he can make his own statement.

And how difficult this process is. Even more so since the storm. The stress level. It's almost as if there's a big clock ticking, pushing us. There's a timeline to get our city back to where it was. That's the FEMA model: you can't do any further building on what wasn't there before. Which makes no sense to me. So if you have a broken pipe you can fix it but not improve it even if it may be less efficient and more expensive. I really don't want the city back where it was, but better.

Interview with Don Marshall
Executive Director of the New Orleans
Jazz and Heritage Festival Foundation

Conducted by Amy Koritz

AMY KORITZ: I'M HERE WITH DON MARSHALL, executive director of the Jazz and Heritage Foundation in New Orleans. Don, could you say a little about this organization?

DON MARSHALL: I feel very fortunate to be the head of a major organization in New Orleans post-Katrina. The major mission of the Jazz and Heritage Festival and Foundation really is to promote, support, and stimulate the music culture and heritage of New Orleans and Louisiana. It's a very broad mission that allows us to do quite a few things. Most people know about our organization primarily because of the New Orleans Jazz and Heritage Festival, which has been going on for more than thirty-five years, presenting, promoting, and stimulating this music, art, and culture. We also present cultural heritage traditions, from Mardi Gras Indians to Social Aid and Pleasure Clubs, demonstrators of folk art and crafts from around the state. It was early on that the festival itself, back in the seventies, was presenting Mardi Gras Indians and Social Aid and Pleasure Clubs when a lot of New Orleanians didn't even know that those things existed, unfortunately. So we had this wonderful event. It actually is a fund-raiser for us, which most people don't understand, and we then return that money, like most nonprofits do, to our mission. This ranges from our Heritage School of Music, which provides after-school music programs, to our

Raising the Roof program, which is helping with housing initiatives in the city. We have lecture series, we have all kinds of concert series, we have a micro–economic loan program, and we own a major radio station. So we're all across the board, including even helping to found the Musicians Clinic. It's a pretty broad mission.

AK: Maybe we'll talk more about some of those specific programs in a little while. How did the aftermath of Hurricane Katrina affect you and your organization?

DM: Well, for the organization, I think, like for most organizations and individuals in this city, it was a total shutdown. Communications were broken down, and while we were able to communicate with our diaspora though e-mails and things, it was hard to get a consensus of what to do and how best to respond. And, quite frankly, this organization had gone through some difficult years prior to Katrina, which was one of the reasons I was brought in, to fix some of the financial issues. So the organization's programs were shut down, and we were just on the verge of bringing them back. We had finally a financially successful Jazz Fest the year before Katrina, and so there was starting to be some money that we could then put back into the community. Katrina comes along, and even the plans for opening up our Heritage School of Music were put on hold. I think initially it was very hard for me because we are such a large organization we were not really able to respond to many of the individual needs. Another reason was we were really focusing in on how we could carry off a Jazz Festival months after Katrina, which I think was a very important thing for the community, employment for musicians, and just sort of spiritually. While it was difficult right after Katrina not to be really responding, being a first responder, I think ultimately it has allowed us to take a broader view, and we're in much better financial shape, and we're able to help the community in many ways now and are finding that many of the organizations that immediately came and stepped up to the plate after Katrina, they're now out of money. I almost feel like we're the second wave, not dealing with the initial disaster but how can we help with the long-term rebuilding and bringing stability to the community.

AK: But you did participate in some of the early recovery efforts in terms of planning. Could you talk a little about those?

DM: I was fortunate to be able to move back to New Orleans before Rita and immediately contacted and came across the few that were here and began working closely with the wonderful people at the Tipitina's Foundation. I'm a big fan of inviting the community to come together. Let's talk, see what issues we have, how we resolve them. So we began doing a sort of weekly meeting at Tipitina's, inviting musicians, club owners, interested parties—the whole process was very interesting. I think first identifying who's here, who is available to even start the rebuilding process, and once you do that, then you can start coordinating and collaborating and figuring out solutions. We had a series of meetings. It brought a lot of people together, made connections, helped people find each other, helped find funding sources, made funding sources for housing, replacement of instruments, all kinds of things available, and it culminated actually in a sort of opportunity fair at Tipitina's in the fall right after Katrina where we had FEMA, we had insurance agencies, we had all kinds of service agencies there so that the people from the music community could come together and access information. From there each organization kind of went off on its own, and Tipitina's has done wonderful things, and we're now back to being a major player. There were some other initiatives: I had lists of visual artists, lists of theater artists, the dance community, photographers, and I began calling them together at Ashé Cultural Center and community centers.

My feeling is that often when we have these gatherings and we share information and knowledge we're all then leaving these meetings and going back to our real worlds where we've got fifty thousand things waiting for us, and without any kind of infrastructure, without any kind of funding for administration, collaborations really don't happen. Occasionally nice things, or an event, will happen, but to build it into any kind of long-term stability you need that, and I think has been the biggest failure post-Katrina, of not being able to support and fund these collaborations. New Orleans is a poor city. We have great, great resources, and we can put them all on the table and come up with some great things, but we lack that kind of administrative support and know-how that keeps things growing.

AK: Would you like to say anything about your participation in the mayor's Bring Back New Orleans Commission?

DM: That was a very interesting situation. The mayor had called together the Bring Back New Orleans Commission. I read in the paper that there was a cultural committee that had been formed and went to the first early meeting down at the Sheraton and sat in, and you know it was interesting because before Katrina you would know exactly who would be at the table, and after Katrina it was like whoever was back, and where was so-and-so, and who was that person. And it kind of got into . . . because when you bring a new group of people together each person has their own story or their own interest, and, I guess, being a long-term, seasoned professional in my field, I usually like to cut to the chase. I'm very supportive of grassroots activities and always looking for ways those activities can be funded and stabilized, but I was at meeting after meeting sitting in the room and listening to someone wanting to create a music festival in April. And I was like, well, there's the Jazz Festival and the French Quarter Festival, and that's not really what we need. Or so-and-so wanted their own theater or whatever. There wasn't an overall understanding of the community, what does the community need. I attended those meetings as an alternate for a board president who was officially on the committee but who was living in Dallas, and I made a couple of efforts to help formalize it, saying we've got to look at these issues in terms of housing and health care and education and economic development. And that wasn't of interest to anybody there. It was more about their particular projects—so-and-so wanting to put on a parade, so-and-so wanting to do this. So I personally became very frustrated and thought, okay, I just can't deal with this anymore.

With the mayor's group, it was very fortunate that Jay Weigel, who was head of the Contemporary Arts Center (CAC), and a few others realized that outside help was needed. So funding was found, and AEA consultants were brought in, who then, of course, put everything in terms of housing, education, etc. Anyone looking at things logically would realize that these were the issues. I was pleased that it had finally evolved into some kind of logical plan. Unfortunately, by that time people were just getting frustrated, and I don't think enough attention has been paid to the plan, and then ultimately, of course, there's no money to fund the plan. So there's been even less interest, but the plan has some pretty good stuff. We can all sit there and find things to add or take out, but this city has never been a city for planners. You know we're very intuitive, or just laissez-faire—whatever happens happens—and some planning can be a total disaster or come up with things we don't need, but I think there is just a real void in planning and follow-through in this community; that's not part of our nature.

AK: I would say the follow-through more than the planning.

DM: Yeah, the planning can get done, but then it's like, well, that's very nice, I'm going home.

AK: Or that's very nice, but it doesn't include the theater I wanted.

DM: Exactly, there is in a strange way a lack of community, of inclusiveness. I think a lot of that has to do with poverty. I mean, if you do not have the financial resources to exist, then you become very focused on your own survival. And what happens in a city like this is that if I'm in a position where I can give a contract to a company or an individual or a friend I expect something back. I'm not being paid enough to survive, so if I am with this organization and I give you a contract to fix a road, I'm going to expect you to come fix my house.

AK: Well, that's the patronage culture.

DM: There's a very big patronage culture, maybe a little bit tied into old Europe or wherever we're coming from culturally, but because there isn't a real clear, strong, business sense and business community we depend on bartering and patronage. We look at what happens to our politicians—it's a pervasive element in our culture. It adds to our charm and our indigenous ways but does not allow us . . . I mean I'm all in favor of grassroots culture, but I'd like people to be paid enough so that they can get health care, those kinds of basic things that are not really here for a lot of New Orleanians.

AK: So that really brings us to our next question, which concerns the challenges faced by the arts and culture more generally and your organization specifically.

DM: Again, I think we have so many resources. We have so many opportunities. I do feel that there is still a lack of leadership in our cultural community. There's a lack of awareness of best practices in how things can be done, there's a certain amount of naveté in how we do things among certain boards, and sometimes I'll just scratch my head and wonder what I'm doing there. Seeing incredible resources and realizing how much that is just being wasted. At the same time, just personally, because of my commitment to this community, being a native, and my years and years and years of experience, I've gotten to the point where I'm no longer interested in sitting around meeting after meeting just letting things wander off into different directions anymore. So for me post-Katrina New Orleans has opened up so many more opportunities. Now there are so many challenges, but things that you could not get people to pay attention to pre-Katrina, or they were very defensive or hesitant about any change, now it's almost an open book.

AK: Can you give an example?

DM: Well, when I first came to this organization I was looking for ways to employ musicians, build the cultural economy, the tourist economy, and festivals are one thing that we do very well. The Jazz and Heritage Festival is a major American phenomenon. I'm talking to my board about starting a new blues festival, and they're, like, do you think we're ready for that, we don't do this, we don't do that, and immediately after Katrina I was able to access funding for all kinds of things. I mean the American public, unlike the government, has been very good about responding to their fellow Americans, and the foundations and businesses and individuals that were willing to send money allowed us, in that first year, to create new events. We did a Festiva Latina; we're very committed to seeing how we can rebuild our relations with Latin and Central America, bringing our Latin jazz and Latin musicians together, creating a celebration, and we did that.

AK: Do you think there are sufficient resources around to keep the artists, and perhaps you want to speak especially to the musicians since that is closest to what you do, in town? Can they make a living?

DM: Well, there's always been that challenge of earning a living here whether you are a visual artist, or certainly actors and dancers or musicians. The double-edged sword of New Orleans is that we are so rich in artistic talent but so poor. So before Katrina there was always that grumbling from the music community that "we have to leave New Orleans to make a living, we have to travel." Well, that's the reality of the situation. Even if you're a musician in New York, you have to get out of there if you are going to make a living, so certainly right after Katrina there was this major awakening to what had happened. The clubs were down. There were no audiences. I think we're seeing certainly, a year and a half, two years after Katrina that all that's coming back. Now there will be musicians and artists who have moved away, have found other realities, other lifestyles; maybe they want to get back. We have so many houses that are still ungutted and unfinished, but it's amazing, I think, at this point when you look at the music community right today it's pretty phenomenal that 80 percent of it, 85 percent of it is back. The challenge is going to be more of . . . the musicians have access to touring, they have access to creating a product that sells for $15.99 or 99 cents on iPod, local performances—people do like to go out and party—but when you are a visual artist and you're trying to go out and sell a unique product that you've created that reflects *you* finding your market is very difficult, and I think that the decline in conventions, more than tourism, has had a brutal impact on the visual arts community. Theater seems to be coming back. Now theater has never really funded the performers properly. We do a lot of community theater here, we do a lot of twenty-dollar-a-night type things. I think one of the major reasons theater has never grown to be a major force in New Orleans, in spite of Tennessee Williams, Lillian Hellman, and everyone else, is that we're not looking at the economics of it so that there is sustainability. Some of that is changing, and we do have Southern Rep and Tulane Shakespeare, but there still needs to be a little bit more there.

AK: You talked about some of the new festivals you had created after Katrina, and I know you've been involved in a number of educational and other kinds of initiatives. So maybe you'd like to talk about some of those other plans that you've got?

DM: I think arts education is critical. I think if we really look at the rebuilding of New Orleans education has to be at the center of it all. We are fortunate that a lot of the schools have come back up, particularly some of the charter schools where you have parental involvement and all kinds of engagement of the community. We're seeing bright spots of schools. I just came from a meeting of people involved in music education, and traditionally you go around the room and people say what they're doing and you think, you know, this is amazing. This must mean we have the world's best music education program because this group's doing this and working with these schools. And, you know, everybody's doing their thing but not in a coordinated manner. Getting back to how do we take all these wonderful resources and all these wonderful people, particularly after Katrina, who are trying so hard, and adding so many layers of responsibility onto their jobs, how do we help manage that? The management of cultural resources, so that we maximize the benefit, whether it's students or the public or the neighborhood, is the biggest challenge. We have more cultural resources here than is normal in a city of this size. Again, can we take those resources and put them together so that people are employed properly and don't have to take five other jobs to exist? That's where we're really challenged.

AK: There was an article in the paper not too long ago claiming that New Orleans was not a music-friendly city, which sounds extraordinary. Do you know where that perspective is coming from?

DM: We still fall very short. There is a lack of professionalism in the industry here, I mean from the ground up, and it is our challenge to figure out what is a professional music industry for New Orleans. It's not going to look like Austin, Texas; it's not going to look like Los Angeles, Memphis, or New York. It's going to look a little like part of those. We can get everybody in the room, and we can hear what everybody's doing and say, well, we're 70 percent there in this area, but again, whose responsibility is it? This organization is moving towards that, but can we or anyone commit the resources for the follow-through?

AK: Would that job have naturally fallen to the Arts Council to do?

DM: Definitely there's a role for Arts Councils to do certain aspects of this. You would think an Arts Council would include everything. Often an Arts Council will focus on a visual arts community or music. I would love to see the Arts Council take on that role of responsibility for coordination—a council of music educators, a council of whatever the art form is. I think that it would make sense to go that route, it's just whether or not that particular organization here has the resources, but, you're correct, it would really be logical for an Arts Council which is broad based, to take on that responsibility.

AK: Let me go back to the question of professionalism that you just raised because I can imagine somebody saying, well, but yes, if we become professionalized, though, we lose the grit, the character, the funkiness that is so much part of what New Orleans culture is.

DM: I don't think we'll ever lose that funkiness. I think Katrina made us even funkier. When people say "we're turning this place into Disney World," I'm, like, "Excuse me? Yes, we finally learned how to pick up the trash in the French Quarter." I don't know how much that's costing, but we will never be Disney World. We will never be overprofessionalized. It's just not in our nature. I'm a big believer that the professionalism only helps because working as much as I do in neighborhood cultures my heart goes out to those who are struggling. Someone may be a Mardi Gras Indian; you don't want to change what they're doing, but it would be nice if they had health care or if they could afford to feed their family.

We recently just went through about three hundred applications for our community grants program, which is exciting. Our range went from the Louisiana Philharmonic and the New Orleans Ballet, the bigger organizations that have the infrastructure—not enough, and not enough staff, but they do have grant writers—down to I'm a Mardi Gras Indian, there are kids in my neighborhood, I want to pass on these traditions. Well, how do you do that? Do you just give somebody a check or do you try to figure out some structure so that the things we take for granted as administrators or businesspeople we can help with. My role is to think about how we can create a program that in working with tradition bearers like the Mardi Gras Indians to say, you want to teach in your neighborhood, that's where it needs to be taught, you want to bring people into your living room, we provide x amount of funding for materials, so that the teacher and the students go to the supplier and pick out their rhinestones and their feathers and here's that money. And is there a photo book of Mardi Gras Indians with some educational information for the kids to each get and have as a reference? Can we put in those basic necessities but still allow the individual creativity and the indigenous, neighborhood feel to still be there but give them the resources that everyone should have.

AK: There's always going to be a tension, though, between that approach and [the] need of anybody who is putting resources into anything to have accountability and reporting mechanisms and all that. So that goes back to the need for some kind of coordinating structure to enable people to do what they do well with the resources that they need to do it without forcing them to become something that they have no interest in becoming.

DM: And for us it's a learning process. I announced to the staff that we are giving money to a hundred different individuals and groups. I want to meet with all of them. That's a lot of time, but I'm very comfortable with all the major organizations. I know they've got all their things, but I'm very interested in sitting down with that Mardi Gras Indian and learning about their needs so that my organization can be much more sensitive and responsive and professional, perhaps offering resources that aren't included in that grant. We were looking at some of the little minifestivals that are going on—some for twenty years—that have never built an audience, that are struggling every year. How do we assist them?

AK: How unusual do you think you are as a leader in the arts and culture world in New Orleans to want to do that? To want to sit down with the individual Mardi Gras Indians, to want to work with the small neighborhood festivals?

DM: Very. Why? I think it's being from this area; continually learning about our culture is pretty important to me personally. And, because I have a pretty good business background, I realize the needs of our community, given the lack of education and awareness of best practices. We in New Orleans should have the best music education program in the country. We have so many wonderful musicians who are underemployed. We have children in our school systems who desperately, desperately need creative stimulation on all levels, not as after-school programs only but in the classroom during the regular school day. I mean, can you teach the LEAP [Louisiana Educational Assessment Program] test, if you are forced to teach the LEAP test, can you do it through music? Schoolhouse rock—let's learn the history lesson, let's sing it! Let's write it and sing it! And also, I guess, just because of my commitment, I'm willing to be at my desk until ten o'clock at night.

AK: But it also sounds to me like you might have a different analysis of the problems, the solutions, the opportunities than some of the other leaders of major arts institutions or initiatives in the city. What do you think is the gap?

DM: I think it's a feeling of responsibility to what you do. So I feel responsible for the Mardi Gras Indian culture—not totally—but I understand that as part of my job description. And it may not be written there, and my bosses on the board may not think that's my responsibility—some do, some don't—but just because of my interest in my field. I've gone from a purely visual arts background into a heavy focus on theater, with dance, and now I'm in this hugely music environment, but it also includes cultural traditions, so to me it's a wonderland. I feel like a kid in a candy store, so, just personally, that's what keeps me going. Plus having that side of the brain that thinks in business terms about how we can be the best.

AK: But can we do that if our other cultural leaders don't think the same way you think?

DM: It's a huge challenge. We do have cultural leaders in town, and they are doing wonderful things with museums and in specific areas. But there are very few who feel the responsibility to cover all the bases in the arts.

AK: But you see them all as connected, so you spread yourself thin, but not randomly.

DM: The arts are very holistic, and I've never seen the difference between dance and theater and the visual arts and spoken word and literature. It's just part of our expression. We're fortunate to have New Orleans; it's a community that's unique, and I don't think—there may be some radical changes in the business world or finance—but for the next fifty years a city like this is never going to be able to go backwards as far as becoming a manufacturing center. Our product is really the arts.

AK: Do you think the business sector understands that?

DM: Well, unfortunately I don't think we have a business sector. I think that's been one of the biggest challenges to the city. What's fascinating to me in New Orleans is that, regardless of whether you consider yourself a white person or a black African American or a Creole, there are three different social systems at work, there are three different educational systems, there are three different debutante systems, there are three different business systems, and the segregation of the races has been a cultural thing as much as anything else and has kept the Social Aid and Pleasure Clubs and the Mardi Gras Indians and the Boston Club and Rex and Comus alive, and Zulu, and they are fascinating to the outside world, and they are pretty spectacular. The fact is if you are an African American student or a Caucasian student, from pre-K through college in this city you will very seldom cross paths. We have three predominately, historically black colleges, and the others, UNO [University of New Orleans] and Loyola and Tulane, have an integrated student body to some extent. We are not encouraging integration until after people graduate from college. It's too late. It's way too late. I mean to learn to play a musical instrument, to learn to love to go to theater, to learn to do anything, you know, third grade, fourth grade, fifth grade. You want people to become comfortable in learning, experiencing, in going to new places, in talking to different people.

It's a double-edged sword for this community to have that kind of segregation, which has kept us with these unique cultural traditions but at the same time you've also developed three different economic systems, which really negatively impacts any economy. There's no sharing of the wealth here, and if you're not sharing the wealth there's no wealth creation, and we have become a poorer and poorer and poorer city. One of the reasons I'm very committed to doing things, say, with Festiva Latina, is that you would want people of different cultures to feel welcome in New Orleans and that we are celebrating their culture as opposed to turning our back on them.

AK: People want to stay in their comfort zones.

DM: Yes, it's very easy, and you know when I was running the Contemporary Arts Center we would have Dashiki project theater going on and a visual arts thing and there was the black audience and the white audience. There was no antagonism—everybody's friendly—but, just as you're saying, you go where you feel comfortable, the restaurants you go to. I mean, I'm shocked when I go to Essence Fest, particularly at the Convention Center. It's one of the most amazing art markets, and you're learning about things and you realize that you may be one of three non–African Americans in the Convention Center. Isn't anybody intellectually curious?

AK: Do you think that the influx of Hispanic workers after Katrina . . . sometimes when Hispanic workers come into an environment tensions increase, particularly between African Americans and Hispanics.

DM: You know, right now I hear so much about the problem of race relations in New Orleans getting worse. Maybe I'm naive or I'm clueless or something, but I don't pick up on that at all. I don't feel it. One of the things I do feel is that, despite the segregation, New Orleanians are sort of Mediterranean, Caribbean friendly. In New Orleans you have a wealth, a wealth, of underemployed African Americans for low-paying jobs requiring very little skill. That's just been the nature, unfortunately, of our community. Before Katrina you were not going to find Hispanics moving in for jobs where there was an overabundance of potential people. Right now we were very, very fortunate to have workers come into New Orleans of all nationalities, and it seems particularly Brazilian and Mexican have come in large numbers. First, there was no one around to be unfriendly, and thank god they came in. But right now, as things are stabilizing, where are those relationships going to go? Where you have people from different cultures now living in poorer neighborhoods, will there be a feeling that people are not getting jobs because of that ethic group?

AK: Following up on the festival you mentioned earlier, do you think there is a role for the arts and culture in getting ahead of the curve on that issue?

DM: Definitely. My fantasy is that there will be a Latin American Cultural Center. A version of the CAC where we are putting on exhibitions and classes and performances and making sure that . . .

AK: Okay, so let me ask a question then. So then we have CAC for the white folks, Hispanic Cultural Center for the Hispanic folks, Ashé for the black folks?

DM: Yeah, we're back to that segregated thing. It's a tough thing. Ultimately you . . . I ran the Contemporary Arts Center. For an organization like the Contemporary Arts Center I think it's very important for them to be multicultural. Then you look at an organization like Ashé or, say, a hypothetical Latin American Cultural Center. There are points in the evolution of cultures and particular communities where you need that safe space to develop and nurture things because major arts institutions will say, "We want to attract African American audiences, and we're going to start advertising for a year, and gosh darn none of those people—those people— ever came to our events, and we gave away free tickets." Well, those people were not comfortable coming to your event or it was of very little interest. So there is that challenge of separation, but I think that in poorer and emerging situations you need the support systems there. I mean, we look at the Jazz and Heritage Festival. Every year we scratch our heads and say, "Where are the African Americans? What have we done wrong?" And to me it's primarily the programming. Just because we put a Ludicris on the day's activities doesn't mean that someone who is interested in that music or culture is going pay to see one act. We have to look at what people are looking for, those experiences that they want, their comfort zones.

AK: But, also from the other direction, how are we educating our young people in terms of their cultural literacy so that a young black person could be interested in a white artist, a young white person could be interested in a black . . .?

DM: Well, a lot of it is really through the school system. We have a festival that is produced by professional festival producers and we have a foundation, and our education programs started to fall apart a couple of years ago, first for financial reasons and then post-Katrina. While the foundation's role had never been to produce or to coordinate busses or anything for the festival, I was, like, I'm not going to let this happen, so all of a sudden the two of us who were back were on the phones and making sure that we got free tickets to every school that was up and running. So all of a sudden we were the most knowledgeable group in the city who knew where the schools were, the phone numbers, etc. And there is a possibility that we may take on the role of the educational component of the festival in the foundation, which I'm very excited about because I think you need to have a group in charge of something that's passionate to make sure it expands, to reach more people. I think educating our young people to all the diverse cultures is important—you want a diverse student body ultimately. I think your point's very well taken, you have to educate all along. The exposure at an early age is so critical.

AK: A lot of that work now is falling on nonprofit groups that are all very stretched in terms of staff, in terms of resources. What should the government be doing—city, state, federal—we talked a little bit about state-level initiatives. What should the government be doing that it's not doing?

DM: To me, it all comes down to education. I feel very strongly that every school needs to have an arts coordinator, an office. It can take different shapes, but I look at, say, Frederick Douglass school in the Ninth Ward and one of the most beautiful art deco auditoriums that's just sitting there rotting away, a resource for the community which would be wonderful. All of our schools built in the twenties and thirties have these glorious auditoriums in a city now that has no auditoriums. How can we take those resources, how can we benefit the school? If there was an arts coordinator who was looking at those resources that the school has, plus the community—I mean, living in the Bywater, we formed an artists' discussion series at the library every other Tuesday, paying small stipends to musicians. Those same people are very interested in helping with the schools, and if there was someone coordinating that, that community relationship with the schools, there would be writers, there would be painters. We have some fashion designers in our neighborhood who are looking for a place to have a workshop. Could that be part of a school program, teaching kids about design? Again, it's not having the people in place who can coordinate the resources. Cultural resource management is a critical, critical area.

AK: What do you think might be the role of the higher eds in town in that, the colleges and universities?

DM: I think there's huge potential, and certainly different universities have taken different stances and some more successful than others. It would take a real commitment by universities. If we have to look to our resources in this community for change, it is the universities, but you know how difficult that is.

AK: There's been a lot of talk about community service and civic engagement in the universities. I know Tulane put out a lot of language about that; they're now requiring all students to fulfill a public service requirement to graduate. Do you think that's sufficient?

DM: It's a very good start. And certainly the three interns that we had this summer [from Tulane] were amazing, and I'm hoping that they benefited from it. I think that, number one, viewing the students as resources to the community is great because we can all use help. There has to be a structure. A lot of organizations are so overworked that the idea of having . . . the initial reaction when we said we have these three interns coming was that everybody said, I don't have time for this. I said, well, let's just work through this. The archivist didn't want anybody. Well, once that person showed up, it was like can I keep him the rest of my life? So you have to work through those things. But it would be great if there was some bigger overall coordination. Ultimately there should be something, somebody, coordinating Loyola, Tulane, etc., interns going into the community: here are the resources of students, here are the needs. That's in a perfect world. Initially there was that "We're all going to do this, it's startup program. It was like you had too many resources and too few organizations able to handle them to sort of start from scratch like that. I'm hoping that we will be building these longer-term relationships if this is going to happen every year at Tulane or Loyola, or Xavier, that we'll know and we can plan for that relationship and develop better learning experiences.

AK: But it almost requires ongoing projects, an awareness over time, so that when I have students I know what kind of work is ongoing, I know something about what my students' interests and capacities are, so there is some way of making that match that is informed rather than being driven by an administrative edict, right?

DM: Right, we're trying to develop something. Again, that's a huge challenge. Ultimately I would love to have a program here that was year-round, that might even be something new and different, that the students . . . that might bring us into . . . let's say if it was going to be the Mardi Gras

Indian tradition . . . that this is a program and we built into it that it really . . . the success of the program depends on three interns every other semester or whatever it's going to be. That takes thoughtful planning, that takes time, that takes commitment. But I'm more than happy to really sit down and figure out what is it that the students would be interested in in relationship to what we do, and how do we make it so that it's seamless. They just come in, they do it, they're learning about it, they love it. We benefit from it. The community benefits from it. And there's not that startup time.

AK: Yes. That's what takes the time frequently. One of the problems we have on the university side is that we're always feeling like we've got to create projects, which is hard to do. And at the same time we know that there are a lot of projects ongoing and there's really no reason why we should be doing that. I think it comes down to communication, and it comes down to communication—not simply about logistics but also about mission, goals, values—that needs to be ongoing and probably needs to happen at a higher level than whoever the program coordinator is.

DM: It's got to come from the top and not just lip service. There's got to be a deeper understanding of what this means and how it can function.

AK: What would be the signal to you that it was deeper, that it wasn't lip service? How would you know that if somebody from a university approached you?

DM: That's a tough question. I don't know the right answer. To me it would be the long-term development of the relationship. That it wasn't going to be post-Katrina for a year and then it was going to go away, that I know that this is a continuing program that the university is committed to and if we're smart we're going to take advantage of these wonderful resources. But it's challenging.

AK: Have people, in all sectors, been more open to learning new things, to being engaged in new ways, or the same or less so since Katrina?

DM: I think certainly people are more open to engagement with others as far as coming together, whether it's a neighborhood meeting or working together to fix problems. There's been this camaraderie; everybody's gone through this horrible experience. And so your neighbor who you never spoke with or never saw for five years is now someone you're seeing on a regular basis and talking with. How do you sustain that? It's just getting to that point and then keeping them together and engaging in activities. I just don't know whether we have the visionary people in this community to do those kinds of things. I think the lack of vision in New Orleans is because of the lack of financial resources, and when you're tying to survive its hard to think about the community, what's going on elsewhere, what can be made better.

The lack of support for infrastructure interests me greatly, and I was hoping through this community partnership grant to see how we can develop a partnership with the people we grant money to. We can find a way to work better with the LPO [Louisiana Philharmonic Orchestra] or the ballet or the opera, but how do we provide the resources that we have and take for granted to the organizations that will never have those? Or the individual artists? So that's why we're going to be getting into exhibitions and figuring out a way to do a film festival of New Orleans–made documentaries with outdoor screenings or something. Now we know the film community: what are your needs? How do we access funding sources?

AK: So if you had all the staff resources you wanted, what would you do?

DM: I would look a little bit heavier into facilities. Some of our programs need key facilities like our Heritage School of Music. I would love it if we actually had a Heritage School of Music, or actually my fantasy is that we have a New Orleans Jazz and Heritage School where arts and culture and music are central to the educational process, not to train musicians and artists but [so] that you grow up with it and it's used. I think we're going to end up with more of a museum, visual arts strength than we've had in the past. I'm hoping that we will have a Jazz and Heritage Gallery or museum within the next six months. I'm looking for ways to focus on dance—I think there's a natural connection between rhythm and dance and jazz and heritage. I just think that right now we're growing in so many different directions.

AK: So as a whole, despite the devastation and the tragedy that it was for so many people, has the aftermath of Katrina been positive for the Jazz and Heritage Foundation?

DM: It has been positive for this foundation. It has given us a clearer purpose. It has allowed for . . . and it's a combination of events. I mean if we were still on the verge of bankruptcy like this organization was four years ago we wouldn't be doing all these things. We're fortunate—maybe there is karma or somebody up there likes us or whatever—that we're in a position where we can, where we have money to give away, and again in an impoverished society like New Orleans, having money is a real luxury. Post-Katrina, my job is much more dynamic and exciting and much more rewarding. It's always been fantastic to be in this field because the people are so wonderful, but it's even nicer to be part of a community where everybody is working hard for everybody else and to actually be in a leadership position where we can help a lot of those people. So that's a nice thing. I'm thankful every day for it.

AK: That's a wonderful note to end on.

DM: Well, good. This has been fun, as always.

Afterword

CIVIC ENGAGEMENT IS A LANGUAGE—WHAT CAN UNIVERSITIES LEARN FROM PUBLIC CULTURAL WORK IN NEW ORLEANS?

Julie Ellison

LIKE AMY KORITZ, coeditor of this volume, I am a literary scholar by training and inclination, a writer of articles and books, a close reader, a cultural historian of print and the word.

Koritz explains that her contributions to this volume tell "the story of how I stopped worrying about whether I was still being an English professor." "It was becoming clear to me," she writes, "well before disaster struck for real, that a slow, nuanced disaster was creeping up on my relationship with my professional identity." And she adds, "Close reading will only get you so far."

But when engaged professional practice and close reading join forces, along with close listening (a first cousin), the results are impressive. This book not only documents acts of civic engagement carried out with the involvement of university-based artists and humanists; it also shows us how to closely write and closely read those acts.

The interwoven labors of talking, writing, and reading are fundamental to the "historic blossoming of civic engagement" that is investigated here, an out-of-season flowering of citizens' voices under conditions of catastrophic inequality and the prospect of metropolitan "suicide."

The editors point to the "real time" qualities of the texts that make up this collection.

> The extreme dislocation of [the authors'] experience surfaces in . . . [the] rhetorical consequences of having to negotiate between personal loss and uncertainty and professional norms of discourse.

But if the "rhetorical consequences" of trauma are here, so are the means to make sense of them. Years ago, at the meeting that led to the creation of the University of Michigan's Arts of Citizenship Program, founded by David Scobey, then provost Nancy Cantor looked quizzically at David as he was laboring to define public scholarship. "Just do it," she said, "and then you'll be able to talk about it." She committed support for the new program on the spot. Here it is, almost ten years later, and the talking about it has reached a new level of ambition and depth.

In February 2007, I attended a conference in New Orleans called "Educating Women for a World in Crisis." It was one of the most strategic events I've been to in a long time, a combination of a teach-in, an organizing meeting, and a global scholarly seminar. In the midst of this conference, I sat down with the editors and authors of this unprecedented volume. The context matters because the conference made palpable for me—an outsider—the times and locations that constitute "the wake of Katrina," the place from which this volume has emerged.

A year after the hurricane, Imagining America sponsored the Hurricane Katrina Web Resource: Creative Community Responses in the Wake of Disaster. Created by staff member Josephine Tsai, this resource provided links to everything we could find that involved responses from colleges and universities, as well as other sectors. So I had some knowledge of the organizations, projects, and people that inhabit this collection. But until the simultaneous experience of the conference, and with the team associated with the book project, Katrina was something I knew about, like most Americans, from afar.

My own civic engagement projects are centered on words in the world. They involve local groups working through cycles of writing, reading, archiving, and searching through archives, performance, and endless talk of different kinds: personal narrative, critical dialogue, structured encounters at meetings, and rhetorics of persuasion in public address.

These projects include a writing workshop with Johannesburg printmakers, a documentary project with high school performance poets, and a multiyear collaboration called The Poetry of Everyday Life in a primary school. The many residency sites of Sekou Sundiata's post-9/11, post-Katrina performance work, *51st (dream) state*, included a collaboration with ten poets and a museum in my home region of metropolitan Detroit in touch with other residency project teams at sites around the country.

I have spent the last ten years working to connect the civic engagement movement as it unfolds in cultural—and intercultural—settings. The civic engagement movement is a profoundly cultural phenomenon that is playing out in and through the places that take responsibility for imagination, memory, critique, eloquence, aesthetic pleasure, and the "dream states" that pervade consciousness and conscience. These places include colleges and universities, public cultural institutions (museums, festivals, heritage sites, and libraries), and community arts organizations. The communicative labors of citizen activism are part of the "public work" that constitutes citizens.[1]

The ripple effects of the democratic imagination, intentionally pondered and acted on, are affecting nongovernmental organizations (NGOs), foundations, and human services professionals who are having doubts about the mind-set of helping and are looking for models of cocreation, partnership, and the politics of coalition. At the same time, changes are flowing in the opposite direction. Growing numbers of artists and humanists—and the contributors to this volume exemplify this impulse—are mastering the demands of relational labor, the fraught topographies of groups and organizations, and the historical inflections of highly fluid intercultural politics that publicly engaged cultural work asks of its participants.

My own efforts aimed at bringing about changes in higher education took the form of helping to found a consortium of over seventy colleges and universities that take culture seriously as a medium of publicness, understanding "public" in Lauren Berlant's sense of politics, "the political as a place of acts oriented toward publicness." That consortium, Imagining America: Artists and Scholars in Public Life (IA, now led by a contributor to this volume, Jan Cohen-Cruz), is an institutional network that supports public scholarship and creative work and campus-community partnerships.

With a strong focus on public scholars, IA squarely addresses the stresses faced by engaged faculty and community leaders. One of IA's most important undertakings, the Tenure Team Initiative on Public Scholarship, addresses the need to establish the intellectual legitimacy of community-based scholarship through new tenure and promotion policies and efforts to effect culture change around these issues on college and university campuses. Legitimation projects involve negotiations around the social power of words and the politics of knowledge. Thus, the effects of words in the world go to the core of these engagement efforts. The humanities are definitely changing, but close reading is far from obsolete.

Consider the dozens of ways in which words form part of the subject matter of this remarkable collection. They are proof, indeed, that the city's near-death predicament "energized public discourse" and now, in the written record of that discourse, brings to bear on it, in this volume, "data-focused exposition . . . personal witness . . . [and] objective analysis."

- The writings in section 1 "embody . . . the tension between the scholarly protocols of analytic distance and the passionate immediacy of circumstance that often motivates civic engagement."
- "Wireless-enabled laptops . . . are the unsung technological heroes of post-Katrina civic engagement."
- The *Times-Picayune* becomes "everyone's darling," introducing special sections on "Meetings" and "Meetings and Contacts."
- A television station "brings back on-air editorials" and "one station launches a nightly civic education and activism forum."
- A radio station switches from classic rock to talk led by local hosts to satisfy "post-Katrina information hunger."

The "documentary impulse" analyzed in this volume by Michael J. Mizell-Nelson in his analysis of the professional and systemic consequences of gathering storm stories complements the communicative impulse described by Richard Campanella in the vignettes just quoted, as manifest in newspapers, radio broadcasts, Internet sites, public meetings, and personal encounters. Those of us wondering what higher education can contribute to the public work of words should take this statement by Mizell-Nelson to mind: "Writing created by high school, community college, and other students provides entry to the experiences of those less likely to have access to the Internet. These are some of the most detailed and valuable objects in the collection."

Mizell-Nelson uses his own family's story as an example of why he wants to convince people that their Katrina narratives are worth recording, especially "the majority of stories that fall between the extremes of heroism and hooliganism." "The mundane signs of life and struggle . . . must survive if we are to create a more representative model" of "post-diluvial" New Orleans, he argues.

Elizabeth Fussell, writing on civic engagement among New Orleans Latinos, conducted over forty oral histories, summoning the "documentary impulse" to illuminate the civic energy of the response to newly arrived Mexican and Brazilian workers. "I'm now learning about becoming civically engaged as a thirty-seven-year-old person," one of her interviewees commented, her explicitness suggesting a considerable degree of deliberateness and intention around the civic research carried out by Fussell who draws on Appadurai's defense of locally scaled but globally networked strategies of narrative and performance.[2]

The copresence of multiple genres in this book enacts the interdependence of different strands of cultural work and professional practice. For example, Rebecca Mark's poem, "Another Evacuation Story," offers an experiential window onto the personal landscapes of displaced intellectual and cultural workers. But it also critically illuminates issues addressed nowhere else in the book: gender and domestic norms made palpable in (and by) disaster, the presence of gay and lesbian support networks, and the testing, in various southeastern towns, of a freer than usual definition of what a family is: "our family is a little different, as I have been telling those people we meet on our journey who want to know or I have the energy to tell."

Telling, as felt in the labor of writing evident through these contributions, is hard work. The poem evokes its protagonists' agency, and the limits of that agency, in inventing their own family culture through rituals, jokes, names, and objects. These cultural strategies are public/private ones, at the intersections of commerce, worship, travel, and the weather. They are fully enmeshed in old news and new news, the posttraumatic reactions constituted by the Holocaust and a conference on Emmett Till. The past floats through the present, and the present arrives through CNN, computers, and cell phones. The poem confesses strategies and tactics, Wal-marts and Home Depots, and defiant aesthetics in the face of the storm: "We are the only people I know . . . who evacuated with their interior designer." Engagement, displaced, extends to the "dailiness" of a life that is at once true and false: "We . . . make a fake life, in a rental home," in the devouring and sanity-preserving embrace of trees.

This poem gives us a vivid sense of the lyric-to-narrative or lyric-to-learning structure of some focused encounters among strangers, including those at the heart of *HOME, New Orleans*, the Gulfsouth Action Corps, and Creative Forces ("this beautiful unfolding puzzle" in a "ghost town"). Language, spoken or sung, was as central to the organizing process as it is to adventurous curricula that are emerging from post-Katrina projects. Dr. Kyshun Webster, D. Hamilton Simons-Jones, and their team have built into the GYAC curriculum—a curriculum that any college campus should be impressed by—multidisciplinary courses that integrate writing, reading, and speaking: Visual Communication, Critical Media Studies, Drama and Social Satire, Culture and Community, and Technology and Community.

Carol Bebelle's "The Vision Has Its Time" demonstrates how speech can work publicly to name disaster as "the federal flood," to follow out, in a rolling conceit, how "the influence, theme, character, and persona of racism were given unrestricted permission to improvise everywhere" and how, again, the "intimate samplings" of close listening "helped us to see the fire of hope." In asserting that "we must not be afraid to . . . be optimistic out of a fear of being disappointed," Bebelle not only speechifies in the face of accounts of discouragement elsewhere in the volume but echoes Cornell West's position as "a prisoner of hope,"[3] invoked also by Sekou Sundiata in 51st *(dream) state*.[4] It is not just enough to "contemporize" the Atlantic slave trade, Bebelle says, summoning the resources of eloquence, "it is the spirit of song, story, memory, image, and creativity that keeps us going on," the "devices of culture" put to work "to create images of what New Orleans will be so that people can envision something they believe is worth putting forth a greater effort." The "spirit" summoned by Bebelle's public speaking carries her listeners (and now readers) forward to a statement of accounts: "There isn't a place for authentic culture bearers at the distribution table; however, often they are a main entrée on the menu."

Bebelle's ensuing call for the "intimacy" of learning focuses on the mediations of voice in narrative and song. In an unexpected dialogue with Bebelle, Carole Rosenstein, after a sustained series of important research-based generalizations about the cultural policies that sustain collaborations between universities and communities, ends with a coda on "cultural longing." Half memoir, half thinking forward into whether "what came before"—that is, what is happening now—will be reintegrated "with what comes after," these pages are characteristic of the multiple temporalities negotiated in these writings. Even those that most resemble policy documents keep circling around to knit together retrospection, realism, and hope—a condition that Geoffrey Hartman, in his readings of romantic poetry, calls "surmise."[5]

I have been constantly struck in the course of doing public engagement work in higher education by how obsessed everyone I meet is with the labor of language, although it is also true that I see the world through language. A recent series of extensive structured interviews with deans, center directors, university presidents and provosts, and leaders of national higher ed and research associations, focusing on how to value public scholarship, bears out this impression. Repeatedly, these individuals stressed the centrality of translation in their work lives—a fundamental part of negotiating among multiple constituencies, each with its own idioms, gestures, and explanatory narratives. Translation is their metaphor for the explanatory activity that forms so much of their working lives: translation everywhere all the time.

One arts dean argued, "Language that is 'broadly communicable' is essential," noting that the translation issues are particularly important among black scholars. For another dean at a West Coast public research university, translation around community-based teaching and research requires a particular kind of administrative literacy: "[Promotion] files need to be contextual. There needs to be translation in the file. There are language issues as well; deans need to know how to talk about community work as research. Translation . . . needs to be everywhere, not just around during tenure."[6] The key to successful community engagement, and to establishing the legitimacy of public scholarship, is to have nimble structures within the university for response. The nimbleness, according to this interviewee, takes the form of translational power.

Furthermore, many of the leaders we interviewed insisted that we had underestimated the substantive analytical demands of public intellectual work, often referred to as public understanding of research (PUR) or the dissemination of knowledge. The head of a national research association stressed the fact that "there is not enough value put into the translation, synthesis and presentation of research. These are also an important part of the engagement process." Legitimizing this form of professional practice "allows for different callings. . . . [We should be saying] 'the university values effective presentations to wider non-academic audiences. What has this candidate done to offer that?'"[7] At this point of institutional process, the work of words becomes inseparable from the politics and economies of professional practice.

Those of us committed to the practices that require the negotiation between hope and critique, a defining feature of the subcultures of public scholarship, need to listen with a keen ear to our own public, personal, and professional idioms—a form of self-critical listening that is modeled in this volume.

Among those who benefited professionally from the crisis were "those connected to the realm of storytellers in a broad sense": journalists, film documentarians, historians, sociologists. Are these professionals "scavengers," as Mizell-Nelson suggests was the case in a number of instances? How do we assess a documentary impulse "that may simultaneously be selfless and self-serving"? What about the tension among public historians, oral historians, and anthropologists, who, Mizell-Nelson feels, were "best prepared" for documentation, and the better-funded arts organizations that fold oral history into performance or visual projects? How do people link "posterity" and "performance" through collaboration? The conversation later in the book among Jan Cohen-Cruz, Ron Bechet, Amy Koritz, and John Barnes about the *HOME, New Orleans* project and the dilemmas of university-neighborhood arts collaborations looks at this question in a different light since these were art projects that certainly tapped—as community-based arts undertakings typically do—the documentary impulse.

The *HOME, New Orleans* project raises another set of questions that surface in Mizell-Nelson's analysis of the documentary economy, questions involving the roles of New Orleans–based cultural professionals and academics and their counterparts from elsewhere, leading to inequalities in employment and grants and, in a few cases, to productive collaborations. How can we have more of the latter, Mizell-Nelson queries. How can oral history and other documentary crafts become "more like house gutting, with . . . groups who reach out to locals and work side by side"?

In Imagining America, we learned through our interviews with civic engagement leaders in higher education what Koritz, Sanchez, and every other author represented in this book learned under much riskier circumstances. It is important to address changing roles, especially roles as constructed in projects, which form the defining work structure for public scholars. Projects are an environment that requires multiple roles, and this multiplicity becomes a defining feature of work and personal identities.

The intervening term between artists and humanities scholars and public scholarship is "the project." Restructuring work around the project, especially under conditions of emergency or crisis, marks a profound change, especially in the humanities. It involves, even during periods of relative normalcy, the reorganization of work, itineraries, schedules, products, language, and relationships. When lives, systems, and cities are in a state of crisis or its aftermath, the freedom to shift teaching and scholarship organized around collaborative projects can arrive suddenly, along with accompanying shocks to the psyche and to academic structures and habits. This book gives us the opportunity to think about this change, at a time when engaged artists and humanists in all sectors of American higher education are starting to use projects as a powerful way of integrating their scholarship, teaching, and public work. Projects are spaces of professional learning and change for faculty and other cultural professionals, as well as platforms for engagement. There are clear project-to-program or project-to-center trajectories as the work gains focus and point. At the same time, projects need to emerge from a larger analysis of assets, opportunities, and challenges.

Once people are in project mode, they negotiate multiple roles. When Koritz recalls how she had sensed "a slow, nuanced disaster . . . creeping up on my relationship with my professional identity" for some time before the shock of Katrina, she points ironically to the way in which working in the spaces between institutions and organizations dismantles the unitary role of the "English professor." For scholars in the humanities and the qualitative social sciences, as well as for artists, the plurality of roles has become a significant trend. It is not a haphazard plurality but a specific mix that is being persistently noticed and felt.

> A number of authors combine the roles of scholar, practitioner, and activist . . . and blur assumed divisions among the museum, the academy, and engaged social action. [Their accounts are] keenly sensitive . . . to different modes of knowledge. (Introduction, Karp and Kratz, *Museum Frictions*)[8]

> We need an "archaeologist-practitioner" to "[give] shape to the project at all levels," including "the circumstances of organization" that reveal the tensions surrounding "the public's protagonism." (George Yudicé, *The Expediency of Culture*)[9]

> I've had conversations with people who know my work in American literature and know nothing about my work with teachers. I've had conversations with people who know my work with school teachers and don't know that I work in the more traditional, within-the-discipline kind of thing. But more and more, what I'm finding is people who know both aspects of the work that I do and people who see the connections. (Sarah Robbins, Kennesaw State University)[10]

People thus find themselves in mediating and combined roles. This growing sense of fluidity and improvisation has become a commonplace in the discourse of entrepreneurship and organizational studies—discourses that humanists and artists often define themselves wholeheartedly against. University leaders and academic administrators, as the interview responses described earlier confirm, also are experiencing the growing complexity and variety of their roles, often under conditions of engagement. As Koritz concludes, underscoring the cross-sectoral and intercultural logic of civic engagement, "The humanities are fundamentally concerned with interconnection" but do not have ways to value the plurality of roles and forms of knowledge that go with being connected.

We need to be clear about two things. First, states of emergency or everyday tension arising from race-based social inequality inspire forms of organized creativity that are strategically intercultural. And, second, multiethnic intercultural engagement requires participating academics to assume plural roles and the translational labor that makes them cohere.

Robert Ibarra presents his research on Latina and Latino faculty members in *Beyond Affirmative Action*. He argues that the way to build a diverse faculty is to foster a specific approach to knowledge. He recommends investing in "context diversity," a model of how educational systems adjust to people rather than the other way around. His arguments in favor of high-context and multicontextual settings, including transformations of libraries, academic fields, and models of community engagement, point toward further research that would look at the impact of practices that favor highly social, relational, and culturally rich environments. Ibarra is looking inside universities, for the most part, but his point applies to the multicontextual arenas of campus-community engagement and the multiple roles that arise from "context diversity" there as well.[11]

George Sanchez's work in multiracial communities in Los Angeles has sparked his powerful analysis of the post–affirmative action university in which "diversity"—now divorced from race—screens a growing divide. What are the terms of engagement between ever whiter research universities and the ever more ethnically and racially mixed cities in which they are located?

In his 2004 Dewey Lecture at the University of Michigan, published in 2005 by Imagining America as "Crossing Figueroa: The Tangled Web of Democracy and Diversity," George J. Sanchez argues that there are two pathways to democracy in U.S. higher education: first, engagement by the university through connections with specific communities and publics; and, second, access to the university for members of all communities and publics through inclusive admissions and hiring policies. In "Crossing Figueroa," Sanchez challenges our understanding of how engagement and diversity are connected and, increasingly, disconnected. How, he asks, will universities "sustain [their] credibility among the urban neighborhoods and organizations that dominate the national landscape?"[12]

That challenge is posed with even greater urgency in *Civic Engagement in the Wake of Katrina,* in which Sanchez and Koritz frame the observations offered by many contributors of how "public engagement" by universities can actually bolster privatization and the shrinking of public institutions and the public sphere.

Katrina, they argue, "exposed the fissures in the community that underlie most efforts at civic engagement and the possibilities of citizen participation." We have to ask ourselves "whether civic engagement work can itself cope with disaster that is . . . rooted in the very fabric of racial injustice, economic disparity, and political malfeasance." They relate the growing privatization of response to crisis—as in Los Angeles after the 1992 riots following the acquittal of Rodney King's assailants—to the "color-blind racism" that blocks direct public investment in city neighborhoods. Race, the retreat from public institutions, and the growth of civic engagement at the interface between university and community are part of a single political economy. Civic engagement, as Richard Campanella argues in his contribution, "blossomed" after Katrina out of a desperate need for New Orleans to survive as a city. Engagement, however civically inspiring, "can be attributed to this failure of government-run institutional and bureaucratic support systems and processes for engaging and communicating with constituents" and to the dysfunctional response of many large relief organizations.

This argument raises important questions of scale for community cultural organizations and universities. Is small better? Are large numbers of passionate, improvising individuals or "small, grassroots groups" that "come together in the face of compelling need" more effective than large organizations? Are universities also hampered, as the editors argue, by "a pattern of institutional shortfalls and individual efforts" that receive high praise but little sustained institutional investment?

Contributors to *Civic Engagement in the Wake of Katrina* note that engagement in colleges and universities often happened at the creative margins of the universities led by people who were loosely bound to standard departmental formations. Marginality can be a position of opportunity, but, as the participants in the dialogue on *HOME, New Orleans* testify, it bears real professional costs, particularly in arts and humanities fields that do not have access to external funding for policy studies, survey research, and program evaluation.

Koritz and Sanchez gather up the evidence pertaining to how universities operated in postdiluvial New Orleans and arrive at some telling generalizations. These are conclusions to which everyone interested in civic engagement in higher education needs to pay attention.

> Higher education enters into this situation primarily as short-term supplementary labor and expertise. . . . [D]ominant models [of engagement] remain single-day service projects and semester-long service learning assignments or internships.

While community-based classes can be transformative "laboratories of practice" for both students and faculty, these models make it "extremely difficult . . . to embark on sustained, reciprocal action with the surrounding community."

> The infrastructure required by such partnerships is beyond the capacity of individual faculty members without external funding, and university units charged with facilitating and overseeing engagement too often focus on short-term experiences. . . . [It is] difficult for universities to integrate students into forms of engagement that model for them what ongoing, collective, and collaborative action looks like.

All the contributors to this volume support the civic engagement movement in higher education, the scale of which is apparent in the existence of almost thirty national associations and consortia dedicated to engagement efforts. But the vanishing of meaningful citizen coalitions with government offices and agencies and the weakening of public investment in schools, libraries, health care, and transportation makes *civic* no longer synonymous with *public*. Tulane's energetic support for the privatization of New Orleans' public schools through the founding of charter schools is an example of how this cycle can work. "To what extent is this . . . advocacy of the civic responsibility of higher education also contributing to the increased privatization of the public sphere?" Clearly the trend is not unidirectional or simple because cultural nonprofits are acting less private and are taking responsibility for publicness in powerful new ways, as the contributions of Bebelle, Marshall, and others demonstrate.

George J. Sanchez, a former president of the American Studies Association, has founded a Center for Diversity and Democracy within the American Studies and Ethnicity department at the University of Southern California (USC). He works nationally in many settings to develop a new politics of engagement centered on the demographic realities of both higher education and American cities. Part of his response to these dilemmas is to give students and members of socially and historically separated communities the capacity for recovering a historically grounded political imagination. He tells the powerful story of his own Boyle Heights Project, a partnership on the history of a multiethnic neighborhood in Los Angeles. The project brought together USC faculty and students, the Japanese American National Museum, public libraries, high schools, and other community organizations over a period of ten years. Sanchez's enterprise reveals the multimission logic of campus-community projects—the way that they bundle together research, teaching, and public engagement. As Sanchez enumerates the chain reactions that structured the work of the Boyle Heights teams, it is important to note that he concludes with his own major scholarly project. This book in progress generated, for example, an article that received the 2005 best article prize from the American Studies Association.

> The exhibition inspired others, from Roosevelt High School students to elementary teachers in Long Beach, to construct their own historical projects looking at multiracialism in the past as a way to understand our 21st century future. In the end, this decade-long project produced a wide range of public scholarship from many of its practitioners: a major museum exhibition, a teacher's guide made free to all teachers, high school student radio projects, undergraduate and graduate research papers, and hopefully, within a year or so, my own next book.[13]

Propelling the chain reaction are highly specific acts of dreaming backward, through rigorous, collaborative, public history, and forward. Campus and community participants could "dream of a multiracial democracy within their midst" by "imagin[ing] [an earlier] time and place where folks lived side-by-side . . . and were forced to work out their problems." They "dreamed of a Los Angeles of the future where this could happen in our lifetimes." Finally, they brought this vision home to the university: "We imagined . . . democratic institutions where access and knowledge would not be limited by one's race or economic circumstance."[14] As for so many of the contributors to *Civic Engagement in the Wake of Katrina*, he links the "documentary impulse" to intercultural and intergenerational partnerships and finally to the formation of a viable public sphere, the civic as a site of learning.

The forms of knowledge production are changing. On campus, things are shifting, although often these new programs are marginal, fragile, underfunded, and not taken seriously as intellectual powerhouses. Nonetheless, new arts and humanities programs and centers are emerging around the country, including new graduate programs where students can get credit for adventurous community-based cultural work. These include the community-based masters program in cultural studies emerging at the University of Washington–Bothell; a new arts curriculum at Rutgers University–Newark; the Visual and Public Art Department at California State University, Monterey Bay; the integration of community-based learning into the curriculum of Columbia College, Chicago; numerous public history programs; and the Professional Development and Public Engagement program run by the Graduate School of the University of Texas.

There is also a striking trend toward founding new public humanities institutes on university campuses and expanding the community engagement of existing humanities institutes and centers. Such institutes are operating at Rutgers–Newark, Texas, Washington, Ohio State, Iowa, Syracuse, Brown, Duke, Florida, and Minnesota, with others in the pipeline. Furthermore, the new Carnegie classification for engaged campuses is creating healthy competition about colleges and universities that are motivated to demonstrate the extent and coherence of their commitment to community-based learning and institutionwide engagement.

These developments—most of them emerging in more stable environments than New Orleans in the wake of Katrina—are encouraging. Concerns remain, however. Some of them relate to the financial bottom line, especially at public campuses. A small focus group survey carried out by Imagining America a few years ago showed that campus-community partnerships in the cultural sector had two main sources of funding: universities themselves and foundations.[15] This only confirms the impression that engagement is a budgetary burden. Can civic engagement attract students? As public universities rely more on tuition, the priorities of students can shape the investment in civic engagement on any given campus.

In my view, civic engagement can attract students when academic leaders are willing to develop flexible, hybrid majors, minors, certificates, and degree programs for this generation of students. Amy Gutmann, president of the University of Pennsylvania, called in her inaugural address for "a truly successful partnership between the arts and sciences and the professions."[16] Connecting knowledge and action in liberal arts fields gives those fields a way to compete against—and collaborate with—professional schools. While the evidence is not yet in, the emergence of new programs, such as those I have mentioned, suggests that a combination of professional development and real world, democratic skill building strongly tied to academic majors appeals to cohorts of students who want to master both critical thinking and project management. It also appeals to and may help to retain key cohorts of faculty.

Some final recommendations are in order, responding to the insistent demands for visionary practicality from every contributor to this book. These recommendations are offered in the spirit of Carole Rosenstein's harvest of best practices for supporting living cultures. They are addressed to colleges and university leaders.

- Create local consortia of colleges and universities driven by the question "What can we do together for the public good of the city?" There is a real need for multicampus coordination within the region. Connect people and programs with similar interests, look for points of convergence, build communications networks, and share information. Be honest about differences in status, resources, and social capital in the region and work across them. Focus together on how universities learn beginning with a close reading of this book paired with, for example, Haridimos Tsoukas's *Complex Knowledge*.

- Develop tenure and promotion policies that recognize and are capable of evaluating public scholarship in the arts and humanities. Nurture civically engaged faculty members across the full cycle of their working lives. For administrators, "the greatest goal is to preserve an individual over the course of a career," one provost told Imagining America's tenure policy research team. At a recent IA conference, one graduate student remarked that, when told to stop doing community engagement while writing her dissertation, "I felt like I had been told to cut off my legs." This feeling may be particularly acute for students and faculty of color, who are seeking to work in the "multicontextual" environments studied by Ibarra.

- Persuade university leaders and campus-based intellectuals to make a vigorous commitment to publicness—to public institutions, public spaces, public servants, and "public work" in Boyte's sense of public work as the action that generates citizenship itself. Practice a politics of coalition, and don't write government off. Particularly at the local, county, and regional levels, the model of government as a (failing) service provider can be challenged. Alternative models are available.

- Develop research policies through national organizations such as the Association of American Universities (AAU) that create guidelines for writing faculty scholars in crisis-afflicted areas into grant and project budgets. Contributors to the volume offer detailed evidence of how outsiders benefited from the surge in public and foundation investment in the Gulf Coast region after Katrina, while local researchers, filmmakers, and others with appropriate expertise were too busy surviving to be writing proposals of their own.

- When drastic budget cuts are required, make decisions that favor the intellectual resources needed for institutional engagement. Sustain and build on strengths in key fields to enable an integrative approach to urban studies, environmental studies, and community cultural development.

- Get the infrastructure for engagement right. Focus on faculty and staff, as well as students, and set up the right reporting relationships so that engagement programs have powerful institutional patronage and intellectual legitimacy.

- Create explicit guidelines to support "the documentary impulse," including ways in which people in the arts and historical fields can build a joint exploration of oral history, personal narrative, photo voice, Story Corps, and related methodologies, and, where appropriate, can collaborate on projects of ambitious scope. Invite archivists, film and video producers, academics, librarians, information professionals, and other documentary professionals to join this undertaking.

- Sustain the small and think hard about questions of scale. Carole Rosenstein focuses her recommendations on neighborhood cultures; I am focusing on the university's capacity to discern, form alliances with, and change in response to places nearby. We need both approaches. Small projects can be sustainable and iterative. There is a widespread, deep intuition that sustainable change tends to begin—

and endure—through face-to-face encounters in small groups. Close to the ground nonprofits can operate at the critical neighborhood level, which is precisely what large institutions and large funders tend to overlook. A center for neighborhood projects and programs might help integrate appropriately scaled work, seek foundation support, and generate an ongoing analysis of the power of the near. Such a center, while engaging in the politics of coalition through neighborhood collaborations, could reach out to global networks of similarly scaled enterprises in order to analyze the relationship and difference between the small, the local, and the nearby.

At the heart of all of these recommendations is my conviction that civic engagement is a social and political phenomenon to which language is central—language in the form of eloquence, demand, story, proposal, analysis, lament, and, above all, translation. Understanding engagement in these terms takes us back, finally, to the question of how university-community partnerships gravitate to the segregated topographies that shape intercultural practice.

Two years ago my students and I worked on a documentary project that focused on two poetry workshops run by the InsideOut Literary Arts Project in Detroit. These workshops were the testing ground for a project of InsideOut's Citywide Poets program. With support from the Skillman Foundation, these workshops—and the participating students' parents—focused on "Boomtown: Detroit Arrival Stories." Family histories sparked poems dealing with urban-suburban racial divides, personal identity, and the meanings of Detroit itself over time.

In one particularly absorbing session, Nandi Comer, the Boomtown program coordinator, gave a Citywide Poets group of six high school poets the following quotation to serve as the spark for individual, on-the-spot "free writes." The quotation highlights 8 Mile Road, the dividing line between Detroit and its northern suburbs. It is a powerful real and symbolic boundary in one of the most profoundly racially segregated metropolitan regions in the United States.

Near 8 mile road in Detroit, which separates the suburbs from the city, almost all the blacks are on one side and almost all the whites are on the other, but all the families nearby are low income. We live on the black side.

One student, J., set the tone, identified the unifying concern, and created the most memorable language in response to this ever-present geopolitical fact: "We drown on separate sides of the same sinking boat," he wrote. This is perhaps the most resonant summary I have heard of the current mood in Michigan, where economic crisis coincided with—and exacerbated—the defeat of affirmative action policies through a state ballot initiative. J.'s poem continued:

> I'm stuck on the black side, where everything is gloomy,
> where our dreams smell like alleys at midnight
> with no streetlights.
> Whites dream the same dreams with a lighter tint
> making their days grey and lonely.
> Fill in the gaps. The devil stands in the empty
> space between us.

J. shows an extraordinary capacity to situate himself firmly in the realities of black Detroit. But he also fully understands the "shrunken imaginings" (a phrase borrowed from a South African writer) of bounded white neighborhoods, and he thinks forward to a different social world, a "melting pot of black and white arrangement / of beautiful delicacies." J. brought into a creative family history project his ability to find language that sees—and sees through—geographical, class, and racial barriers. As the academic partner in the Boomtown project, I am reading J.'s work, and that project overall, more acutely after reading this book. Its authors make us better readers, writers, and practitioners of intercultural engagement in Detroit, Los Angeles, and just about anyplace else.

NOTES

1. Harry Boyte, *Everyday Politics: Reconnecting Citizens and Public Life* (Philadelphia: University of Pennsylvania Press, 2004).

2. Arjun Appadurai, *Fear of Small Numbers* (Durham: Duke University Press, 2006).

3. Cornel West, Commencement Address at Wesleyan University, Middletown, CT, May 30, 1993. See also Sekou Sundiata, *the 51st (dream) state*, http://www.humanity.org/voices/commencements/speeches/index.php?page=west _at_wesleyan.

4. Sekou Sundiata, *the 51st (dream) state* (2006). Conceived and written by Sun-

diata. This multimedia ensemble work included audio recordings by Cornel West, including the "prisoner of hope" passage, excerpted from "Restoring Hope," an address delivered by West at Pasadena Community College, December 2003. Used in *the 51st (dream) state* with permission.

5. Geoffrey Hartman, *The Geoffrey Hartman Reader*, eds. Geoffrey Hartman and Daniel T. O'Hara (New York: Fordham University Press, 2004).

6. Julie Ellison and Timothy K. Eatman, *Scholarship in Public: Knowledge Creation and Tenure Policy in the Engaged University* (Syracuse: Imagining America, 2008).

7. Ellison and Eatman, *Scholarship in Public Knowledge*.

8. Ivan Karp, Corinne Kratz, et al., *Museum Frictions: Public Cultures/Global Transformations* (Durham: Duke University Press, 2006).

9. George Yudicé, *The Expediency of Culture: Uses of Culture in the Global Era* (Durham: Duke University Press, 2003).

10. Sarah Robbins, "Building Feminist Networks for New 'Missionary' Work." Keynote Address, Women's Breakfast of the American Studies Association, Atlanta, November 2004.

11. Robert Ibarra, *Beyond Affirmative Action: Reframing the Context of Higher Education* (Madison: University of Wisconsin Press, 2001). See also "Context Diversity: Reframing Higher Education in the 21st Century," in B. Holland and J. Meeropol, eds., *A More Perfect Vision: The Future of Campus Engagement* (Providence, RI: Campus Compact, 2006).

12. George J. Sanchez, *Crossing Figueroa: The Tangled Web of Diversity and Democracy*, Foreseeable Futures #4 (Ann Arbor, MI: Imagining America, 2005).

13. George J. Sanchez, "'What's Good for Boyle Heights Is Good for the Jews': Creating Multiracialism on the Eastside during the 1950s," *American Quarterly* 56, no. 3 (September 2004), 633–62.

14. George J. Sanchez, *Crossing Figueroa*.

15. Cynthia Koch, *Making Value Visible: Excellence in Campus-Community Partnerships in the Arts, Humanities, and Design* (Ann Arbor, MI: Imagining America, 2005).

16. Amy Gutmann, Inaugural Address, University of Pennsylvania (http://www.upenn.edu/secretary/inauguration/speech.html).

Contributors

Carol Bebelle (aka Akua Wambui) is a native New Orleanian. She received her bachelor's degree from Loyola University in sociology and her master's degree from Tulane University in educational administration. She spent nearly twenty years in the public sector as an administrator and planner of educational, social, and health programs. She is a published poet whose work has appeared in several anthologies and journals over the years. In 1995, she published a volume of her work entitled *In a Manner of Speaking*. Her work appears in the anthology *From a Bend in the River*, edited by Kalamu Ya Salaam; and *Sisters Together*, edited by Nancy Manson and Debra Gould. In 1998, with Douglas Redd, she founded the Ashé Cultural Arts Center, a pivotal strategy and force for the revitalization and transformation of Oretha Castle–Haley Boulevard, formerly known as Dryades Street. Ashé, as it is familiarly known, has become a pivotal focus for change in the city, the state and the nation. *Ashé*, defined in the Yoruba vocabulary as "a divine force, the ability to make things happen, so let it be done," all ways to describe the commitment that Carol Bebelle and Douglas Redd have made to building bridges, accessing resources, and helping to evolve a better world.

Geographer **Richard Campanella** applies mapping sciences and spatial analysis to a wide range of disciplines through his research at Tulane University's Center for Bioenvironmental Research. Among his books are *Geographies of New Orleans*, winner of the Louisiana Endowment for the Humanities 2006 Book of the Year; and *Time and Place in New Orleans*, the 2002 New Orleans/Gulf South Book of the Year. His research has been published in the *Journal of American History*, *Architectural Education*, *Technology in Society*, and *Photogrammetric Engineering and Remote Sensing* and featured on National Public Radio's *All Things Considered*, in the *New York*

Times, and on Public Broadcasting's *American Experience*. His next book, *Bienville's Dilemma*, will be published by the University of Louisiana's Center for Louisiana Studies in late 2008.

Jan Cohen-Cruz is Director of Imagining America: Artists and Scholars in Public Life, based at Syracuse University. She wrote *Local Acts: Community-Based Performance in the U.S.*, edited *Radical Street Performance*, and, with Mady Schutzman, coedited *Playing Boal: Theatre, Therapy, Activism* and *A Boal Companion: Dialogues on Art and Cultural Politics*. As a professor at New York University's Tisch School of the Arts from the late 1980s to 2006, she produced community-based arts projects, codirected Tisch's AmeriCorps on violence reduction through the arts, directed the minor in applied theater and Tisch's Office of Community Connections, and was among the founders of NYU's Department/Center of Art and Public Policy. In 2006–7, she coconceptualized and coinitiated *HOME, New Orleans*, collaborating with Xavier, Dillard, and Tulane Universities, local artists, including the VESTIGES Project, and residents of four neighborhoods in experiments on art's role in the revitalization of "home" as dwelling, neighborhood, and the city itself.

Julie Ellison is Professor of American Culture, English, and Art and Design at the University of Michigan, where she has taught since 1980. She is also Director Emerita of Imagining America: Artists and Scholars in Public Life, a consortium of seventy-five universities that fosters civic engagement through the humanities, arts, and design. She is one of the nation's foremost experts on emergent models of public, community-based, and project-centered scholarship. She has worked with collaborators in South Africa since 2003 on the changing relationship between cultural institutions and universities there. Her current research partnership in South Africa focuses on expanding communities of writing, focusing on urban adults working in the cultural sector and on the public role of university writing centers. She recently completed a speaking tour of New Zealand universities as a Fulbright Senior Scholar and keynoted a national humanities congress. Before founding Imagining America, she served for four years as Associate Vice President for Research at the University of Michigan. She received her bachelor's degree from Harvard University in American history and literature and her doctorate in English from Yale University. Her scholarly work ranges across the literature and culture of the eighteenth and nineteenth centuries, with particular emphasis on gender, emotion, politics, and genre. The University of Chicago Press published her third scholarly book, *Cato's Tears and the Making of Anglo-American Emotion,* in 1999. Her current research project focuses on the new politics of cultural knowledge, particularly the reframing of the imagination as a democratic condition by black intellectuals and artists and other scholars of color. She has published poems in a number of quarterlies and small magazines. In fall 2007, she was Distinguished Visiting Scholar at Syracuse University where she completed a national report on tenure policies that are responsive to the work of engaged scholars.

Pat Evans specializes in consulting for nonprofit and government organizations. For over thirty years, she has worked in the public, private, and nonprofit sectors. Her areas of expertise include strategic planning, community organizing, collaboration, communications, marketing, organizational development, crisis management, and conflict resolution. In 1999, she founded and currently directs the International Project for Nonprofit Leadership at the University of New Orleans. The project provides a continuum of capacity-building offerings, including graduate education, certificate training, technical assistance, and consultancy to the nonprofit sector locally, nationally, and internationally. At the same time, she created Urban Routes, a neighborhood-based capacity-building program for nonprofits in low-wealth urban neighborhoods. This program offers skills training in New Orleans' neighborhoods on collaboration, organizational development, conflict resolution, and managing for results.

Elizabeth Fussell is Assistant Professor of Sociology at Washington State University, having left Tulane's Sociology Department in 2007. She studies international migration from Mexico and other Latin American countries and has been studying Latinos in New Orleans since December 2005. She also studies transition to adulthood and is involved in a study of adversity and resilience among a cohort of New Orleans community college students affected by Hurricane Katrina. She is coeditor, with James R. Elliott, of *Displaced City: Hurricane Katrina and the Unequal Recoveries of New Orleans.* She has published her research in *Demography, Social Forces,* the *Journal of Marriage and Family,* and edited volumes.

Keith Knight—cartoonist, rapper, and filmmaker—is part of a new generation of talented young African American artists who infuse their work with urgency, edge, humor, satire, politics, and race. His art has appeared in various publications worldwide, including *Salon.com, ESPN the Magazine, L.A. Weekly, MAD Magazine, Funny Times,* and *World War 3 Illus-*

trated. He won the 2007 Harvey Award and the 2006 and 2007 Glyph Awards for Best Comic Strip. Three of his comix were the basis of an award-winning live-action short film, *Jetzt Kommt Ein Karton,* in Germany. His comic art has appeared in museums and galleries in the United States and Europe. His work has been anthologized in four collections of his multipanel strip, the *K Chronicles,* and two collections of single-panel strips. He cowrote and illustrated *The Beginner's Guide to Community-Based Arts.*

Amy Koritz left Tulane University in 2008 to become founding director of the Center for Civic Engagement at Drew University. Since 1998, she has been developing programs and courses for undergraduates that connect the humanities to the community beyond the university. Her scholarship has addressed topics in performance studies, urban studies, community cultural development, and the role of the humanities in higher education and the public sphere. She is the author of *Gendering Bodies/Performing Art* (University of Michigan Press, 1995) and *Culture Makers: Urban Performance and Literature in the 1920s* (University of Illinois Press, 2009). She has written about civic engagement in the humanities for *Diversity Digest,* the Modern Language Association's *Profession,* and other journals. As Associate Director for Community and Culture at the Tulane/Xavier Center for Bioenvironmental Research, she developed projects and partnerships in New Orleans that integrated the arts and culture into efforts to build and strengthen sustainable communities.

Sarah Lewis is Cofounder and Codirector of Common Knowledge, a New Orleans nonprofit that helps citizens to effectively engage in local decision-making processes. She runs the Citizens' City Hall project, which tracks New Orleans social networks and provides free video recordings of community meetings on the Internet. She spent three years as a graduate assistant with the Louisiana Regional Folklife Program, where she helped document the region's traditional culture. In particular, she worked with staff at the New Orleans Museum of Art to design *Raised to the Trade: The Creole Building Arts in New Orleans,* a major exhibition that used oral histories to highlight the work of the city's skilled artisans. While with the Folklife Program, she assisted community groups in efforts to document, interpret, and present their own traditions at community centers and local festivals. She is pursuing a doctorate in urban studies at the University of New Orleans. She holds a bachelor's degree in political science and art history from Emory University and a master's degree in urban and regional planning from the University of New Orleans. Her recent research focuses on the nexus of heritage preservation, social networks, and disaster recovery. At the University of New Orleans, she has taught classes on urban studies and the New Orleans metropolitan region.

Rebecca Mark is a literary scholar whose articles, editions, and books, *The Dragon's Blood: Feminist Intertextuality in Eudora Welty's Fiction* and *The Greenwood Encyclopedia of American Regional Cultures: The South*, address southern writing and women's fiction with a special focus on the work and life of Eudora Welty. She is currently completing two books. *The Radical Welty: A Private Address* is a study of the fiction of Eudora Welty. *Ersatz America* is about false histories and how and why the American cultural imagination holds on to and perpetuates these myths. She was a founding member of the Deep South Regional Humanities Center at Tulane University and served there as Director of Special Projects for two years. In 2005, together with Alferdteen Harrison from Jackson State University, she received the Public Humanities Achievement Award from the Mississippi Humanities Council for codirecting Unsettling Memories, a landmark conference on the civil rights movement in Jackson that took place in June 2004. From 2006 to 2008, she served as Interim Executive Director of the Newcomb College Institute.

Don Marshall is Executive Director of the New Orleans Jazz and Heritage Foundation, where he manages a range of programs and initiatives, including the Community Partnerships Grants Program, the Don Jamison Heritage School of Music, and several community festivals. He was the first director of the Contemporary Arts Center in New Orleans from 1977 to 1986, where he built a successful membership and fund-raising program. His other job titles have included Executive Director of Le Petit Theatre du Vieux Carre, Executive Director of the Saint Tammany Art Association, Director of the Cultural Resource Management Program at Southeastern Louisiana University, Director of the Graduate Program in Arts Administration at the University of New Orleans, and Manager of the Louisiana Division of the Arts' Percent for Art program.

Michael Mizell-Nelson is Assistant Professor of History at the University of New Orleans. His research interests center on the social history of New Orleans, and he is completing a book-length study of race relations within the city's neighborhoods during the Jim Crow era. A New Orleans native born in Saro Mayo Hospital, he first became interested in the city's history while conversing with older residents on the transit system. The school transit pass unveiled the community and neighborhood histories overlooked by scholars who for decades privileged the city's colonial, antebellum, and architectural histories. Stories of everyday life in this extraordinary city occupy his interests as a teacher, scholar, and video documentarian. Since 1992, he has worked with his students to record the histories of their families, neighborhoods, churches, and other institutions they deem significant. Each year his students contribute hundreds of additional oral histories and new media projects that help to document a singular city.

Carole Rosenstein studies cultural policy, public culture, and cultural democracy. Her contribution to this volume was written while she was a 2007 Rockefeller Humanities Fellow at the Smithsonian Institution's Center for Folklife and Cultural Heritage. From 2000 to 2007, she worked as a cultural policy researcher and analyst at the Urban Institute in Washington, DC., where she is currently an affiliated scholar. She is now Assistant Professor of Arts Management at George Mason University. She is the author of *Diversity and Participation in the Arts* and *How Cultural Heritage Organizations Serve Communities*, and she has contributed to numerous other Urban Institute research publications on the arts and culture. Her work has been published in *Semiotica, Ethnologies,* and the *Journal of Arts Management, Law, and Society.* She is currently completing a study of government funding for museums in the United States for the Institute for Museum and Library Services.

George J. Sanchez is Professor of American Studies, Ethnicity, and History at the University of Southern California. He is the author of *Becoming Mexican American: Ethnicity, Culture, and Identity in Chicano Los Angeles, 1900–1945* (Oxford University Press, 1993), and coeditor of *Los Angeles and the Future of Urban Cultures* (Johns Hopkins University Press, 2005). His "'What's Good for Boyle Heights is Good for the Jews': Creating Multiracialism on the Eastside during the 1950s" appeared in the *American Quarterly* in 2004. He served as president of the American Studies Association in 2001–2 and is a coeditor of the book series American Crossroads: New Works in Ethnic Studies at the University of California Press. He currently serves as Director of the university's Center for Diversity and Democracy and Director of College Diversity. He works on both historical and contemporary topics of race, gender, ethnicity, labor, and immigration and is currently working on a historical study of ethnic interactions among Mexican Americans, Japanese Americans, African Americans, and Jews in the Boyle Heights area of East Los Angeles in the twentieth century.

Mat Schwarzman is the founder of the Creative Forces Youth Educational Theater Corps and Director of the Crossroads Project for Art, Learning, and Community. He has been an administrator, artist, student, instructor, and writer in the field of community-based arts since 1985. A veteran teacher, presenter, facilitator, and workshop leader, he holds a doctorate in integral studies, with a concentration on learning and change in human systems, from the California Institute for Integral Studies and has helped establish instructional programs in community organizations, high schools, and universities across the country. He is coauthor of the *Beginner's Guide to Community-Based Arts* (New Village Press, 2005), which is used as a textbook in universities and community organizations internationally.

D. Hamilton Simons-Jones is chief development officer for Operation REACH in New Orleans. He is involved in a wide variety of community organizations and efforts focused on youth leadership, volunteerism, social entrepreneurship, and community service. His work focuses on developing community-focused leadership and connecting people and resources with meaningful opportunities for community impact. He has professional experience in academia and sports philanthropy, as well as the corporate and nonprofit sectors. He received a bachelor's degree from Tulane University and a master's degree in urban studies from the University of New Orleans' College of Urban and Public Affairs. His recent research has focused on ownership in public education in New Orleans, as well as the state of youth services and social entrepreneurship in New Orleans post-Katrina.

New Orleans native and public school graduate **Dr. Kyshun Webster** is a nationally recognized educator and certified teacher who has worked in the nonprofit sector as a community educator since he was twelve years old. He grew up in the St. Bernard Housing Development and returned there to launch his first after-school tutorial program in 1998, which was later recognized by the Tiger Woods Sharing and Caring Award Program, which declared him a "local hero." He most recently has studied the implementation of parental involvement programs required under the federal No Child Left Behind policy. Additionally, he has served as a policy consultant and expert witness for legislative initiatives on parental involvement in education for the Minnesota and Louisiana legislatures. He is founder and Chief Executive Officer of the nonprofit Operation REACH, Inc., a youth development organization in New Orleans.

Index